# Microsoft Windows NT 4.0
## Security, Audit, and Control

Microsoft Technical Reference

**James G. Jumes, Neil F. Cooper,**

**Paula Chamoun, and Todd M. Feinman**

**of PricewaterhouseCoopers**

PUBLISHED BY
Microsoft Press
A Division of Microsoft Corporation
One Microsoft Way
Redmond, Washington 98052-6399

Library of Congress Cataloging-in-Publication Data
Jumes, James G.
   Microsoft Windows NT 4.0 Security, Audit, and Control / James G.
   Jumes.
      p. cm.
   Includes index.
   ISBN 1-57231-818-X
   1. Microsoft Windows NT.   2. Operating systems (Computers)
3. Computer security.   I. Title.
QA76.76.O63M52434   1998
005.8--DC21                                            98-38727
                                                      CIP

Printed and bound in the United States of America.

2  3  4  5  6  7  8  9   WCWC    4  3  2  1  0  9

Distributed in Canada by ITP Nelson, a division of Thomson Canada Limited.

A CIP catalogue record for this book is available from the British Library.

Microsoft Press books are available through booksellers and distributors worldwide. For further information about international editions, contact your local Microsoft Corporation office or contact Microsoft Press International directly at fax (425) 936-7329. Visit our Web site at mspress.microsoft.com.

**Acquisitions Editor:** David Clark
**Project Editor:** Michael Bolinger
**Technical Editor:** Nick Cavalancia

# Contents

List of Tables   viii

Acknowledgments   xi

Introduction   xiii

## 1   The IT Security Control Model   1

| | |
|---|---|
| Objectives | 2 |
| Corporate Business Objectives | 3 |
| Corporate IT Objectives | 3 |
| IT Security Objectives | 4 |
| Controls | 5 |
| IT Security Controls | 6 |
| IT Security Controls and Windows NT Security  Features | 7 |

## 2   A Typical Environment of Windows NT Implementations   9

| | |
|---|---|
| Domain Controller | 10 |
| File and Print Member Server | 11 |
| Application Server: Web Server | 12 |
| Application Server: Database Server | 12 |
| Application Server: Remote Access Server | 12 |
| Workstation | 13 |

## 3   Effective Security Management   15

| | |
|---|---|
| Approach to Developing Corporate Security Culture | 15 |
| Corporate Security Policy | 16 |
| Legal Notice | 26 |
| Understanding C2 | 27 |
| Is Windows NT C2 Compliant? | 27 |
| Making Windows NT C2 Certified | 28 |

## 4   Effective Security Monitoring   29

| | |
|---|---|
| Performance Monitor | 29 |
| Chart View | 30 |
| Alert View | 31 |
| Log View | 32 |
| Report View | 34 |

Recommended Settings 34

Windows NT Diagnostics 36

Windows NT Diagnostics Information 37

Recommended Settings 37

Network Monitor 38

Capturing Data 39

Recommendations 43

Auditing 43

System Auditing 44

Recommended System Auditing Settings 44

File and Directory Auditing 47

Recommended File and Directory Auditing Settings 48

Registry Auditing 49

Recommended Registry Auditing Settings 50

Printer Auditing 51

Recommended Printer Auditing Settings 52

Remote Access Server (RAS) Auditing 53

Event Viewer 54

Recommended Event Viewer Settings 57

Securing the Audit Logs 58

## 5 Securing Physical Access to All Critical Systems 61

Physical Security 61

Physical Security in the Computer Room 62

Physical Security in the Communications Room 62

Physical Security on the Workstation 63

Physical Security on the Network Access Points 64

## 6 Securing All External and Internal Network Connections 65

Network Security Management 65

Domain Administration 66

Trust Relationships 66

Protocols 72

External Networking 79

RAS Authentication 80

Secure Remote Access Services 82

Administering Users 83

Recommendations Considerations and for Securing          90
External Networking

---

**7   Implementing Security through User Management   93**

Group and User Accounts                                   93
   Groups                                   94
   Users                                   105
Creating and Modifying Accounts                          108
   Group Accounts                          108
   User Accounts                           113

---

**8   Securing Accounts with Account Policies   123**

Account Policy                                           123
   Password Restrictions                  124
   Account Lockout                         127
   Recommendations for Account Policy      129
User Rights                                              131
   Standard Rights                         132
   Recommendations for Securing Standard User Rights   135
   Advanced User Rights                    136
   Recommendations For Securing Advanced User Rights   139

---

**9   Managing Resource Security   141**

File Systems                                             141
   NTFS                                    142
   FAT                                     143
   Converting between File Systems          143
   Recommendations for Choosing a File System   143
File and Directory Permissions                          144
   Implementing Permissions                144
   Ownership                               152
   Recommendations                         153
   Shared File and Directory Permissions   156
Managing Printers                                        160
   Permissions                             161
   Ownership                               162

**10    Managing Server Security    163**

Computer Properties                                            164

Users                                                         165

Shares                                                        167

In Use                                                        168

Replication                                                   169

Alerts                                                        174

Services                                                       175

Changing Startup Accounts for Services                        176

Recommendations                                               177

Promote to Primary Domain Controller (PDC)                     181

Considerations and Recommendations                             181
for Using Server Manager

**11    System Security Management    183**

The Registry                                                   183

HKEY_LOCAL_MACHINE                                            186

HKEY_CURRENT_CONFIG                                           188

HKEY_CLASSES_ROOT                                            188

HKEY_USERS                                                    188

HKEY_CURRENT_USER                                             188

HKEY_DYN_DATA                                                 188

Registry and Security                                          188

Securing the Registry Files and Directories                   189

Securing the Registry Keys                                    189

Registry Key Values                                           193

Workstation Lockout                                            202

**12    Ability to Recover from Operational Failure    202**

Environmental Protection                                       203

Backing Up the Registry                                        204

Viruses                                                        205

Fault Tolerance                                                206

Disk Mirroring                                                206

Data Striping                                                 208

Uninterruptable Power Supply (UPS)                            208

Data Backup and Recovery                                       209

Backups                                                       210

Backup Media 210
Backup Types 210
Recovery 214
Recovery Recommendations 215
Last Known Good Configuration 215
Emergency Repair Disk (ERD) 215
ERD Recommendations 216
Disaster Recovery and Business 216
Continuity Planning

**13**    **Auditing Windows NT Security Features and Controls 221**

The Systems Security Audit Process 222
PricewaterhouseCoopers' Windows NT Security 222
Audit Program (PwC-NTSAP)
Background of the IT Environment 223
Effective Security Management 226
Effective Security Monitoring 227
Securing Physical Access to All Critical Systems 230
Securing All External and Internal Network Connections 232
Securing the System 234
Auditing User Rights 241
Server Security Management 243
Ability to Recover from Operational Failure 248

## Appendixes

**A**    **Baseline Security Configurations 253**

**B**    **Service Pack 3 Features and Enhancements 269**

**C**    **Option Pack 273**

**D**    **Windows NT Commands 277**

**E**    **Resource Kit Security Programs 283**

Glossary 293
Index 305

# Tables

**1**
1-1. General Corporate IT Objectives ... 4
1-2. IT Security Controls ... 6

**3**
3-1. Sample of a Corporate Risk Assessment Matrix ... 19
3-2. Example of a Corporate Risk Assessment and Cost/Benefit Analysis ... 20

**4**
4-1. Chart Options ... 30
4-2. Alert Options on the Add to Alert Dialog Box ... 32
4-3. Alert Options on the Alert Options Dialog Box ... 32
4-4. Alert Recommendations ... 35
4-5. Windows NT Diagnostics ... 37
4-6. Windows NT Diagnostics ... 38
4-7. Network Monitor Capture Filter ... 41
4-8. Capture Triggers ... 42
4-9. Domain Users' Audit Policy ... 46
4-10. Data Files Audited for Domain Users' Access ... 49
4-11. Registry Auditing Options ... 50
4-12. Registry Options ... 51
4-13. Printer Audit Options ... 52
4-14. Printer Audit Recommendations ... 53
4-15. Detailed Event View ... 55
4-16. Event Viewer Categories ... 56
4-17. Event Log Settings Options ... 57
4-18. Event Log Wrapping Setting Recommendations ... 58
4-19. Log Settings Size Recommendations ... 58

**6**
6-1. Denial of Service Attack Fixes ... 79
6-2. Remote Access Admin Dialog Box ... 82
6-3. Communication Ports Dialog Box ... 83
6-4. Remote Access Permissions Dialog Box ... 84
6-5. Remote Access Users ... 86
6-6. Remote Access Setup ... 87
6-7. Network Configuration Dialog Box ... 89
6-8. RAS Security Configurations ... 92

**7**
7-1. Local and Global Group Scenarios ... 105
7-2. New Local Group ... 110

| | | |
|---|---|---|
| 7-3. | Add Users and Groups | 111 |
| 7-4. | New Global Group | 113 |
| 7-5. | The New User Dialog Box | 115 |
| 8-1. | Security Configurations | 131 |
| 8-2. | Recommendations for Securing Standard User Rights | 135 |
| 8-3. | Recommendations for Securing Advanced User Rights | 139 |
| 9-1. | NTFS vs. FAT | 142 |
| 9-2. | File Permissions Dialog Box | 145 |
| 9-3. | Special Permissions and the Associated Actions They Allow | 146 |
| 9-4. | Standard File Permissions and the Associated Actions They Allow | 146 |
| 9-5. | Directory Permissions Dialog Box | 147 |
| 9-6. | Special Directory Access Permissions and the Associate Actions They Allow | 149 |
| 9-7. | Standard Directory Permissions | 151 |
| 9-8. | Standard Directory Access Permissions and Associated Actions on Directories | 151 |
| 9-9. | Standard Directory Access Permissions and Associated Actions on Files | 152 |
| 9-10. | Recommended Permissions | 153 |
| 9-11. | The Sharing Tab of the Properties Dialog Box | 157 |
| 9-12. | Share Permissions | 158 |
| 9-13. | Share Permissions and the Associated Actions on Directories and Files They Allow | 159 |
| 9-14. | Printer Permissions | 161 |
| 10-1. | Computer Properties | 165 |
| 10-2. | User Sessions | 166 |
| 10-3. | Shared Resources | 167 |
| 10-4. | Open Resources | 168 |
| 10-5. | Replicator Account Settings | 170 |
| 10-6. | Manage Export Directories | 172 |
| 10-7. | Windows NT Services Recommendations | 179 |
| 11-1. | Registry Edit Commands and Data Types | 185 |
| 11-2. | Recommended Permissions for Registry Directories | 189 |
| 11-3. | Recommended Permissions for Registry Directories | 190 |
| 11-4. | Registry Permissions: Standard and Special | 191 |
| 11-5. | System Policy Profile for Users | 201 |

**8**

**9**

**10**

**11**

11-6. System Policy Profile for Computers 201

**12** 12-1. Backup Information Options 213

**13** 13-1. Domain Controllers Rights and Capabilities 235

13-2. Non-Domain Controllers Rights and Capabilities 237

# Acknowledgments

We would like to thank all the following people for their effort and hard work in making this book a reality:

John Benge, Partner, PricewaterhouseCoopers, New York, NY

Bob Gardner, Partner, PricewaterhouseCoopers, New York, NY

Bruce Murphy, Partner, PricewaterhouseCoopers, New York, NY

Michael Compton, Manager, PricewaterhouseCoopers, Detroit, MI

Bill Moore, Manager, PricewaterhouseCoopers, San Francisco, CA

James Ott, Manager, PricewaterhouseCoopers, Raleigh, NC

Cindy Smith, Manager, PricewaterhouseCoopers, Pittsburgh, PA

Robert Lofblad, Senior Manager, PricewaterhouseCoopers, Boston, MA

Kevin Reardon, Senior Associate, PricewaterhouseCoopers, San Jose, CA

Maurice Schilder, Senior Associate, PricewaterhouseCoopers, New York, NY

Jason Booth, Associate, PricewaterhouseCoopers, San Francisco, CA

Jonathan Stearn, Associate, PricewaterhouseCoopers, New York, NY

Helen Cooper

We would also like to thank the following Microsoft employees for their contributions:

Peter Brundrett, Program Manager, Microsoft

David Clark, Acquisitions Editor, Microsoft Press

Jason Garms, Product Manager, Microsoft

Ed Muth, Group Product Manager, Microsoft

# Introduction

This *Microsoft Windows NT 4.0 Security, Audit, and Control* book is designed to assist Chief Information Officers, Information Technology Managers, Systems Administrators, Security Officers, Security Administrators, and Information Technology Auditors understand how to build and audit a secure Windows NT 4.0 environment. The objective of this book is not to be a definitive resource on the multitude of Windows NT features or a guide in installing Windows NT. Microsoft offers publications and white papers that focus on these topics. The objectives of this book are discussed in the following section.

## Just Another Windows NT Security Book?
## What Makes This Book Different?

A trip to the bookstore reveals a large number of books focusing on Windows NT, and several books focusing on Windows NT Security. Many of the Windows NT security books do a great job describing Windows NT Security features, so why write another? We wrote this book because our clients continuously ask us to assist beyond identification and use of Windows NT Security features. When designing this book, we listened to our clients' questions and organized the book's major parts around these questions. The following presents our clients' most-often-asked questions and how this book addresses these questions.

- How do Windows NT features support corporate IT Security control objectives and corporate business objectives?

  This book is based on and organized by security control objectives. Chapter 1, "The IT Control Model," presents the Information Technology Security Control Model. This model describes the relationship between corporate business objectives, IT Security controls, and Windows NT Security features, as well as all the links in between. These links include corporate IT objectives, corporate IT Security objectives, IT control objectives, and IT Security control. Chapters two through twelve present the Windows NT Security features based on the security control objectives supported.

- How can I build a secure Windows NT environment?

  Chapters three through twelve are structured on the IT Security control objectives in Chapter 1. Each Windows NT Security feature, which is also a security control, is presented with details on its configuration and implementation. Implementing Windows NT Security features in this manner ensures that the necessary controls for securing a Windows NT environment are met. In our experience, we have seen many corporations with different implementations of Windows NT. For example, Windows NT has been used as a web server, application server, and file server, to name a few. Chapter 2 begins by presenting some common implementations of Windows NT in a business environment. When features are presented, and when appropriate, the implememmentation of the feature is discussed in relation to each of the six common implementations. In addition, throughout the book, we use fictitious corporations to exemplify concepts and the application of Windows NT Security features. Chapter 3 also provides guidance on assessing risk, developing security policies and procedures, creating security awareness, getting senior management commitment, managing security, and monitoring security.

- How can our corporation audit our Windows NT environment to assess the strength of our security configuration?

    Chapter 13, "Auditing Windows NT Security Features and Controls," includes PricewaterhouseCoopers' Windows NT Security Review and Audit Program. This program describes the systems audit and the systems audit process; it also includes a comprehensive security review program that can be used by itself or with one of the automated tools available in the marketplace, to evaluate the security of a Windows NT environment.

- Can you provide me with a baseline security configuration?

    Appendix A, "Baseline Security Configurations," provides baseline security configurations for each of the common implementations of Windows NT presented in Chapter 2. The baseline configuration is structured, as in Chapter 2, around each of the IT Security control objectives and the six common implementations of Windows NT. The appendixes also provide information about security enhancements and implications found within service and option packs, the resource kit, and command line features.

## Who Should Read This Book

The following table outlines the chapters within this book and the intended primary and secondary audiences. One should note there are also many other tertiary audiences that this book may benefit.

| Chapter | Primary Audience | Secondary Audience |
|---|---|---|
| Chapter 1—IT Security Control Model | CIOs, IT Managers, Security Officers | System Administrators Security Administrators IT Auditors |
| Chapters 3 through 12—Security Controls and Security Objectives | Security Administrators System Administrators | IT Auditors |
| Chapter 13—PricewaterhouseCoopers Windows NT Security Review and Audit Program | IT Auditors | Security Administrators System Administrators |

# Conventions Used in This Book

Before you read any of the chapters, it is important that you understand the terms and notational conventions used in this book.

## Notational Conventions

- Characters or commands that you type appear in **bold lowercase** type.
- Italic is used for terms that are introduced for the first time and defined.
- Names of files and utilities appear in ALL CAPITAL letters.

## Notes and Icons

Notes appear throughout the book. This table identifies the icons that mark these notes and the type of text contained within these notes.

| Icon | Description of Note |
| --- | --- |
| | Notes marked Caution contain warnings about possible loss of data. |
| | Notes marked Note contain supplemental information. |
| | Notes marked Tip contain explanations of possible results or alternative methods. |

# About PricewaterhouseCoopers

PricewaterhouseCoopers refers to the US firm of PricewaterhouseCoopers L.L.P. and other members of the worldwide PricewaterhouseCoopers organization. PricewaterhouseCoopers, the world's largest professional services organization, helps its clients build value, manage risk, and improve their performance.

Drawing on the talents of more than 140,000 people in 152 countries, Pricewaterhouse-Coopers provides a full range of business advisory services to leading global, national, and local companies and to public institutions. These services include audit, accounting, and tax advice; management, information technology, and human resource consulting; financial advisory services including mergers & acquisitions, business recovery, project finance, and litigation support; business process outsourcing services; and legal services through a global network of affiliated law firms.

PricewaterhouseCoopers has recognized the risks and threats to information since the early stages of information technology development. Their original approach to auditing computer-based systems included the study and evaluation of controls over the security of information. The firm has since established the Technology Risk Services (TRS) national practice dedicated to serving their clients' needs in addressing security over one of their most important resources—technology generated and resident information. The TRS professionals are recognized leaders in the fields of information technology, telecommunications, logical and physical security, and auditing. They are knowledgeable in the latest security tools and methods, and in reviewing, analyzing, developing, and implementing security and control solutions.

Services offered by the TRS practice include Electronic Commerce Security Implementation and Assessment, Enterprise Security Assessment, Penetration Testing, Internet Connectivity Reviews, Firewall Reviews, Operating System Security Reviews, Information Security Risk Analysis, Security Plan Development, Policy and Procedure Development, Business Continuity Planning Review, and Training.

## Disclaimer

This book presents certain discussions and recommendations concerning the operating system, Windows NT 4.0 (Windows NT), developed and marketed by Microsoft Corporation (Microsoft), and suggestions for establishing and maintaining a secure environment for its use. Security problems and vulnerabilities are continually changing and becoming more complex over time. Businesses and their software systems are continuously being assaulted by hackers and other criminals who are increasingly sophisticated and resourceful. Security analyses and recommendations, and the related audit procedures and tools, can remain no more than a small step ahead of rogue technology and security hackers. PricewaterhouseCoopers and the individual authors of this Guide (collectively "PwC") have used their collective skills, experience, and expertise in evaluating Windows NT, and have relied to a large extent upon technical documentation and other information developed and supplied by Microsoft. PwC believes that the methodologies, software, information, and philosophical approaches used by PwC in preparing this Guide are reliable and appropriate. However, PwC makes no representations or warranties concerning the methodologies and recommendations presented in this Guide or the results obtained from their use. While PwC believes that the material in this Guide presents a fair and reasonable approach to securing and auditing Windows NT, the information in this Guide is not meant to be comprehensive or definitive, and should be used only for general guidance. The information provided does not necessarily apply to any particular situation and should not be used as a substitute for each reader's own professional and business judgment, independent investigations, and research into the subjects covered. Nothing herein constitutes an endorsement by PwC of any product or company.

PwC cautions each reader of this book that it is impossible to interpret the effects of all possible permutations of security features and Windows NT configurations. Some combinations of security features and Windows NT configurations may cause detrimental effects to your system or files on that system. All system changes should be fully tested in a test environment, separate from the production environment, before being implemented in production.

# Chapter 1
# The IT Security Control Model

Information Technology (IT) Security is the protection of data from malicious or accidental destruction and loss. Protecting data not only entails configuring the system (such as setting up passwords) but also having good security policies and procedures. Many corporations do not implement any of these strategies and are, therefore, unable to properly secure their system environments.

However, our clients continue to ask the same questions: What is the appropriate level of security and how much time and effort shall we spend on security? This question is critical, as it is the catalyst for the rest for this book and the security future of the corporation. The answer to this question is different for every corporation. What corporations fail to realize is how tightly integrated IT Security is to their business objectives. This book explains that correlation and helps senior management, IT management, and systems administrators understand how it all must work together.

The IT Security Control Model depicts the relationship between corporate business objectives and IT Security controls or Windows NT Security features, as shown in Figure 1-1. IT Security should support corporate business objectives. By understanding a corporation's business needs, systems administrators can assess the proper level of IT Security needed and implement the proper security controls or Windows NT Security features to help meet its business objectives. By creating a link between corporate business objectives and IT Security controls, the corporation is not only assured that the necessary security steps have been taken but also that a secure IT environment (which can be easily monitored, audited, and modified to meet changing business needs) has been created.

Although the objectives and controls concepts may seem confusing and unnecessary at first, you will come to understand their relevance to Windows NT Security in the following sections. Some of the material may be a bit dry and dull at times. However, rather than skipping the next sections, we recommend that you (systems administrators especially) attempt to read and understand the concepts in order to implement Windows NT Security features to meet your business needs. We use IT Security controls and Windows NT Security features interchangeably because, for the purpose of this book, they are the same.

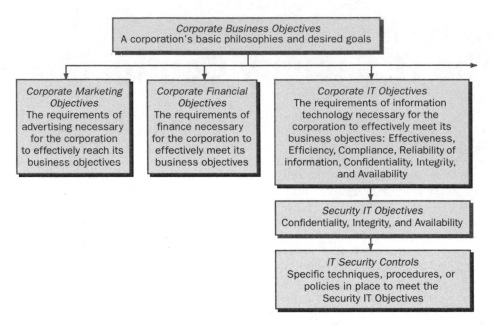

**Figure 1-1.** *The IT Security Control Model illustrates the relationships between business and security objectives.*

## Objectives

IT Security involves developing objectives that you would like your IT Security to achieve. These IT Security objectives are not created in a vacuum, rather they are built from objectives that support the business. To successfully create value-added IT Security objectives, you must understand how they support, and are linked to, the overall business objectives. The mistake that many corporations tend to make is that they develop IT Security objectives independent of their corporate business objectives. The Megan's Children Hospital (MCH) may provide a good example of this situation. The IT department of MCH may determine that an important security objective is the confidentiality of patient data. If the department's patient data resides on the Patient Data Windows NT system, the department should spend the extra time and effort creating permissions and users rights to limit access to this system in order to meet its security objective.

Now, if you go to the MCH boardroom and ask the CEO, What are MCH's corporate business objectives? their answer may be, Provide quality care. They may also respond, Provide the best medicine possible. To meet the second business objective, he needs to ensure that the research and medicine information stored in MCH's Research and Development (R&D) Windows NT system is secured so that its integrity is intact at all times. MCH cannot risk having medicinal information being tampered with. The CEO asks the head of IT, Is my system secure? The head of IT responds, Yes. However, they are not talking about the same system. The CEO is talking about the R&D Windows NT system, and the IT Manager is talking about the Patient Data Windows NT system. They have spent a great deal of effort securing the Patient Data system, while the R&D system is not secure. This is a prime example of where the IT Security controls do not meet the corporate business objectives.

To rectify this problem, both the IT Manager and CEO need to understand and explain the relationship between the MCH's business objectives and IT Security controls. An explanation of each step in the relationship and how it can be developed for a corporation is described in detail in the following sections.

## Corporate Business Objectives

All corporations are founded on basic philosophies and desired goals. These elements combine to form corporate business objectives. A good corporation will define and communicate to its employees and shareholders its corporate business objectives and modify them as the business strategy changes. That same corporation will use these objectives to measure its achievements.

Many corporations develop a mission statement but usually do not clarify the detailed corporate business objectives. Sometimes it is hard for a corporation to clearly explain to its employees and shareholders its corporate business objectives; and, most employees probably would not be able to tell you what the corporate business objectives are if you asked them. For example, employees of Enright Bank may think the corporate business objectives are to service each customer to the highest quality level. However, a closer analysis reveals that Enright Bank's corporate business objective is to "secure customer assets." These corporate business objectives need to be developed by the business managers, documented, and circulated throughout the corporation.

## Corporate IT Objectives

Having defined its corporate business objectives, a corporation may now examine its various functional divisions, such as finance, marketing, information technology, and so on. Each functional division should also develop objectives that support the overall business objectives—that is, corporate financial objectives, corporate marketing objectives, and corporate IT objectives. This task will help strengthen the corporation's overall business objectives. Because managers from each of these divisions helped document the corporate business objectives, they can fully understand them and are able to go back to their own functional areas and develop their own departmental objectives.

The corporate IT objectives can be defined as the Information Technology requirements that a corporation adheres to for effectively meeting its overall corporate business objectives. In general, the IT department needs to meet minimum objectives to support the business. For example, they should provide fast, reliable, and available systems. Table 1-1 defines the minimum objectives that usually comprise a corporation's IT objectives.

**Table 1-1. General Corporate IT Objectives**

| Corporate IT Objective | Definition |
| --- | --- |
| Availability | Information is available when required by the business process now and in the future. |
| Compliance | Information is complying with those laws, regulations, and contractual arrangements to which the business process is subject—i.e., externally imposed business criteria. |
| Confidentiality | Information is protected from unauthorized disclosure. |
| Effectiveness | Information is relevant and pertinent to the business and is delivered in a timely, correct, consistent, and usable manner. |
| Efficiency | Information is provided through the optimal (most productive and economical) use of resources. |
| Integrity | Information provided is accurate and complete as well as in accordance with business values and expectations. |
| Reliability | Information provided to management is complete and accurate so that they can operate the entity and exercise its financial- and compliance-reporting responsibilities. |

However, as previously stated, each corporation is different and should not simply follow these general IT objectives. Instead, a corporation should use these generalized objectives as a foundation to build its own unique corporate IT objectives. This is done by varying the degree of emphasis placed on each of these objectives and by combining them with the corporate business objectives, the individual's needs, and any business regulations. When they are formulated, these corporate IT objectives will constitute the goals of a corporation's Information Technology systems strategy.

Enright Bank has already documented one of its corporate business objectives as *secure customer assets*. Because the IT manager was on the team that developed the corporate business objectives, he or she can use them to create the corporate IT objectives. Rather than managers simply saying that their systems will be secure, they can now define unique, detailed IT objectives. Understanding the needs of the business, the IT objective should be defined as, "The systems that support our client accounts will be secured from unauthorized access." With this definition in mind, the IT department now has specific goals to work towards.

## IT Security Objectives

Because the focus of the book is security, we will not spend time reviewing all the general IT objectives. Rather, we will focus on the objectives that relate to security. Of the general IT objectives, the following three are necessary for effective security: Confidentiality, Integrity, and Availability. When your corporation formulates its own unique IT Security objectives, it will take these three objectives and modify the emphasis placed on each according to its business objectives. For example, because a highly sensitive system (such as a national defense system) has a greater need for the confidentiality of classified information, more emphasis is placed on confidentiality. An electronic funds transfer system or a medical system has a greater need for strong integrity controls. An automated teller machine has a need for all three objectives.

### Confidentiality

Confidentiality is the protection of information in the system so that unauthorized persons cannot access it. Enright Bank uses Windows NT file permissions to secure its customers' asset data from anyone not directly associated with the account. It may also be important for some businesses to protect their financial, marketing, and research and development data from competitors.

### Integrity

Integrity is the protection of information in the system from unauthorized, unanticipated, and unintentional modification ensuring data is accurate and complete. The means to establishing data integrity are listed as follows:

- Ensuring consistency of data values within a computer system
- Recovering to a known consistent state in the event of a system failure
- Ensuring that data is modified only in authorized ways
- Maintaining consistency between information internal to the computer system and the realities of the outside world

Megan's Children Hospital will rely on Windows NT's auditing features and review logs to ensure their research and development data remains unaltered. Integrity also includes protecting not only the data within a computer system but also the process or program used to manipulate the data from unauthorized modification. Any changes made to programs that manipulate data must also be correct and authorized.

### Availability

Availability is ensuring that information and vital services are accessible when required. Availability to data can be denied through purposeful malicious ways or through natural disasters such as fires, storms, and earthquakes. Enright Bank will implement Windows NT disk mirroring to ensure the customer account data will be available at all times.

## Controls

Controls are specific techniques, procedures, and policies that ensure corporate objectives are met, regardless of whether they are business or IT objectives. In an IT environment, developing IT control mechanisms helps ensure that the systems are meeting the corporate IT objectives, which are meeting the corporate business objectives.

## IT Security Controls

Specific security controls can be implemented to meet the IT Security objectives. Good security controls use the Windows NT Security features that the IT department of Enright Bank will implement to secure its customer data, such as placing restrictive permissions on the directories and files and implementing disk mirroring.

There are three different types of security controls:

- Preventative
- Detective
- Corrective

Preventative controls ensure that security vulnerabilities are not exposed. Placing restrictive permissions on directories and files are preventative controls. Windows NT provides many other preventative controls such as encrypting data over a network, giving users and groups restrictive rights, and supporting strong password policies. Detective controls ascertain when security holes are in the process of being exploited. There are many reports and alerts that can be generated within Windows NT that would provide good detective controls. The Security Log provides a report where suspicious information can be filtered and tracked and Performance Monitor can be configured to send alerts when a hacker may be attempting to compromise security. Corrective controls correct security holes that have been exploited—for example, installing a service pack that is known to fix existing issues.

IT Security controls are vehicles for meeting IT Security objectives. Table 1-2 lists the IT Security controls, including their descriptions and the corporate IT Security objectives to which they correlate.

**Table 1-2. IT Security Controls**

| IT Security Controls | IT Security Controls Description | IT Security Objectives |
| --- | --- | --- |
| Ability to Recover from Operational Failure | Controls should be in place to ensure business operations continue if the systems should go down or Availability is disrupted due to natural or other disasters. | Availability |
| Manage Security Effectively | Controls should be in place to ensure system security is being managed and maintained correctly. Controls that may be implemented include developing a security policy and procedures that help employees understand security. | Confidentiality, Integrity, and Availability |
| Monitor Security Effectively | Controls should be in place to monitor whether a secure computer environment is maintained. These | Confidentiality, Integrity, and Availability |

*(continued)*

**Table 1-2.**  *(continued)*

| IT Security Controls | IT Security Controls Description | IT Security Objectives |
| --- | --- | --- |
| | controls will help senior management determine whether steps have been taken to secure the systems. Good controls include violation and exception reports that help management determine at-a-glance whether their systems are being compromised. | |
| Secure All External and Internal Network Connections | Controls should be in place to prevent these external network connections from undermining system security. All network connections should be secured to ensure data is secured on the system and the network it traverses. | Confidentiality and Integrity |
| Secure Physical Access to All Critical Systems | Controls should be in place to ensure physical access to computer facilities and data are appropriately restricted. | Confidentiality and Integrity |
| Secure the System | Controls should be in place to make sure that all access to the computer system, programs, and data is appropriately restricted. | Confidentiality |

# IT Security Controls and Windows NT Security Features

When the corporate IT Security objectives are defined and the IT Security controls needed to achieve these objectives are understood, you may be asking yourself, What are the security controls in Windows NT and how do I implement them?

Windows NT has many security features, options, and configurations. Trying to understand or implement all of them can be a daunting task for any systems administrator. However, by focusing on the controls, a systems administrator can understand and implement Windows NT Security features in a systematic way.

For example, to ensure confidentiality, a systems administrator may want to implement System Security controls—or all the controls that ensure access to the computer system, programs, and data is appropriately restricted. Within Windows NT, this may entail such tasks as ensuring that proper groups are created, implementing the Windows NT File System (NTFS), providing appropriate file permissions, or granting proper user access rights.

For Enright Bank, the systems administrator may want to ensure availability and implement the controls of recovery from operational failure. To meet this objective, the systems administrator may implement a fault tolerance strategy, such as disk mirroring, and implement a backup strategy that includes a full backup one time per week. The backup strategy may also focus on the Registry, which is NT's database of all system information

Many books on the market describe how to implement Windows NT features. However, these features are not organized in any way. In this book, we organize the features by IT Security controls and recommend how to implement them. The structure of this book and the security recommendations conveyed within the material will help the systems administrator ensure that security meets the overall business objective.

# Chapter 2
# A Typical Environment of Windows NT Implementations

Windows NT Server and Workstation have been implemented in a variety of configurations for a number of different uses in the corporate computing environment. It is unlikely that two corporations will have identical Windows NT implementations and for this reason, it is often hard to provide "cookie-cutter" security configuration recommendations. Depending on the Windows NT implementation, different security features or security controls will be utilized to protect the environment. This chapter illustrates the most common Windows NT implementations we have come across.

We provide these common Windows NT implementations and refer to them throughout the book to illustrate various security controls that can be implemented through Windows NT Security features.

For the purpose of this book, we have created a fictional corporation, Fecha, based in Springfield, Colorado. Fecha manufactures and distributes the web widget, a useful tool in computer system repair and operation. Fecha has eight locations within the United States and Canada as well as operations in the United Kingdom and South America. All of its facilities are connected with a high-speed private network. All of the facilities run Windows NT as the principal local Network Operating System (NOS). Each facility has an internal LAN with routed connections to the other locations.

Although Fecha is a fictional corporation, the network structure described here is based on actual experience with our clients. From the domain model to the described functional uses of the servers and workstations, all descriptions are based on actual implementations that we have seen or security controls that we have reviewed. They are derived from many different client implementations and have been synthesized into this one fictitious corporate entity.

The Windows NT implementation at Fecha is based on the master domain model: The headquarters location operates the master domain, while each of the other installations operates a local resource domain that has a trust relationship established with the headquarters master domain as shown in Figure 2-1. The remaining sections in this chapter will continue to explain the diagram found in Figure 2-1.

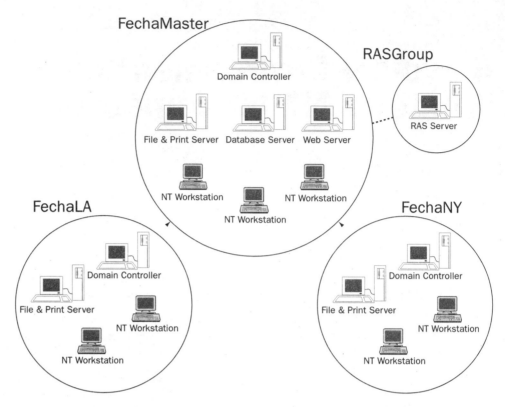

**Figure 2-1**. *How Fecha organized its domain structure for their United States operations*

Each Windows NT server at Fecha runs version 4.0 with Service Pack 3 installed on x86-based machines. Each of the servers has several of the post-SP3 hot fixes installed depending on their usage and implementation on the network.

## Domain Controller

Domain controllers serve two purposes in the Windows NT environment: to authenticate users and grant them access to other resources within the network, thus meeting the authorization objective. Several instances of domain controllers are implemented at Fecha. The master domain, FechaMaster, contains 11 domain controllers. One functions as the *primary domain controller (PDC)* and is the computer where all account information is created and controlled; this account information is stored in the User Account database. The other 10 domain controllers, known as *backup domain controllers (BDC)*, are installed at each corporate location and provide local authentication services for users at those locations. These controllers contain replicated copies of the User Account database from the PDC. Although they are physically located in many different locations, they all belong to the master domain.

Each site within Fecha hosts a local resource domain. Each local resource domain requires a domain controller to manage any accounts created within the domain. Any account created on the local resource domain's controller is not a master domain account. Each local resource domain has a trusting relationship with the master domain in Springfield. Each local resource domain, such as the FechaLA domain in Figure 2-1, supports local application servers that may be used by users resident at that location or by users that work within the corporation.

Domain controllers, as a general rule, should not be running any other applications than those described in this section. It is best to restrict a domain controller from running any other software because it contains extremely sensitive user information that is used for authorization purposes. If applications are run on the domain controller, the controller may be exposed due to the lack of security controls within the application. However, in our experience, we often see corporations running applications on the domain controllers, rather than on a dedicated application server. This choice is usually due to budgeting and resource constraints.

## File and Print Member Server

Each domain within the Fecha environment provides file and print services for the users at each location. Each user authenticating to the master domain is provided a home directory share for their daily work. This directory exists on a file server in the master domain if they work in the Springfield headquarters. Users resident at Fecha locations outside of Springfield receive their home directory share at a file server within their local resource domain. The individual home directory shares are set up as hidden shares (shares that have a $ symbol at the end of the share name) and are secured by assigning permissions for the user to have full control rights over the shared directory. Fecha home directory shares are always mapped to the H drive on any user station.

Users who only authenticate to the local resource domain receive their home directory share on the file server in their local domain. All the security controls governing the home directory for master domain users apply to these local domain users as well, including share permissions and backup policy.

Each file server also contains group folder shares. These are made available to users based on group membership and are mapped during the logon process. Individual user permissions in these shares are set at the Change level RWXD for folders and files. Specific files within the folders may be set at lesser permission levels. Group shares are typically mapped to drives I through L.

User home directories and group share directories are backed up nightly in the domain where they reside.

The file server in each domain controls the printer queues for that domain. Each user is mapped to three printer queues upon logging in to the network. Queue assignment is based on the user's group membership and physical location.

The typical file and print server is a rather fast processing computer system with ample amounts of disk space available for storage of data. To protect the data from loss, recoverability controls (such as disk mirroring or Redundant Array of Inexpensive Disks (RAID)) should be implemented.

## Application Server: Web Server

There is one web server installed at Fecha: an intranet server located in the master domain. Fecha's intranet is available to all authenticated domain users from the master domain. Users who have only authenticated to a local resource domain may access the Intranet server as well, by means of the anonymous user account.

The internal web site contains information regarding corporate policies and procedures, marketing information, employee benefit guides, and other relevant information. Future plans include employee access to their savings and pension plan information. The internal web server runs the Web Publishing service only. It uses Internet Information Server (IIS) 4.0. All users' workstations run Internet Explorer 4.01 as their active web browser.

## Application Server: Database Server

A database server at Fecha used to support several different types of applications. The typical database server at Fecha runs the SQL Server 6.5 product integrated with Windows NT Security. As with the file and print server, the ability to process long transactions rapidly and the capability to store large volumes of data is critical. To protect the data from loss, the disk should be mirrored or be part of a RAID array.

## Application Server: Remote Access Server

Fecha allows employees to access certain resources while traveling away from their offices. The principal uses for this methodology are accessing mail systems for sending and receiving messages, to provide certain users access to their data, and for system support when the administrative staff is offsite or the needs are after normal business hours. There are a number of security controls and implementations of Remote Access Server (RAS). We describe a few here, but there are even more expounded in Chapter 6, "Securing All External and Internal Network Connections."

Fecha has one implementation of the Remote Access Server as a workgroup member RAS server in a segregated workgroup, RASGROUP. This server's dial-in access number is provided to those members of the user community who travel for business and who are authorized to send and receive mail while outside the office. Other users, such as the marketing department, are given access to market analysis tools.

Users who have been granted dial-in access to the RAS server must authenticate to the machine upon making their connection. After authentication, the login script and user policy files for remote access take over and restrict the user's access to the mail server. The policy is based on the assigned TCP/IP address of the connecting machine, which is recognized as being from outside the internal network. There is a limited predefined pool of external TCP/IP addresses that is used, along with a limited pool of modems, to restrict the number of concurrent remote access users. The RAS server is configured to support the Microsoft Challenge Handshake Authentication Protocol (MS-CHAP), which is an encrypted login protocol, and the encrypted sessions. The callback feature is enabled for those traveling users who only use one standard remote location.

## Workstation

Fecha has chosen to implement the Windows NT Workstation for its standard user desktop environment. All workstations are implemented using NT Workstation 4.0 with Service Pack 3. All workstations are configured as members of the master domain because all users are required to authenticate to it. In certain locations, some workstations are defined as members of the local resource domain, because the specific connecting users or the applications accessed from the workstations do not require access to the master domain.

To provide stronger security controls, no local user accounts outside of the built-in administrator and guest accounts are defined on the workstations. All user authentication processing occurs on a domain controller. After logon, user access to the local workstation is severely limited through the use of Windows NT policies. It should be noted that we usually observe user accounts on a workstation, although they are not needed and do not provide any benefit.

These policies are defined to control what a user can do on the local workstation and also control the look and feel of the desktop. Based on the user's group definitions, applets will appear on the desktop for use during the current session. These policies also control the mapping of the shared network drives, including the home directory and any group shares.

# Chapter 3
# Effective Security Management

*Effective security management* is an important security control that is usually overlooked. This control ensures that system security is being managed and maintained correctly. Some good controls that may be implemented include developing corporate security policies and procedures that help employees understand security.

*Effective security management* is also made up of intangible controls, such as having a good corporate security culture and security training. Many corporations do not take the time to generate reports such as Windows NT audit logs, or if they do, no one has the time to review them. They also do not take the time to train or create security awareness. However, many security risks occur because of misinformation, lack of knowledge by the employees, and carelessness with confidential information. These security risks can be mitigated with the proper security management, which we often see lacking at corporations. The following section describes some security controls and recommendations that we advise clients of to help them achieve security management effectively.

## Approach to Developing Corporate Security Culture

An important piece of effective security management is what we like to call *corporate security culture*. The security culture of a corporation includes many layers and defines security for the corporation. A corporate security culture includes a corporate security policy that defines the assets of a corporation, risks to those assets, owners of the assets, and how to protect those assets. It also includes creating security awareness among employees and having senior management support.

Many times we see corporations that fail in their security endeavors for the same reason: They have not created a corporate security culture. Because the corporate security culture entails intangibles such as security awareness, many times the corporate security culture is overlooked or deemed wasteful and unnecessary. However, this is an important part of security, which will help ensure that the security is being managed throughout the corporation and to one area where we usually suggest improvement. Windows NT security features, by themselves, are not sufficient controls and must be coupled with a good corporate security policy.

## Corporate Security Policy

Security is made of policy and system controls. Security policies must be established and documented before systems can be configured in order to achieve the best security possible. A *corporate security policy* not only embodies the security needs of the corporation, but it also lays out the framework under which the entire corporation treats and reacts to attacks on its resources. The purpose of a corporate security policy is to inform employees of the corporation's regard for security, the standards to abide by, and the procedures to use to keep up security. A solid corporate security policy both reflects and helps to define your entire corporate security culture.

In the development of such a document, the input of several voices should be considered and a team should be established for the writing of its content. These tasks will help to ensure proper coverage of content. They will also empower those who will have to follow the stated guidelines. Members of the development team should include the management from each functional area, the representatives from the audit department, the systems programming area, the applications programming area, the legal arena, and the human resources department.

The corporate security policy consists of several security policies, all of which should include the following:

- Mission Statement
- Objectives and Scope
- Definition of Assets
- Analysis of Threats to Your Assets (Risk Assessment)
- Protection of and Values Placed on the Assets
- Awareness of and Commitment to the Policies Created to Protect the Assets
- Management and Review of the Security Policies

### Mission Statement

A corporate security mission statement, which summarizes the corporation's overall security values, is an important part of the corporate security policy. A good corporate security mission statement should include general broad-based security information for the corporation, information on how security supports the overall business objectives, and management's regard for security.

### Objectives and Scope

The corporate security policy should include the objectives and scope of the policy. This inclusion will clearly document what and whom the policy affects and the reasons why the policy was written.

## Definition of Assets

The term *assets* should be applied in its broad sense to mean anything that is of value and needed for the operation of the corporation. This application will most likely include tangible objects such as people, computer hardware, and data, but it may also include intangible elements such as a business process and your corporation's working environment or reputation.

Although this step is probably the easiest to complete in the development of a corporate security policy (and the easiest to overlook), it is nonetheless an extremely important first step. Unless a corporation agreement (as to what is important for the corporation) and a listing of all that should be protected is reached, the final policy will be incomplete and will not reflect the entire operating culture of the corporation.

Upon completion, your list of assets should be a constant reference point as you decide what is important to protect and how it should be protected. Although this seems simple enough, experience with our clients has repeatedly shown that a corporation's security policy is usually defined by their current technology. In many cases, a corporate security policy is defined and written down only after the IT department has discovered a problem and implemented a solution. This method leads to an ad-hoc type of policy development and does not achieve the goal of a strong corporate security policy, which is to protect a corporation's valuable assets and clarify the rights and responsibilities of users with regard to those assets.

This list will, therefore, help to ensure that all assets are considered in the development of a corporate security policy and that technology does not define your policy, but rather is defined as an asset itself and as a possible tool for the protection of your other valuable assets.

## Threats to Your Assets

As every corporation is different in the types of services or goods it provides, so are the risks and threats it faces. An example would be that of national defense applications or fund transfer systems in financial institutions. These examples of systems are at greater risk, from a wider array of threats, and would require a higher degree of security than an order-entry system in a small business. However, all corporations have the same basic need: the protection and effective use of the entity's assets to help ensure the continued successful operation of the corporation's business.

Although it is generally agreed that threats do exist and that measures must be taken to protect against them, it is also well accepted that these security measures can be expensive and if not properly controlled, crippling. Careful consideration must be given to weighing the importance of an asset, the risks that threaten the asset, and the security measures that will provide for a sufficient level of protection for the asset. This consideration is usually made through a risk assessment. A risk assessment is a crucial piece of your corporate security policy.

## Risk Assessment

Risk assessment is the measurement of exposure to possible harm or loss. Risk is not always easy to define, as the threat could be from a variety of sources, including market forces, disgruntled employees, competitors, or one's own inefficient/outdated processes. When analyzing threats, it is often important to remember that they can easily come from within, as well as external to the corporation such as through a network or modem connection.

Major actions to consider in assessing and managing risk are identifying and ranking the assets of the corporation. These assets should include the critical systems and data that the corporation deems necessary to operate the business. Without these critical systems, the corporation may face financial failure. For example, the accounting and financial applications of the funds transfer system have a higher rate of criticality than the employee name and address database. From this analysis, you can begin to rank the importance and criticality of all the assets. After the assets are defined, as described earlier, the following steps can be taken to rank their importance:

1. All assets should be assessed for all the possible vulnerabilities that can be exploited and the probability of their exploitation. These vulnerabilities should range from the generic to the consideration of unique attacks against specific types of systems or processes. Within the Windows NT environment, common threats would include unauthorized access (usually as a result of a poor password policy), denial-of-service type attacks, and disclosure of information (usually through poor/default access control settings). Additionally, given the importance (and exposure) of networks, a proper study of network vulnerabilities for all platforms should be conducted.

2. In this step, you begin by assuming the worst. If an asset has been exploited, what are the possible resulting costs to operation, reputation, and competitiveness? The purpose of this step is merely to identify and reenforce which assets are critical, and lay out the consequences and costs that may result from an exploited vulnerability. From this, one can begin to sort assets from the most important to the least important, and sort exploits from the most dangerous/costly to the least dangerous/costly.

3. Assets need to be assessed for the corporation's viable protection mechanisms against the most probable or common type of vulnerabilities (that is, viable steps to take that will minimize risk). Special attention should be placed on the word *viable*, as the protection mechanism must not only be technologically feasible, but also enforceable. If a protection mechanism goes against a corporation's culture, then either workers will be disgruntled or, as is most often the case, the resulting corporate security policy will be ignored. To be viable, the protection mechanisms must fit smoothly into a corporation's security culture and must be transparent, which is possible with many Windows NT type controls, or a conscious effort to modify the corporation security culture must be made.

The resulting data generated from the major risk assessment steps can be mapped into a matrix. This will simply and graphically present the universe of options available to the corporation, as illustrated in Table 3-1.

**Table 3-1. Sample of a Corporate Risk Assessment Matrix**

| Critical Applications | Vulnerabilities/ Probability of Occurring | Viable Solutions |
|---|---|---|
| General Ledger | Data Forging/.80 | Access controls using Windows NT NTFS and share permissions |
| | | Audit trails using Windows NT audit trails |
| | Floods/.75 | Raised floor in computer room |
| | Earthquake/.45 | Not probable |
| Order Entry | Input Error/.90 | Field checks |
| | Data Forging/.80 | Independent reconciliation Windows NT access controls |
| | Floods/.75 | Raised floor in computer room |
| | Earthquake/.45 | Not probable |
| Accounts Receivable | Data Forging/.80 | Independent reconciliation Windows NT access controls |
| | Floods/.75 | Raised floor in computer room |
| | Earthquake/.45 | Not probable |

Engaging in this risk assessment exercise will help to identify high-risk assets, the likelihood of vulnerability occurring in the high-risk assets, and the possible methods of preventing, detecting, or correcting these vulnerabilities.

Although we realize that assessing all vulnerabilities and possible solutions can be a daunting task, we hope that the main body of this book will provide you with the necessary knowledge and tools to easily make this assessment for the Windows NT 4.0 environment.

## Cost/Benefit Analysis

Protecting against security vulnerabilities can be costly. The cost of security is not only measured in financial terms, but also in reduced performance, increased management, administrative overhead, and possible user aggravation.

When a corporation has mapped protection options available for its security risks, a cost/benefit analysis can be conducted. Using the previously built matrix, a corporation can assess the cost of each possible protection mechanism. A fourth column should be added to the matrix, which contains the monetary cost of implementing the option. This cost should include software purchases and training classes, as well as other opportunity costs such as increased management time and lost productivity.

Finally, a fifth column should be added to the matrix that assesses the long-term benefits of implementing the options. The benefits should be measured in dollars and should include such gains as continuous productivity, and efficiency and accuracy of critical data. It should also include intangible rewards such as increased competitive advantage, positive corporate reputation, and high user morale. Factored into this matrix should also be the benefit of retaining the asset and its integrity. Table 3-2 provides an example.

**Table 3-2. Example of a Corporate Risk Assessment and Cost/Benefit Analysis**

| Critical Applications | Vulnerabilities/ Probability of Occurring | Viable Solutions | Cost ($) | Benefit ($) |
|---|---|---|---|---|
| General Ledger | Data Forging/.80 | Windows NT access controls | 100K | 500K |
| | | Windows NT audit trails | | |
| | Floods/.75 | Raised floor in computer room | 50K | 250K |
| | Earthquake/.45 | Not probable | 0 | 0 |
| Order Entry | Input Error/.90 | Field checks | 50K | 100K |
| | Data Forging/.80 | Independent reconciliation | 50K | 500K |
| | | Windows NT access controls | | |
| | Floods/.75 | Raised floor in computer room | 50K | 250K |
| | Earthquake/.45 | Not probable | 0 | 0 |
| Accounts Receivable | Data Forging/.80 | Independent reconciliation | 50K | 500K |
| | | Windows NT access controls | | |
| | Floods/.75 | Raised floor in computer room | 50K | 250K |
| | Earthquake/.45 | Not probable | 0 | 0 |

Although the preceding discussion on cost/benefit analysis and risk assessment tools is brief, it does point out that these tools are the primary tools by which a corporation can assess and manage risk. Numerous management books and guidelines exist within this area of study, and it is beyond the scope of this book to examine it much further. However, an accurate summary and rule of thumb would be that one should never *spend more on protecting an asset than what the asset is worth*—where cost and worth are measured by tangible, as well as intangible, matrix.

## Protection and Values

With the data gathered from the previous steps, and the analysis performed, we are now ready to formulate a working corporate security policy to address the following:

- Asset Owners
- Roles and Responsibilities
- Procedures
- Security Standards
- Employee Rights and Responsibilities

When moving forward in the draft of your policy, it is important to realize that there will always be exceptions to a policy rule. However, rather than ignoring this fact, it would be far more advisable to include the exceptions simply as part of the policy. In this way, the level of risk associated with the exception is known and properly managed.

### Asset Owners

Every asset should have a clearly defined owner (either an individual position or group) that is both responsible and accountable for that asset. The owner should be fully aware of the rights and responsibilities with regard to that asset, and all policies pertaining to its use.

In addition to the data owner, the policy should state the groups or individuals that require access to the asset in order to complete their job functions. Furthermore, access should be controlled, if possible, to allow only the level of access needed for that person or group to complete their tasks.

For example, within the Windows NT environment, access control is accomplished primarily through physical security, share security, authentication controls, effective group definitions, and the setting of file and directory permissions using shares and NTFS. The last two points are particularly important, since our experience has repeatedly shown that clients fail to limit access to key directories, and instead keep the default permission settings on all directories. The result of this accomplishment is that data classified as an asset is not being protected. The establishment of data owners and access controls would help to alleviate this risk.

### Roles and Responsibilities

Clear roles and responsibilities should be defined and documented. A Security Administration group, whose purpose is to maintain and monitor security, should be established. The roles and responsibilities of any user involved in security should also be documented.

### Procedures

Security procedures are the formal steps to be taken by employees to abide by security policies. For example, because roles and responsibilities are constantly changing within a corporation, clearly defined procedures for the granting of and removal of access rights must be established for your assets. An access right procedure is especially helpful when new employees are brought on or, even more importantly, when employees leave the corporation. We see this situation far too often with our clients, as system administrators are constantly bothered to quickly grant access to new users, and at they same time they are the last to know when an employee has left the corporation.

To effectively combat this situation, a well-defined and accepted policy (with its accompanying procedures) needs to be put into place. For example, a policy regarding the granting of new users their necessary access rights could be as follows: All new system users should be authorized users with access that is commensurate with their job responsibilities. To maintain this policy, procedures, such as providing users with log-on IDs and appropriate rights, need to be developed. These procedures might include the following steps:

1. User completes a System User Access form and submits to his or her supervisor.
2. User's supervisor indicates, on the form, the appropriate level of access depending on the user's job responsibilities.
3. User's supervisor signs the form and submits the form to the security officer.
4. Security officer creates the ID in the system, granting the user the necessary access rights as requested.

If these procedures are diligently followed, the corporation can be assured that authorized users accessing the system have access rights that are commensurate with their job responsibilities. In addition, an audit trail has also been created so that all users can be traced back to an original User Access form. Having the supervisor sign off on the form has also created accountability.

If any exceptions exist, they must be clearly spelled out with the necessary reasons for performing the exception provided. This step is to ensure that exceptions do not become the "norm," and that the integrity of the corporate security policy is maintained.

Policies should be far more stringent, with few (if any) exceptions, when granting administrator or administrator equivalent rights. These individuals have the power to grant or remove all access rights that the end user will possess. Without stringent security controls (such as limiting access to the Administrator account), all protection obtained in the preceding policy will be lost. Therefore, as always, administrator-type accounts need to be granted to as few trusted individuals as possible. Within Windows NT, domain administrators have access to the entire system and must be fully and completely trusted.

## Security Standards

After a person has been granted access to an asset, the proper usage of that asset must be clearly identified by standards. The goals of this section are to inform the end user what constitutes an abuse of the asset and to encourage efficient usage. These goals are most often achieved through the statement and enactment of standards, which often include such areas as application, system, hardware, network, remote access, and Internet security standards.

As in many areas of a corporate security policy, the needs of security must be weighed against the requirements of usability and openness. This is particularly true in the area of security standards, where standards are often considered as ideals that the corporation is to work towards but are counterproductive in getting the job done. We have often seen this attitude in the field, with the resulting negative impact that the overall strength and response to all the security standards is weakened. The result of viewing standards as ideals is that people do not believe that the standards are truly in effect either today or in the future.

This effect can be minimized through careful preparation. It is important in the development of a security standard to ensure that it does not go against the working environment and culture of the corporation. Standards that do so will fail. After the elements of the security standard are developed, they should be graded based on the importance of protecting the asset and clear penalties assigned for employees who disregard the standard. This grading will clarify to the employees the risks (and possible costs) they take in disregarding a security standard, and will spell out the possible consequences to them of those actions.

For example, a security standard might state that remote access to computer resources may only be done through properly approved and secured corporation-provided facilities. However, the definition of the standard may not be enough in preventing employees from attaching personal modems to their machines, unless they are also aware of the security risk that they have now personally placed on the corporation's entire network.

### Defining Employee Rights and Responsibilities

A corporate security policy should describe the rights of every employee, based on the use of a corporation asset to which they have been granted access. Specifically, the corporation must make clear the personal and privacy rights the individual has in the use of corporation assets.

The last part of the corporate security policy concerns itself with the responsibilities of every employee in the use and operation of corporation assets. Security procedures must be followed in order to ensure the protection and continued safe operation of the corporation's assets.

This last point is key, because we often find that a corporation will fail to address the need of having procedures to help ensure that the corporation's asset will be protected into the future, as well as the present. This does not simply mean that a goal of rewriting the security procedures every six months should be made, but rather that consideration should be given to developing procedures that are effective in the long run, as well as the short run.

For example, it is well known that operating systems are frequently open to new forms of attack and that vendors periodically release fixes to patch these security weaknesses. However, we have rarely seen a procedure to address this all-too-common issue. Ideally, it would be the responsibility of an appropriate staff member to regularly review operating system patches, to decide on the appropriateness of implementing the fix (the risk of not implementing it), and to test the fix before moving it out into production. Above all, the individual would be responsible for documenting the entire process to help ensure that the current level of security and risk to the assets is known and acceptable for the corporation.

## Awareness and Commitment

Awareness and senior management commitment to a secure environment are social-based controls that equal the importance of the previously presented controls. Awareness and senior management commitment can prevent security risks due to misinformation, lack of employee knowledge, and carelessness.

### Creating Security Awareness

It is important that the users are aware of and follow the developed security policies. Security policies and procedures are useless if not practiced. Policies can sometimes be more of a burden to follow, and it may be easier to circumvent the procedures in order to complete the job. However, this practice also circumvents the purpose of the policies, which is to protect your assets. This phenomenon emphasizes the importance that users realize their responsibilities in adhering to the policies, and the consequences that may result if they do not.

Users should be provided a booklet or manual that outlines both general security policies and the procedures that are specific to their job function. In addition, training should be given to the users so that they are not only aware of the policies and procedures, but also understand their purposes. Training will ensure they have the requisite knowledge, while the booklet or manual will be available for reference purposes. Users should sign off, indicating that they have received the booklet and the training, and that they understand their responsibilities for security and the implications of not adhering to the policies and procedures.

One-time training is not enough to ensure compliance with the security policies. At a minimum, regular general security seminars should be offered to and attended by all employees. Employees who have security-related functions, should attend intensive security seminars. In addition, periodic distributions of security updates should be distributed to employees.

To further ensure compliance and awareness, security requirements and management's expectations of the employee could also be included as an integral part of the performance evaluation process for each employee.

### Senior Management Commitment

Awareness of security policies is not always sufficient to gain user compliance. An important factor in effective security management and gaining compliance is senior management's commitment to the policies. If the employee feels security is important to the corporation, it will become important to them. Therefore, management of security must start by showing management's commitment to security.

As with any corporate-wide policy, if senior management does not commit to providing support, it will most likely fail. The risk assessment and cost/benefit analysis steps (described in previous sections) will assist senior management in understanding and committing to the benefits of security. Ideally, senior management can even be involved in the initial steps of asset definition, risk assessment, and the cost/benefit analysis. This commitment can then be permeated throughout the corporation by having senior management sign off on the corporate security policy manual, attend the security training with all the employees, and continually communicate the policy's goals and importance through periodic security memos distributed to all employees.

## Management and Review

Management and review of the security environment is essential to ensuring the procedures are implemented and followed. These controls are often the vehicle for closing the gap between standards and ideals.

### Managing Security

To aid in the process of awareness, training, and overall management of security policies, a functional security group should be created. The security group's main responsibilities would include the implementing, developing, and monitoring of the corporation's security policies. The security group should not report to the programming group, the CIO or CFO, but instead to a department where no conflict of interest is possible, such as the risk management group. The security officer whose only responsibility is to manage corporate security should head the security group. This placement ensures that the security group will implement and enforce all necessary controls without fear of any repercussion.

Depending on the size of the corporation, the security group could be anywhere from one part-time person to a whole department. Roles and responsibilities for this position should be clearly defined, otherwise there is a high risk that controls may not be either implemented or enforced. In addition, clear roles and responsibilities will provide for accountability.

### Monitoring Security

One of the key tasks of the security group will be to monitor the progress and effectiveness of the security policies. Additionally, the group would be responsible for performing high-level reviews of the security policies in place to ensure compliance with the documented standard.

The importance of this role cannot be overstated. Because policies are a compromise between absolute security and the openness needed for people to complete their jobs, monitoring must be employed to ensure that this openness is not being abused or taken advantage of. Furthermore, effective monitoring will help to ensure that policies are not being circumvented by weaknesses in the technology you have employed in implementing your policies.

We would suggest that the security group focus on reviewing the audit logs using automated tools and creating automatic alarms to aid in this process. For example, the Windows NT Performance Monitor can send alerts to the security officer to warn him of suspicious behavior. More often than not, clients either do not keep logs or they keep extensive logs that are rarely reviewed. Automating this process, and clearly defining the roles and responsibilities based on audit logs and alarms, will help to guarantee that the log files are being used effectively in the protection of your assets.

**Policy Development**

A corporate security policy manual is not a static document that can be written once, distributed, and then forgotten. Nor is it guaranteed to be the most effective or efficient means of securing your assets from the first implementation. A corporate security policy is a dynamic document that needs to evolve, expand, and transform with the business and technology. The group responsible for creating the policy should conduct a regular review of the corporate security policy manual. Any changes in the business strategy, such as reorganization or addition of new systems, should be reflected in the security policy. Reviews of this document should be conducted approximately every six months.

Although the preceding text serves as a guideline to the development of controls and policies for the protection of your assets, there are many additional sources of information to help you in this process.

# Legal Notice

Another important part of effective security management that many corporations tend to overlook is the legal notice. The *legal notice* is the message that appears whenever a user logs on the system. It warns that only authorized users may access the system and that they are being monitored. The legal notice is an important control that will strengthen security management in many ways. First, it provides the employees with a general security awareness. Seeing the notice every time they sign on reinforces the notion that security and confidentiality is extremely important to the corporation. Second, the legal notice strengthens the legal liability of individuals who may attempt to access a system without authorization. Some corporations have been hacked into and were unable to prosecute because instead of a legal notice, they had a welcome banner.

In Windows NT, the feature displays a message when the Secure Attention Sequence is invoked (Ctrl+Alt+Delete is pressed at logon). This feature requires the user to acknowledge the notice by clicking the OK button in the message box before continuing. The Legal Notice message box contains a corporation-specific message and caption.

Implementing this control and enabling the legal notice is an easy security control that makes a big difference. The legal notice is set through the Registry Editor or System Policy Editor.

Choose Start ➪ Run, type **REGEDT32.EXE** in the open field, and then click OK to run the Registry Editor. The legal notice is defined under the following keys:

| Registry Key | Value |
|---|---|
| HKLM\Software\Microsoft\WindowsNT\CurrentVersion\ Winlogon\LegalNoticeCaption | "Legal Notice" or "Warning" or other acceptable heading |
| HKLM\Software\Microsoft\WindowsNT\CurrentVersion\ Winlogon\LegalNoticeText | Approved Message |

The Windows NT legal notice is available to Windows NT users logging on to a workstation or Windows NT Server console. All other network users should receive the warning message by way of the log-on script.

The Legal Notice message must include a statement about being a proprietary system (such as, unauthorized access is prohibited) and that the network is monitored. A typical message is as follows:

"You have connected to a monitored proprietary system. Only authorized users may access this system. Access by unauthorized individuals is prohibited."

Remember that these changes will not take effect until the system is restarted. Also, be sure to update the Emergency Repair Disk after making changes to the Registry.

As stated earlier, an important reason for having a warning banner is more for legal precedence in the event that an unauthorized user tries to gain access. Previous criminal proceedings have used the "excuse" that the "...screen said welcome." This is simply another level of precaution, although not fully a means of prosecuting a hacker in any case. With a welcome message, the courts may uphold a hacker's attack on your system. The Electronics Communications Privacy Act (ECPA) prevents you from eavesdropping on the activities of an intruder, even if you own the system, unless you post a message to indicate that all activities are subject to being monitored. So warning messages should be displayed whenever possible.

# Understanding C2

C2 is a security evaluation level assigned to a specific product by the National Computer Security Center (NCSC), a division of the National Security Association (NSA), after a period of detailed product review and attestation. The C2 level of "trust" is one level that can be granted to an evaluated product. The defined levels of trust, in increasing levels of trust (or security), are D, C1, C2, B1, B2, B3, and A1. All of these trust ratings are defined in a document entitled the "Trusted Network Interpretation (TNI)," also known as the "Red Book." You can find more information about C2 certification on the National Computer Security Center's (NCSC) web page, http://www.radium.ncsc.mil/tpep/index.html.

## Is Windows NT C2 Compliant?

As of August 1995, Windows NT 3.5 (both server and workstation), with Service Pack 3, passed the C2-level evaluation process as a stand-alone system. The network components in Windows NT 3.5 were not evaluated, and Windows NT 4.0 is still under evaluation.

Windows NT 3.5, with Service Pack 3, has passed the Orange Book criteria for C2 evaluation. Windows NT 4.0 is currently being evaluated in a configuration with full network support.

More information on the specification requirements of the Windows NT 3.5 evaluation process are available in the Final Evaluation Report (FER) for Windows NT, accessible on the NCSC web site.

Windows NT 3.51 has also passed the European Commission's Information Technology Security Evaluation Criteria (ITSEC), or an F-C2/E3 rating. This rating is similar to the NCSC's class rating C2. Information on the ITSEC can be found on the Internet by searching for "Information Technology Security Evaluation Criteria" with a major Internet search engine.

## Making Windows NT C2 Certified

When considering the C2 evaluation level, or any other trust rating, one must consider the relevance and effectiveness of the security rating to the desired IT Security objectives. The C2 rating may or may not fully meet a corporation's security needs; in general, it does not. In either case, a trust rating is but one part of an effective security policy—as emphasized throughout this book—that must include such things as physical security, operational controls, monitoring procedures, and continued maintenance.

However, the fact that the underlying security and system architecture of the Windows NT platform has been evaluated to meet C2 criteria is certainly a valuable element in the trust needed to develop a secure operating platform.

In practice, it would be impractical and unnecessary for most corporations to install Windows NT in a C2-compliant node. One reason is because the Windows NT 3.5 evaluation did not include networking components.

# Chapter 4
# Effective Security Monitoring

Controls should be in place to monitor whether a secure computer environment is maintained. These controls will help upper management determine whether steps have been taken to secure the systems. Some good controls include violation and exception reports that help management determine, at a glance, whether their systems are being compromised. Many times, corporations run reports that log violations; however, running these reports in itself does not satisfy this control. Either the report is gathering too much information, the proper violations are not being filtered, or no one is reviewing the reports.

These reports are another set of controls that help mitigate security risks throughout the corporation, but we often see them overlooked. Windows NT has the capability to log a great deal of information. The ability to log a lot of information is very good, however, sometimes too much information is logged and not analyzed properly. This section lists the monitoring and auditing tool that should be utilized, the data that should be gathered, and the information that should be analyzed.

## Performance Monitor

You can use the Windows NT Performance Monitor to monitor system performance, to gather vital information on system statistics, and to analyze and graphically display information. In addition, Performance Monitor can be configured to alert systems administrators when certain events occur. *Alerts* are critical security controls that help perform real-time monitoring. Instead of reviewing a violation report once a week and finding a security breach after the fact, alerts warn a systems administrator of a potential security violation.

Windows NT Performance Monitor utility tracks objects such as processors, memory, cache, threads, processes, and services running on the Windows NT Server. Every object has counters that keep track of specific events or activities. The Performance Monitor may be used to monitor selected security-related events. The counters' data can either be gathered and monitored over a long period of time for analysis or tracked for certain values.

Performance Monitor provides a variety of ways to view the information that is gathered for analysis. The four different types of viewing options are as follows:

- Chart
- Alert
- Log
- Report

To start the Performance Monitor control, choose Start ⇨ Programs ⇨ Administrative Tools ⇨ Performance Monitor. The Performance Monitor screen is launched.

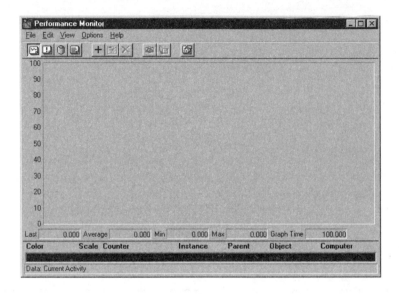

## Chart View

You will want to build charts in order to collect data related to the performance of the objects you select. This allows you to analyze the data in real time. To begin building charts, choose Edit ⇨ Add to Chart.

The fields within the dialog box are described in Table 4-1.

**Table 4-1. Chart Options**

| Fields | Description |
|---|---|
| Computer | Choose a computer to track. You can monitor the performance of any computer in the network. |
| Object | Choose an object to track. Each object has its own set of counters. |
| Counter | For each object, choose the specific event or activity you want to track. |
| Instance | Some object types have several instances. For example, the processor object type will have multiple instances if a system has multiple processors. Some object types, such as Memory and Server, do not have instances. If an object type has multiple instances, each instance may be used with the same set of counters. The data is then tracked for each instance. |

On the right side of the dialog box is the Explain button. Click this button to display the lower Counter Definition field. The Counter Definition field explains what each counter is measuring so you can determine if you need to add it to your chart. Click Add to start tracking the event on the chart. You can continue to add other events or click Done to close the dialog box.

Charts are important and should be used for monitoring performance, especially on highly critical machines. For example, at Fecha Manufacturing Corporation, we would recommend more chart views of system performance monitors on the database server. Choose Logical Disk ⇨ % Free Space to monitor hard drive space and ensure that the database does not get full and crash the system. Fecha should also implement Memory ⇨ Available Bytes to ensure that physical memory is not too low and to avoid possible system crashes.

## Alert View

Alerts track certain events and warn systems administrators when they occur. Choose View ⇨ Alert to get to the Alert screen. Choose Edit ⇨ Add to Alert to begin tracking events and alerting the administrator or security officer of the occurrence of events. The Add to Alert dialog box appears.

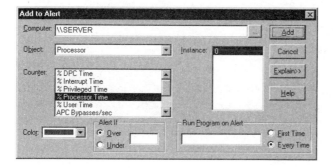

The procedure for adding alerts is similar to the procedure for adding charts. In addition to the tracking processes, it is possible to add high- and low-threshold values so the system will send alerts when the thresholds are met. On one system, Fecha tracks % disk space and has an alert established if available disk space is less than 20%. Table 4-2 lists the fields that are available in the Alert Options dialog box.

**Table 4-2. Alert Options on the Add to Alert Dialog Box**

| Fields | Description |
|---|---|
| Computer, Object, and Counter | Enter the appropriate information as described previously in Chart View. |
| Alert If | Click on Over or Under and then enter a threshold value in the field. |
| Run Program on Alert | Enter the name of a custom program that will run when the threshold value is met. Also click First Time or Every Time, depending on whether the program should be run only once or every time the threshold is met. |

In addition, Alerts can be further configured in the Alert Options dialog box, which you can open by choosing Options ⇨ Alert. Table 4-3 presents and describes the Alert options.

**Table 4-3. Alert Options on the Alert Options Dialog Box**

| Fields | Description |
|---|---|
| Switch to Alert View | Brings the Alert Log area into the foreground when an Alert occurs. |
| Log Event in Application Log | Creates an entry in the Application Log of the Event Viewer. |
| Network Alert | Allows a message to be sent to the specified user when an Alert occurs. |
| Update Time | Specifies how often the Alert Log screen is refreshed. |

When counters exceed the threshold values set, the date and time of the event are recorded in the Alert Log area window. One thousand events are recorded before the oldest events are discarded.

## Log View

Logging allows the system to capture data in a file and save it for later viewing and analysis. The same type of information captured in Chart View can also be captured in Log View.

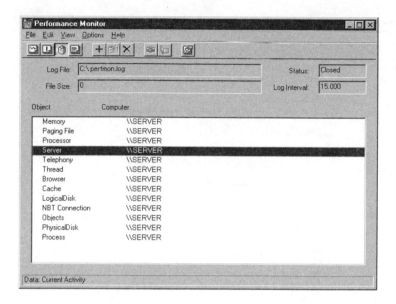

Choose View ⇨ Log to access the Log View. Choose Edit ⇨ Add to Log to begin log-ging an object. The option to choose a computer and the objects to trace is available. Choose Options ⇨ Log to launch the Log dialog box. This dialog box will prompt for a log name. If you use an existing file, data is appended to it. Choose either Manual Update or Periodic Update in the Update Time box. If you choose Periodic Update, you can set the interval for the updates. If Manual Update is chosen and you want to get updated information, choose Options ⇨ Update Now. Click the Start button to start logging. When you want to stop logging, choose Option ⇨ Log and click the Stop Log button.

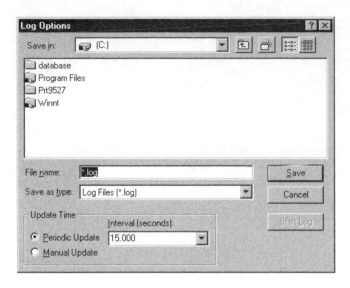

## Report View

You can use Report View to capture changing information (such as processor usage) and display it in a report format. The options available to Report View are similar to Chart View, except you do not have the ability to select different graphical ways to display information.

To build a report, choose View ⇨ Report and then Edit ⇨ Add to Report. The following fields can be filled as described in Chart View: Computer, Object, and Counter. A list of selected objects appears in the reporting area. As the system changes, the values are updated. Choose Options ⇨ Report to determine how often you want the options updated. Select Periodic Update for an automatic update of information and set the time interval for the updates. Each displayed value is usually an average over the last two data reads, which are separated by the length of the time interval. Choose Manual Update if you want to manually update the settings. If Manual Update is chosen and you want to get updated information, choose Options ⇨ Update Now.

## Recommended Settings

Windows NT contains many objects, and each object contains many counters that you can track. As previously mentioned, tracking and logging everything is not only infeasible and inefficient, but it defeats the purpose of proper security monitoring. It is also important to remember the type of Windows NT implementation set up.

At Fecha Manufacturing Corporation, the web server has been running extremely slow and even crashing in some instances; therefore, it has begun to monitor Logical Disk ⇨ % Disk Time, Processor ⇨ % Processor Time, and Memory ⇨ Pages/sec. This step is not to say that these three counters are the problem, but it may provide insight as to the problems Fecha is experiencing. In the event nothing is learned from the analysis, Fecha can monitor a new set of counters.

Also at Fecha, its database server contains very important, real-time data, and it must be available 24 hours a day, 7 days a week. Therefore, Fecha has implemented the same controls that are on its web server (for the database server) to monitor system performance. This step provides a control for Fecha to ensure the availability of the database server. This is because the systems administrators are able to observe when the server is getting to a critical point of low system resources.

Alerts are important controls for providing real-time monitoring and detecting possible compromises of confidentiality. For example, Fecha has alerts set on its administrative RAS server for Server ⇨ Errors Logon, with a threshold of 100 bad logons. Because only the administrator should be logging in the Administrator account, when 100 bad logon attempts occur, an alert is initiated. The system administrator who receives this alert knows that someone is trying to hack in.

You can set alerts (such as Errors Logon and others) by choosing View ⇨ Alert, and then choosing Server in the Object field. Send these alerts to the system administrator and security officer. Often a third-party software utility is used that will receive the alert, and then page the appropriate personnel. Table 4-4 contains a description of the counters that should be monitored for attempted security breaches.

**Table 4-4.  Alert Recommendations**

| Counter | Description |
| --- | --- |
| Errors Access Permissions | Indicates whether somebody is randomly attempting to access files in hopes of finding an improperly protected file. |
| Errors Granted Access | Logs attempts to access files without proper access authorization. |
| Errors Logon | Displays failed logon attempts, which could mean password guessing programs are being used to crack security on server. |

Alerts are powerful Windows NT security controls that we do not see used often. Fecha implements Errors Logon on its domain controllers because this is where all authentication occurs. Fecha wants to monitor hacker attempts of logging in the domain. Fecha also is monitoring Errors Access Permissions and Errors Granted Access on its file and print server, and database server. This monitoring assists in detecting when a user might randomly be attempting to access files for which they do not have authorization. Errors Logon does not need to be monitored on these machines because all authentication takes place on the domain controllers. Fecha's web server and domain member RAS server are set to monitor all three counters because users log in and access files on those machines. Lastly, workstations monitor nothing.

You can save Chart, Alert, and Log information in files for further analysis and tracking of illicit activities (or activities that may be degrading the performance of a system). These files are critical controls in monitoring security and should be printed and reviewed on a regular basis. Again, depending on the type of Windows NT system implemented, the review basis will vary. In our experience, most clients will not review audit logs. If they do, it is not done on a regular basis.

For Remote Access Servers that allow employees to connect externally, you should review exception reports and bad logon attempts daily. You should also review these reports for any private web server that is set up. For database servers and domain controllers, weekly or biweekly reviews should be sufficient. However, real-time monitoring through the Chart and Alert views is highly recommended.

## Windows NT Diagnostics

You can use the Windows NT Diagnostics utility to view various system, resource, and environment information. You can also use Windows NT Diagnostics not only to troubleshoot problems, but also to monitor possible breaches of security. You can implement these features as security controls to monitor your system. To begin using Windows NT Diagnostics, choose Start ➪ Administrative Tools ➪ Windows NT Diagnostics.

Choose File ➪ Computer to pick the computer you want to diagnose. You can print a report of the various settings by choosing File ➪ Create Report. This step is an easier way of viewing all the data at the same time in a text file format.

## Windows NT Diagnostics Information

There are nine tabs displayed in Windows NT Diagnostics and each contains in-depth information about your system. Click each tab in the dialog box to view various diagnostic information. Table 4-5 describes the information located on each tab.

**Table 4-5. Windows NT Diagnostics**

| Tab | Description |
| --- | --- |
| Version | Click this tab to view the current version and build  the operating system. |
| System | Click this tab to view BIOS and processor information. |
| Display | Click this tab to view video adapter and display information. |
| Drives | Click this tab to view information about disk drives, including whether they are NTFS volumes and whether security is preserved. |
| Memory | Click this tab to view Paging, Physical, and Kernel memory information. |
| Services | Click this tab to view what services are running or stopped. |
| Resources | Click this tab to view the settings of hardware devices in the system. |
| Environment | Click this tab to view the system environment variables. |
| Network | Click this tab to get detailed network information such as: |
| | **General**—Displays current network settings, such as workgroups or domain, network version, logon domain, logon server, and name of the current user. Use this page to view your current logon account in case you forget whether you logged on as an administrator or regular user. |
| | **Transports**—Displays a list of current network transport protocols and the addresses of the network adapters to which they are bound. |
| | **Settings**—Shows the current value of network parameters, such as session timeouts, buffers, caches, pipes, and encryption. |
| | **Statistics**—Shows current statistics for the network, such as bytes received, requested, and transmitted, as well as many other parameters. |

Click the Refresh button to get the latest statistical information on pages with values that require more frequent updates.

## Recommended Settings

Windows NT Diagnostics contains helpful monitoring information for maintaining a system. It is not feasible to monitor every variable within the system.

Table 4-6 indicates some statistics that are important to monitor for security reasons. Click the Network tab and then click the Statistics button to access these statistics. These statistics are critical in monitoring system security. Although these settings are important, they are very similar to those discussed in the "Performance Monitor" section. If the Performance Monitor alerts have been set, these controls are redundant.

**Table 4-6. Windows NT Diagnostics**

| Statistic | Description |
|---|---|
| Server Password Errors | This statistic tracks the number of failed logon attempts to the server. This value may indicate that someone is running a password-guessing program in an attempt to crack the security on the server. |
| Server Permission Errors | This statistic is the number of times that clients have been denied access to files they were trying to open. This value may indicate that somebody is randomly attempting to access files in hopes of getting at something that was not properly protected. |

# Network Monitor

The Network Monitor utility monitors network traffic to and from the server at the packet level. You can capture Network traffic for later analysis, which will make it easier to troubleshoot network problems.

**Note**   Network Monitor comes with Windows NT 4.0 Server. This utility can only be used to monitor packets of information that are sent from or received by the computer where you are running the program, including broadcast and multicast frames. This section discusses the Network Monitor that comes with Windows NT 4.0 Server.

**Tip**   Microsoft System Management Server includes an advanced Network Monitor utility. This version allows users to capture frames sent to and from any computer on the network, edit and transmit frames on the network, and capture frames from remote computers running Network Monitor Agent (included in Windows NT Workstation 4.0 and Windows 95) on the network.

To use this tool, choose Start ⇨ Administrative Tools ⇨ Network Monitor. The Network Monitor dialog box appears.

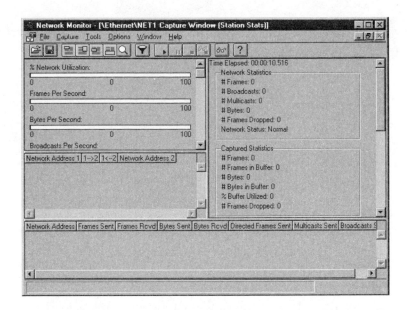

## Capturing Data

To begin capturing data that is being transmitted over the network, choose Capture ⇨ Start. It is also possible to enable dedicated capture mode, which will capture data with the screen minimized, thereby freeing resources for capturing data.

To view captured data, choose Capture ⇨ Stop and View or choose Capture ⇨ Stop and then Capture ⇨ Display Captured Data. Both methods will invoke the Captured Data screen.

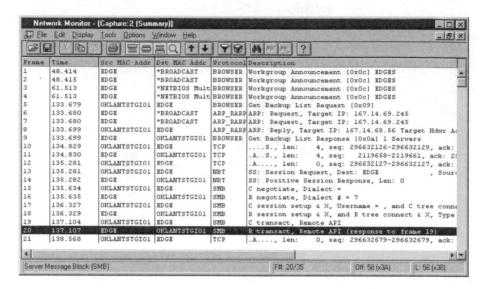

The Network Monitor gathers a great deal of information. The data gathered can be filtered so only the relevant information is displayed. To filter data, choose Capture ⇨ Filter, which displays the Capture Filter dialog box.

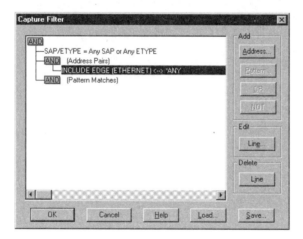

The information can be filtered by protocol or by network address. Filtering is an important feature that you can use as an Effective Security Monitoring control. As previously said, systems administrators will turn on Network Monitor and will then be inundated with tons of information, most of which they will not go through. Filtering allows the system administrator to be creative and come up with good expressions to capture the correct data. The Capture Filter dialog box shows the filter's decision tree. A *decision tree* is a query-like structure that graphically represents the filter expression.

In a decision tree, statements are linked together by colored AND, OR, and NOT tabs. Combined, these statements specify the kinds of data you want to capture or display. The Capture Filter dialog box has four main categories, which are described in Table 4-7.

**Table 4-7. Network Monitor Capture Filter**

| Category | Description |
| --- | --- |
| Expression | Shows the expression line that you want to locate or add to the display filter's decision tree. It changes as you select items in other areas of the dialog box. This category cannot be edited directly. |
| Address | Specifies the address you want to find. |
| Protocol | Specifies the protocols you want to find or filter. |
| Property | Specifies the protocol properties to filter. |

To filter the information by protocol, double-click on Protocol Expression and the Protocol Expression dialog box appears. For example, Fecha Manufacturing Corporation may want to monitor all the FTP requests to its internal web server. It can create an expression to do just that and then review the information on a daily basis.

The network addresses monitored can also be filtered in a similar manner. Double-click an address to launch the Address Expression dialog box. In the Station 1 and Station 2 boxes, select the computer addresses between which you want to monitor traffic, or that you want to locate. In the Direction box, select the arrow key that indicates the traffic direction that you want to monitor or locate. Click the Edit Address button to edit the currently selected network address.

The Address Database dialog box is a list of all network addresses captured and their friendly names. The friendly name would be the NetBIOS machine name if available, or one assigned by an administrator. Use this dialog box to add or delete addresses or to save addresses in a file for later use. The Address List displays the following information about each computer: a friendly name, the 12-digit hexadecimal network address, the address type, the name of the vendor who created the network card, and an additional comment.

The Address database is first created when you start capturing data. After capturing data, choose Capture ⇨ Find All Names to associate the captured computer addresses with the friendly names of the computers from which the frames have been captured. Then choose Capture ⇨ Address to display the names that have been added to the Address Database. To use these addresses to design a filter in the future, click the Save button to save it to a file.

Triggers, which are conditions that must be met before an action occurs, can also be set. For example, Fecha wants to capture data on its web server when a specific Telnet command is issued. Fecha sets up a trigger that starts Network Monitor, capturing data if a pattern (such as a code or sequence used by a hacker) is found. Triggers are good controls because they work on set conditions.

Choose Capture ⇨ Triggers to launch the Capture Trigger dialog box.

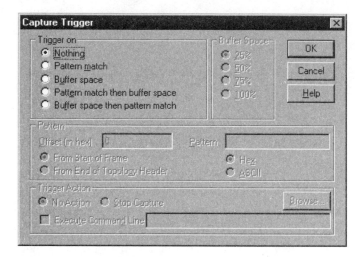

Table 4-8 describes the options that are available in the Capture Trigger dialog box.

**Table 4-8. Capture Triggers**

| Option | Description |
| --- | --- |
| Nothing | Indicates that no triggers are set. |
| Pattern Match | Initiates a trigger when a particular pattern occurs. |
| Buffer Space | Initiates a trigger when a specified percentage of the capture buffer is filled. |
| Pattern Match Then Buffer Space | Initiates a trigger when a particular pattern occurs, and then a specified percentage of the capture buffer is filled. |
| Buffer Space Then Pattern Match | Initiates a trigger when a specified percentage of the capture is filled, and then a particular pattern occurs. |

In the Trigger Action box, specify the actions you want to occur when the trigger conditions are met. You can choose to Stop Capture by clicking the Stop Capture radio button or by clicking Execute Command Line and typing the name of a command or executable file.

Choose Tools ⇨ Identify Network Monitor Users to identify who else in the network has installed and is using Network Monitor. Only the Network Monitor tool will be detected; other network monitoring tools will not.

It is possible to use the Network Monitor Agent services on other Windows NT computers to capture statistics on those computers and have them sent to the server running Network Monitor. Network Monitor Agent is a service that would run on those workstations.

## Recommendations

Network security control is extremely important for confidentiality. If other users run an installation of Network Monitor on their computers, they could use it to watch packets on the network and capture valuable information. To protect a network from unauthorized use of Network Monitor, this tool provides security controls such as password protection and the ability to detect other installations of itself on the local segment of the network. To change the password, click Start ⇨ Setting ⇨ Control Panel. Double-click the Monitoring Agent applet and then click the Change Password button.

FTP and Telnet send passwords over the network in clear text, that is, readable without requiring any additional interpretation like deciphering; therefore, someone monitoring the network can capture and view these passwords.

Network Monitor will detect other Network Monitor installations and display the information about them, such as the name of the computer, user, adapter address, and whether the utility is running, capturing, or transmitting information. However, it cannot detect third-party monitoring software and/or equipment. Be aware that other third-party software may be sniffing data. This is why it is important to secure the data as it traverses the network.

## Auditing

Auditing is an important component of the Effective Security Monitoring controls. *Auditing* means measuring the system against a predefined system setting to ensure no changes have occurred. Changes may indicate possible security breaches. If no auditing is being conducted, then the Effective Security Monitoring controls will not be satisfied and thus confidentiality, integrity, and availability of data is at risk.

Auditing takes time and effort to implement and it uses a lot of resources; therefore, many corporations do not even turn on auditing on their Windows NT systems. The audit services of a Windows NT operating system provide a chronological record of events in the audit logs. These logs support individual accountability by recording user actions. The audit log is also potential evidence for legal or administrative actions. It also serves as an assurance tool, revealing how well the security mechanisms are working.

All audit events are logged and can be viewed through Event Viewer; thus, you can trace the security threats to their origin and rectify the weaknesses. However, effective audit options must be enabled in order to achieve this.

## System Auditing

System auditing tracks system-level events such as logons and file and directory access. To enable System auditing choose Start ⇨ Administrative Tools ⇨ User Manager for Domains ⇨ Policies ⇨ Audit. The following dialog box appears:

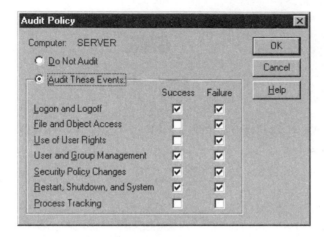

Audit events are recorded in the Security Log. The Security Log can be viewed in the Event Viewer discussed later in the section entitled, "Event Viewer." If the Do Not Audit option is highlighted, all Windows NT auditing is disabled and the Security Log will generate no entries.

## Recommended System Auditing Settings

Click the Audit These Events button to enable the auditing system to track the events. You can choose from a variety of events, and you can choose to audit the success and/ or failure of these events. However, tracking all events will consume a lot of resources so you need to carefully decide what to audit.

Auditing is a critical and important security control that you need to plan and think through carefully. The recommendations made here may not fit all corporations exactly, so use them only as a guide. We will use Fecha Manufacturing Corporation and its Windows NT environment to recommend what we believe are baseline security configurations.

Because the file and print, database, and web servers are members of the domain, the following audit policies set on the domain controller level for the entire domain affect all these servers: Logon and Logoff, Use of User Rights, User and Group Management, and Security Policy Changes.

Fecha has determined that it wants to enable auditing of the Logon and Logoff server for failure on all Windows NT machines that authenticate users, which are the domain controllers and the RAS server. This is because Fecha wants to audit when a hacker may be trying to guess a user's password and gain access to the system. Successful logons and logoffs do not need to be audited in Fecha's environment because Fecha has no need to control users who are properly authenticating.

Fecha audits the failure of Use of User Rights on the machines with User Account Databases so administrators can determine which users have been attempting to do things beyond their privilege. For example, a user may try to take ownership of files they do not have access to in order to edit them. Or, a user who somehow got physical access to a Primary Domain Controller (PDC) might try to log in locally. For similar reasons, Fecha audits Security Policy Changes for success and failure. Administrators will then be able to review which individuals may be trying to establish trust relationships or modifying their user rights.

Fecha also wants to audit User and Group Management for success and failure on all Windows NT machines that authenticate users, because it is important to know which individuals modified or attempted to modify the User Account Database (only administrators and account operators have this capability). For example, an account operator may have added a user without following the corporate security policy and a security officer wants to know who performed this procedure.

File and Object Access auditing is enabled for failure on the domain controllers, remote access servers, and file and print servers, as well as for failure and success on the database server. This is because Fecha wants to be able to implement Object auditing on these servers, especially the servers that contain critical business data, such as the database server. (Discussions on the objects that should be audited are in the "Recommended File and Directory Auditing" section.) In addition, Fecha has determined that the cost of a virus outbreak would be too high and so will also enable auditing the success and failure of write access for program files such as files with .EXE and .DLL extensions. Therefore, whenever a program file is written to, an audit event will be generated stating which user wrote to the file.

The Restart, Shutdown, and System audit feature is selected for success and failure on all machines except workstations because workstations can be restarted as many times as necessary and no security implication exists. This audit feature provides administrators a log of the individual who committed the shutdown or restart. If a machine is down, an administrator will want to check the Event Viewer and see who shut down the box.

Lastly, the Process Tracking audit event does not need to be enabled for success or failure under normal circumstances. Perhaps during a troubleshooting scenario this might be useful, although it does fill the log quickly.

Table 4-9 presents the Audit Policy features, a description of the features, and how auditing should be implemented.

**Table 4-9. Domain Users' Audit Policy**

| Audit Feature | Description | Domain Controller | RAS Server | File and Print | Data-base | Web Server | Work-station |
|---|---|---|---|---|---|---|---|
| Logon and Logoff | Enables auditing of logon/off attempts, and breaking of network connections to servers. | Select Failure | Select Failure | Do not select | Select Failure | Do not select | Do not select |
| Use of User Rights | Enables auditing of attempts to user rights that have/have not been granted. | Select Failure | Select Failure | Do not select | Do not select | Do not select | Do not select |
| User and Group Management | Enables auditing of creation, deletion, and modification of user and group accounts. | Select Success Select Failure | Select Success Select Failure | Do not select | Do not select | Do not select | Do not select |
| Security Policy Changes | Enables auditing of granting or revoking rights to users or groups, and establishing or breaking trust relationships with other domains. | Select Success Select Failure | Select Sucess Select Failure | Do not select | Do not select | Do not select | Do not select |
| File and Object Access | Enables the ability to turn on the auditing of access to a directory or file that is set for auditing. | Select Failure | Select Failure | Select Failure | Select Success Select Failure | Do not select | Do not select |
| Restart, Shutdown, and System | Enables auditing of shutdowns and restarts of the computer, the filling of the Audit Log, and the discarding of audit entries if the Audit Log is already full. | Select Success Select Failure | Select Success Select Failure | Select Success Select Failure | Select Success Select Failure | Select Success Select Failure | Do not select |
| Process Tracking | Enables auditing of the starting and stopping processes. | Do not select | Do not select | Do not select | Do not select | Do not select | Do not select |

## File and Directory Auditing

File and Directory auditing, like System auditing, provides good controls for security monitoring. File and Directory auditing allows you to monitor what resources are being accessed. For files and directories deemed critical, this is extremely important. Reviewing the reports is also very important. Without reviewing the reports, the security controls will not be effective. File and Directory auditing tracks detailed activity for selected users on individual files and directories. For each directory or file, you can define users or groups to audit.

File and Directory auditing is granular because it is possible to choose to track a specific user's access to a specific directory or file. This type of auditing helps minimize the events that are tracked and reduces the use of system resources, such as the disk space required to store the auditing events.

To enable File and Directory auditing, choose Start ➪ Programs ➪ Windows NT Explorer, highlight a directory, right-click the object to open its drop-down menu, and then choose Properties. The Properties dialog box appears. If you highlight a file, right-click it and choose Properties from its drop-down menu, the File Properties dialog box appears. Click the Security tab and then click the Auditing button. A Directory Auditing dialog box appears.

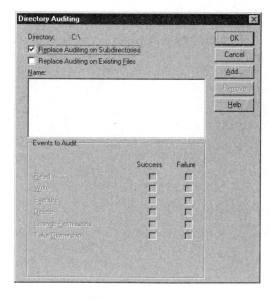

The dialog box for Directory auditing differs slightly from the dialog box for File auditing. The Directory Auditing dialog box contains two additional options: Replace Auditing on Subdirectories and Replace Auditing on Existing Files. These options are described in the following table:

| Fields | Description |
| --- | --- |
| Directory | Displays the logical drive and NTFS directory to which auditing is to be applied. Multiple directories can be simultaneously selected. |

| Check Box | Description |
| --- | --- |
| Replace Auditing on Subdirectories | Allows the user to make changes and apply them to all subdirectories. By default, this option is not selected. |
| Replace Auditing on Existing Files | Allows the user to make changes and apply them to the files in the directory. This option is enabled by default because auditing applied to the directory affect the files in that specific directory. |

| Section | Description |
| --- | --- |
| Name | Displays the name of the user or group accounts and the type of auditing enabled. If multiple directories are selected, the auditing displayed will be common to the selected files. |

| Button | Description |
| --- | --- |
| Add | Opens the Add Users and Groups dialog box. |
| Remove | Deletes the selected account from the Names list. |

The Replace Auditing on Existing Files check box is not a state; it is an option that you can execute at a specific time. If it is checked, all files within the directory inherit audit settings at that moment and the box becomes unchecked. The files will not inherit permissions again until this box is rechecked.

To view the audit events that were logged, choose Start ⇨ Programs ⇨ Administrative Tools ⇨ Event Viewer ⇨ Log ⇨ Security. To save these events to an external file (that is, if you need to archive them or open them in another application), choose Log ⇨ Save As.

## Recommended File and Directory Auditing Settings

To audit files and directories on a particular server, the File and Object Access audit event option must be enabled in the Audit Policy for that server. Selecting to audit events relating to file and directory access is a critical control and should be carefully thought out and planned. Table 4-10 lists some important audit recommendations for the Fecha database server's data files.

These settings are for domain users. Because auditing takes up a lot of resources, Fecha has decided that it is only cost-effective to audit these data files because they contain critical business information. Fecha does not want to audit the Windows NT system files on its domain controllers because only administrators have access to those files.

Fecha audits failure on read because it wants to know who attempted to access a file they should not have. In addition, Fecha wants to know who successfully deletes and attempts to delete any data files. Lastly, because the Change Permissions and Take Ownership items are very sensitive, Fecha audits who completes and attempts to complete those operations.

**Table 4-10. Data Files Audited for Domain Users' Access**

| Item | Success | Failure |
| --- | --- | --- |
| Read | Do not select | Select |
| Write | Do not select | Do not select |
| Execute | Do not select | Do not select |
| Delete | Select | Select |
| Change Permissions | Select | Select |
| Take Ownership | Select | Select |

## Registry Auditing

Auditing the Registry is an important aspect of auditing because the Registry contains important system configurations. Noting any changes that take place in the Registry is crucial for maintaining the integrity, confidentiality, and availability of your systems. You can audit changes made to specific Registry keys. If someone manages to gain physical access to a domain controller or if there are many administrators in a corporation, it is highly recommended to implement Registry auditing as a security control to determine who made the modifications.

Registry auditing is set up in the Registry Editor utility. To launch the Registry Editor, choose Start ⇨ Run and type **REGEDT32.EXE**. Choose Security ⇨ Auditing and the Registry Key Auditing dialog box appears.

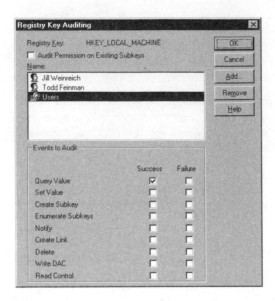

Click the Add button to add a user, and then set the Success or Failure options in the Events to Audit area. Table 4-11 describes these Registry options.

**Table 4-11. Registry Auditing Options**

| Permissions | Description |
|---|---|
| Query Value | Attempts to read the settings of a value entry in a subkey. |
| Set Value | Attempts to set the value in a subkey. |
| Create Subkey | Attempts to create a new key or subkey within a selected key or subkey. |
| Enumerate Subkey | Attempts to identify all subkeys within a key or subkey. |
| Notify | Attempts to receive audit notifications generated by the subkey. |
| Create Link | Attempts to create symbolic links to the subkey(s). |
| Delete | Attempts to delete selected keys or subkeys. |
| Write DAC | Attempts to modify the discretionary access control (DAC) list for the key. |
| Read Control | Attempts to read security information within selected subkey. |

To view the audit events that were logged, choose Start ⇨ Programs ⇨ Administrative Tools ⇨ Event Viewer ⇨ Log ⇨ Security. To save events to external files, if you need to archive them or open them in another application, choose Log ⇨ Save As.

## Recommended Registry Auditing Settings

To audit the Registry, the File and Object Access audit event must be enabled in Audit Policy. If changes to a particular key by a user or application are to be audited, you can turn on auditing for that key. Sometimes it is prudent to audit only those events that fail. Auditing successful events may produce many entries that the Security Log will quickly fill up. As with File and Directory auditing, careful planning should take place before you turn on Registry auditing.

Table 4-12 provides recommendations for Fecha's Registry auditing scenario. These recommendations are not comprehensive, so just use them as a guide when you set up your Registry auditing policies. Fecha administrators want to be able to log who made Registry modifications that may bring the system down or make harmful system changes. Therefore, Fecha implemented its Registry auditing settings on the Administrators and Domain Admins groups. In addition, to monitor individuals who obtain physical access to the domain controllers and attempt to make changes to the Registry, Fecha will audit the Everyone group. The following Registry keys and their existing subkeys should be audited:

> HKEY_LOCAL_MACHINE\System
>
> HKEY_LOCAL_MACHINE \Software
>
> HKEY_CLASSES_ROOT

**Table 4-12. Registry Options**

| Item | Recommendation |
| --- | --- |
| Query Value | Do not select |
| Set Value | Select Success and Failure |
| Create Subkey | Select Success and Failure |
| Enumerate Subkeys | Do not select |
| Notify | Do not select |
| Create Link | Select Success and Failure |
| Delete | Select Success and Failure |
| Write DAC | Select Success and Failure |
| Read Control | Do not select |

## Printer Auditing

Windows NT Server provides the ability to secure and audit printer access. These controls can also be important depending on where employees print and what is being printed. Color printers that are on the network but only to be used by the marketing department, for example, should have the proper permission on them. In addition, they should have auditing controls so you can track any attempt by unauthorized users. Printer auditing can audit the success or failure of attempts by users to print, change job settings for documents, pause print jobs, restart print jobs, and reorder and delete documents in the print queue. In addition, it is possible to audit user attempts to share printers, delete printers, change printer permissions, and change printer ownership.

Choose Start ⇨ Settings ⇨ Printers. Double-click the printer you want to audit. Choose Printer ⇨ Properties, click the Security tab, and then click the Auditing button to access the Printer Auditing dialog box.

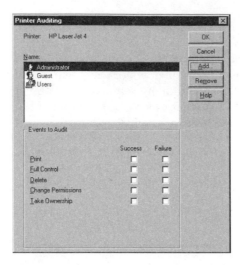

Table 4-13 presents and describes the printer options to audit:

**Table 4-13. Printer Audit Options**

| Option | Description |
| --- | --- |
| Print | Printing documents |
| Full Control | Changes to document settings, pausing, restarting, moving, and deleting documents |
| Delete | Deleting a printer |
| Change Permissions | Changing printer permissions |
| Take Ownership | Taking ownership of a printer |

## Recommended Printer Auditing Settings

To audit printers, the File and Object Access audit event must be enabled in the Audit Policy.

Auditing printers is not a common practice that we see because it consumes system resources. However, in some circumstances (such as when a printer is dedicated to printing checks), it is a security control to audit anyone who may attempt to print a check. For example, Fecha's file and print server has a check printer, FechaCHECK that only the accounting group should use. Table 4-14 details how all print attempts are audited in such an example.

**Table 4-14.  Printer Audit Recommendations**

| Printer | FechaCHECK | | |
| --- | --- | --- | --- |
| **Name** | Everyone | | |
| **Option** | | **Success** | **Failure** |
| Print | | Do not select | Select |
| Full Control | | Select | Select |
| Delete | | Do not select | Select |
| Change Permissions | | Select | Select |
| Take Ownership | | Select | Select |

## Remote Access Server (RAS) Auditing

Windows NT Server can log the activities of remote users accessing Remote Access Servers. Auditing events that may indicate attempts to break into your system through a dial-up connection can be viewed with Windows NT Event Viewer.

Before auditing can take place, a parameter must be enabled in the Registry. Changing this Registry value is outlined in the following steps:

1. Choose Start ⇨ Run and then type **REGEDT32.EXE** in the text field.
2. Select the HKEY_LOCAL_MACHINE window.
3. Open the following key:
   SYSTEM\CurrentControlSet\Services\RemoteAccess\Parameters
4. Highlight Parameters and double-click Enable Audit in the right pane.
5. Make sure the value in the DWORD value is 1.

**Caution**   Monitoring and auditing RAS is important from a network security control perspective as intruders often attempt to dial in and breach system security.

Fecha Manufacturing Corporation, as do most of our clients, has a RAS server for allowing its employees to dial in from remote locations. This is a critical server for Fecha, because most employees dial in to check e-mail and access data files from home or from the road. RAS creates another point of entry and should be audited appropriately to mitigate this risk. Although many RAS audit messages appear in the Event Viewer, Fecha will filter only two important audit messages:

"The user has connected and failed to authenticate on port *portname*. The line has been disconnected."

"The user connected to port portname has been disconnected because there was a transport-level error during the authentication conversation."

By reviewing the Event Viewer for these particular messages, Fecha will be monitoring for attempts to guess user names and passwords.

## Event Viewer

The Event Viewer is the tool within Windows NT that you can use to review audited events. Event Viewer has three logs that record system, security, and application-related events, known as the System Log, the Security Log, and the Applications Log, respectively. These are critical controls for monitoring security. Many times, systems administrators turn on auditing, record events, and then never look at the logs. Reviewing the logs and following up on any discrepancies is an important part of the control. Without it, the security control is ineffective. In addition, where other controls cannot be used (such as when files cannot be properly secured), Security Logs and the review thereof can be a compensating control that will help mitigate the risks.

The System Log records errors, warnings, or information generated by the Windows NT Server system.

The Security Log can record valid and invalid logon attempts and events related to the use of resources such as creating, opening, or deleting files and other objects.

The Application Log records errors, warnings, and information generated by application software such as an electronic mail or database program.

The System and Application Logs can be viewed by anyone. Only systems administrators or users with the Manage Auditing and Security Log user right can view the Security Log. For security control, the Security Log is the critical log. If a system administrator had to choose between which logs to review, the Security Log should be top priority.

To start Event Viewer, click Start ⇨ Programs ⇨ Administrative Tools ⇨ Event Viewer. Then choose Log ⇨ System, Security, or Application to view one of the three different sets of logs.

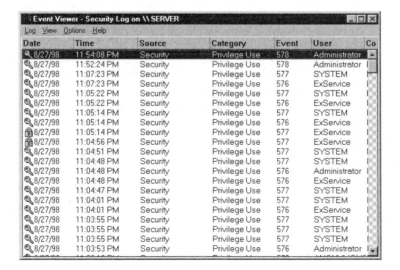

You can choose from a variety of ways to view the information in all the logs. Choose View ⇨ All Events to see everything that has been logged. If this is too much information to analyze, choose View ⇨ Filter events to see only certain events.

When you choose View ⇨ Filter Events, you can analyze events from certain days or only certain types of events. For example, if Fecha Manufacturing Corporation wanted to see only error messages that occurred on January 15, 1999, you would click the Events On button in the View From box, and then type **1/15/99** in the Date field and **12:00:00 AM** in the Time field. Then you would click Events On in the View Through box, type **1/15/99** in the Date field and **11:59:59 PM** in the Time field. Lastly, you would check the Error option in the Types field. In addition, audited events can be filtered by Source, Category, User, Computer, and Event ID (described in Table 4-15).You can also view this information in the Event Detail dialog box. Double-click an event to get its event detail.

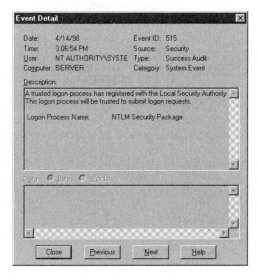

The information contained in the Event Detail dialog box is summarized in the Table 4-15.

**Table 4-15. Detailed Event View**

| Item | Description |
| --- | --- |
| Date | The date the event was generated. |
| Time | The time the event was generated. |
| User | The account name translation of the subject's SID that generated the event. This username will be the impersonation ID of the client if the subject is impersonating a client, or it will be the username of the primary ID. |

*(continued)*

**Table 4-15.** *(continued)*

| Item | Description |
|------|-------------|
| Computer | The computer name for the computer where the event was generated. |
| Event ID | A unique, module-specific ID of the specific event. |
| Source | The name of the system that submitted the event. For security audits this will always be Security. |
| Type | The audit type indicating whether the audited security access attempt was successful or unsuccessful. |
| Category | A classification of the event by the event source. |

You can filter, view, and sort events by their category. The category of the event is also listed in the Event Detail information. Table 4-16 shows categories of events and their definitions. The events in the parentheses are the actual titles of the events listed in the Audit Policy dialog box. To view this dialog box, choose Start ⇨ Program ⇨ User Manager for Domains ⇨ Policies ⇨ Audit Policy.

**Table 4-16. Event Viewer Categories**

| Category | Definition |
|----------|------------|
| Account Management (User and Group Management) | These events describe high-level changes to the Security Account Database (creating a new user or changing a user account). |
| Detailed Tracking (Process Tracking) | These events provide detailed tracking of subject information. Subject information includes program activation, handle duplication, and indirect object access. |
| Logon/Logoff (Logon and Logoff) | These events describe a single logon or logoff attempt and whether successful or unsuccessful. Included in each logon description is an indication of what type of logon was requested or performed (interactive, network, service). |
| Object Access (File and Object Access) | These events describe both successful and unsuccessful access to protected objects. |
| Policy Change (Security Policy Changes) | These events describe high-level changes to the security policy database, such as the assignment of privileges or logon privileges. |
| Privilege Use (Use of User Rights) | These events describe both successful and unsuccessful attempts to use privileges, including a special case when privileges are assigned. |
| System Event | These events indicate that something affecting the security of the entire system or the Audit Log occurred. |

Event logs eventually get full and items will be deleted. To save events to external files (that is, if you need to archive them or open them in another application), choose Log ⇨ Save As. Event logs can also be manually cleared, but be sure the information is not needed because it cannot be retrieved after clearing the logs.

Maintenance of log files is a critical security control that is usually overlooked. Systems administrators take the time to review and implement audit settings. However, a good hacker can create problems that cause the logs to fill quickly and if the proper settings are not set, the logs will overwrite previous log information, essentially erasing the hacker's tracks or crashing the system, causing a denial-of-service attack. Therefore, it is critical that the log parameters for size and event recording for each log are set appropriately. Choose Log ➪ Log Settings to open the Event Log Settings dialog box.

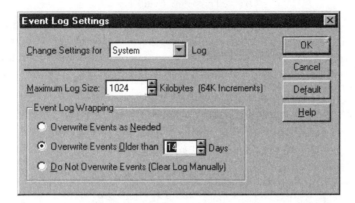

Click on Change Settings for the drop-down list to choose settings for the Security, Applications, or System Log. The options are the same for all three. Table 4-17 describes the options available within the Event Log Settings dialog box.

**Table 4-17.  Event Log Settings Options**

| Option | Description |
| --- | --- |
| Maximum Log Size | This option allows you to choose the log size. The default maximum size of a log is 512K. However, it can be increased to accommodate more auditing. |
| Overwrite Events as Needed | This option allows each new event to replace the oldest event if the log is full. |
| Overwrite Events Older than x Days | This option is the best choice to use in conjunction with a regular archive policy. The default is 7 days. |
| Do Not Overwrite Events | This option ensures a complete Audit Log. When selected, the log must be cleared manually. |

## Recommended Event Viewer Settings

Event logging begins at boot time. If all options in the Audit Policy dialog box, including Process Tracking, are enabled, Windows NT can log a significant amount of activity to the Event Log, thereby filling the log. It is possible to enable system halting when the log gets full. If the system is not set to halt or crash when the Audit Log is full, it will wrap and overwrite older entries. However, you can set when Windows NT will start overwriting older events in the Event Log Wrapping section of the Event Log Settings dialog box. Table 4-18 lists some general recommendations for the Event Log Wrapping option on all Windows NT implementations.

**Table 4-18. Event Log Wrapping Setting Recommendations**

| Log | Overwrite Policy Setting |
| --- | --- |
| Security Log | Overwrite events older that 14 days |
| System Log | Overwrite events older that 14 days |
| Application Log | Overwrite events as necessary |

In addition, Table 4-19 lists the recommended sizes for the log files based on the type of Windows NT implementation. The sizes are also based on estimates that are large enough to contain two weeks of data. For example, five to ten megabytes is large enough to contain two weeks of Security Log audit events.

**Table 4-19. Log Settings Size Recommendations**

| Log | Domain Controller | File and Print Server | Data-base Server | Web Server | RAS Servers | Work-station |
| --- | --- | --- | --- | --- | --- | --- |
| Security Log | 5-10 MB | 2-4 MB | 2-4 MB | 2-4 MB | 5-10 MB | 1 MB |
| System Log | 1-2 MB | 1-2 MB | 1-2 MB | 1-2 MB | 1-2 MB | 1 MB |
| Application Log | 1-2 MB | 1-2 MB | 1-2 MB | 1-2 MB | 1-2 MB | 1 MB |

However, in our experience, for the Security Log, we have noted that the best practice is to make sure that the size of the log is big enough to hold 14 days of events online. This may mean providing bigger spaces for your logs depending on what Windows NT server is being audited and what audit features have been implemented. For example, on a Windows NT domain controller, the log-size setting will probably be set to a bigger size. On the other hand, for a Windows NT workstation, for which no auditing has been implemented, the log size will be very small. Setting the correct log size can only come with testing and experience.

Windows NT provides the "Crash On Audit Fail" flag in the Registry key located in SYSTEM\CurrentControlSet\Control\Lsa\CrashOnAuditFail. When this flag is set to 1 and the system cannot for any reason log an audit record, the system is brought down. If this flag is not set (set to 0), and the Audit log is full, an alert message is displayed to the system administrator warning that the Event log is full. This security feature is a double-edged sword and should be thought out carefully. Hackers like to generate lots of audit messages, fill the Audit log so that it cannot accept any more messages and then commit malicious acts, which are not logged. If the flag is set, the system will halt when the log is full and the hacker cannot commit any malicious acts. However, setting the flag and halting the system also invokes a denial-of-service attack.

## Securing the Audit Logs

Auditing the system is not enough. In addition, the logs that hold the auditing information should be secured and maintained. In other words, security controls should be placed on the actual log files themselves to ensure confidentiality and availability when they are needed. If the files are not protected properly, a hacker may perform some activities and then delete the logs to cover the trail. The following files are the log files, which can be found in the systemroot\System32\CONFIG directory.

**APPEVENT.EVT**—Application Events Log

**SECEVENT.EVT**—Security Events Log

**SYSEVENT.EVT**—System Events Log

The best way to secure these files is to create an auditor group that has access to these files, and then take it away from all other groups. The people assigned to the auditor group will be responsible for maintaining the data within the logs.

# Chapter 5
# Securing Physical Access to All Critical Systems

One of the first steps in system security is securing all physical access to critical systems. Meeting these controls ensures that unauthorized users cannot physically access the systems, which is the easiest way to access data. Controls should be in place to ensure that physical access to computer facilities and data are appropriately restricted. However, many times corporations are lax in implementing or enforcing these controls. Many corporations have locks on their data center's door; however, many of these doors are propped open or left ajar. The following section describes some key recommendations and controls for securing physical access.

## Physical Security

To protect the integrity and confidentiality of a corporation's system and data, physical access to all components of the system that contains critical business data should be appropriately controlled. The goals of physical security are simply stated as follows:

- To prevent unauthorized access to system resources
- To protect assets from harm, including people, data, systems, and facilities

Threats to physical security can be either accidental (that is, human error) or intentional (for example, theft or vandalism). As previously mentioned in Chapter 3, "Effective Security Management," a risk analysis should be conducted on the critical systems to determine the vulnerabilities of IT systems and operations. The vulnerabilities should be assessed and categorized by their relative severity and likelihood. A security risk analysis allows the systems administrator to "expect the unexpected" and to implement the necessary security controls to minimize the impact on a corporation caused by any threat.

The migration from the traditional mainframe environment to the highly distributed systems of today requires that areas outside the central computer room be given equal consideration when evaluating physical security risks. The portability and relative ease in administering Windows NT has, in many ways, contributed to this problem. In the past, it was cost prohibitive to have duplicate computing environments for separate business units. Decreased equipment cost and ease of administration have prompted many companies to move toward empowering individual departments to administer and house their own information resources. This decentralization of resources and responsibility often leads to less stringent controls in the physical environment.

Security awareness of employees is key to maintaining physical security in the workplace. Identification badges should be issued to employees and contractors alike, and staff should be trained and encouraged to challenge anyone without proper identification. Employees should also be encouraged to report unknown persons in buildings, and security training should be a core part of the employee training and evaluation process.

Areas that should be targeted when considering physical security controls include:

- Computer/Server Room
- Communications Room
- Workstations
- Network Access Points

## Physical Security in the Computer Room

Restricting physical access to a computer room is a critical security control to maintaining a secure computing environment. For even unsophisticated intruders, physical access to a device could provide easy access to data. Access rights can be assigned from a console and data can be viewed and downloaded to tape, disk, or CD-ROM. The server can also be removed from the building. Although a standard lock and key are usually sufficient, electronic key cards and push-button cipher locks add a level of convenience for high-traffic rooms, and they can provide the logging of user access. All key access should be controlled by the security officer. Access should be limited to only operations staff and should be reviewed regularly. Security guards, cameras, and alarms are also effective controls for preventing and detecting intruders. Additional provisions should be made for the protective storage of electronic media, such as backup tapes and installation disks. All onsite storage of electronic media should be in a locked, fireproof file cabinet within the computer room.

Although it is infeasible to lock all computers in a corporation, all servers containing critical applications or data should be locked in the computer room. For example, Fecha would need to ensure that all its critical computers including Domain controllers, Web servers, RAS servers, Database servers, and File and Print servers are in the locked computer room.

## Physical Security in the Communications Room

The speed and integrity of data transmissions can be affected by physical factors. Popular transmission protocols, such as Ethernet, are limited in cable length before data cannot reliably reach the receiver. Consequently, communications equipment (such as hubs, switches, routers, terminal servers, and repeaters) is often spread throughout a facility in order to avoid surpassing limitations of the cabling. In addition, short cables are less vulnerable to risks, such as overheating, and do not need to be housed in an environmentally controlled room.

Because all network data travels through this cable, there is a substantial risk of some-one "eavesdropping" on these communications lines and obtaining sensitive data. A net-work "monitor" enables a technician to analyze network performance and utilization by examining the traffic going across a network. Hackers can also use it to scan network traffic for user passwords and login IDs. Although Windows NT login information is relatively safe because it is encrypted, non-Windows NT clients, application logins, and certain communications protocols, such as Telnet and FTP, do not use encryption and could be vulnerable. For this reason, entry to the communications room should be as tightly controlled as the computer room.

In addition to using physical controls to prevent unauthorized access to network data, tech-nologies such as Virtual LANs (VLANs), internal firewalls, and network encryption should be considered. VLANs restrict where the data can travel by configuring communications equip-ment to route data across specific paths. An internal firewall creates a barrier to block un-authorized data from traveling between sites on a LAN. Network encryption encodes data travelling across the LAN into an unreadable form until it reaches its intended recipient, where it is then decoded automatically. Network encryption renders any captured data useless.

## Physical Security on the Workstation

It is often difficult to restrict physical access to desktop computers, especially in today's open work environments. Although security devices, such as cables and alarms, can be used to deter hardware theft, employees' security awareness (as to where data resides and how it is protected) should be of primary concern. Hardware is easily replaced, but loss of critical data can have catastrophic consequences. All critical files should be accessed from a server so that loss or failure of the workstation does not result in lost data. Server file directories should be properly secured through Share and NTFS permissions.

The security architecture of Microsoft Windows NT significantly limits the risk of unautho-rized access to the workstation compared to previous operating systems. Most methods used by hackers to bypass access controls in other operating systems are rendered ineffective by the Windows NT Security Subsystem. For example, access to a workstation's hard drive can be gained by booting the system from a floppy disk. Using NTFS, as opposed to the File Allocation Table (FAT) file system, makes this task slightly more difficult.

Floppy drives also present security issues at the workstation. The risk of unauthorized copying and removal of data has become even more significant in the age of inexpensive and readily available removable mass storage, writable compact disks, and portable streaming tape units. Strong policies limiting the use of such devices or disabling them mitigate this risk. Windows NT allows you to disable floppy drives.

Modems are also used to provide access to desktop computers remotely. If proper authen-tication is not required for the connection, that workstation and network is vulnerable to someone using a dialing attack strategy. Hackers write programs to call random numbers until they reach a modem that provides them with access to a network. Remote dial-in should be limited and tightly secured with proper passwords and logins and by having callback options. Callback options force the user to call from only a certain number, as the modem will call back that number to complete the connection. Strong policies and procedures regarding appropriate use of modems should be implemented and enforced.

## Physical Security on the Network Access Points

Data traveling throughout a network is potentially vulnerable at any point along the cable. Network connections, particularly those in insecure areas such as conference rooms and corporate cafeterias, represent a serious exposure to network data. This danger is due to the relative ease of monitoring network traffic by simply plugging a laptop into the jack and running network analysis software. Unlike someone breaking into a computer room or communications closet, a hacker would rarely be challenged if they quietly connected to one of the usually many exposed network jacks . Network connections should be restricted to active workstations, and connections made for temporary use in shared areas should be disconnected as soon as possible.

Advanced technologies such as wireless network connectors and wireless modems represent a new twist to the traditional physical security model. The devices effectively expand the range of a network such that there are no boundaries to where data can travel. When using these devices, intentional or accidental interception of network data is possible by people using similar equipment or other technologies designed for this purpose. It is, therefore, important that robust data encryption be used to mitigate this risk when using these devices.

# Chapter 6
# Securing All External and Internal Network Connections

Most systems today are made up of many different computers that are networked. Rarely do we see stand-alone systems. These systems are networked to other computers within the same building, in other buildings, halfway across the world, in different corporations, and throughout the Internet. All these connections create potential access points and data that not only resides on the computers, but also must traverse the network to other systems on cables, making the data vulnerable. This type of infrastructure makes security even harder. All network connections should only be used for valid business purposes, and controls should be in place to prevent these connections from undermining system security. In other words, all network connections should be secured so that data is secured as it sits on the system and as it traverses the network.

Security controls should be placed on the connection points so unauthorized users cannot access the system. Other controls should secure data as it traverses the system. In addition, if users are allowed to access the system externally, such as dial-up users, then they should be valid authorized users accessing only their data. Windows NT provides many features for setting up networks, the most notable being the Domain feature. The Domain Administration control is critical in securing the network and should be carefully considered. In addition, Windows NT RAS also allows many external connection features; it also provides many controls for securing those connections. The following sections provide some recommendations for implementing the correct controls to secure the network.

## Network Security Management

Within the Windows NT network environment, it is essential to secure all network components and ensure that information is protected from unauthorized disclosure. Domains, protocols, trust relationships, remote access, and Internet access could be considered a requirement of a network. Therefore, information traversing the network through these network components must be accurate and secure. This section describes the differences between the many security options and features available for networking and how to meet the confidentiality and integrity corporate IT security objectives.

## Domain Administration

*Domains* are tools for allowing data to traverse the network. They are also a point-of-access for authorized users to access the system. Protecting the data and access controls to the data involves domain administration. Domain administration is controlled by administrators who are members of the global group Domain Admins. The administrator may manage properties and services on one or all servers in a domain. The administrator also may promote a backup domain controller (BDC) to a primary domain controller (PDC). The administrator can manage all functions within the domain such as establishing trust relationships, reviewing resources, granting permissions, and disconnecting users for server maintenance.

Windows NT Server can extend administrative authority from the single computer to the entire domain. In a domain, administrators need only manage one account for each user, and each user needs only one account. The PDC maintains the security database for that domain. To avoid a single point of failure for this critical database, Windows NT Server replicates this crucial user and security information to other Windows NT servers acting as BDC. This approach avoids a single point of failure for the network, ensuring that information will be available and authentication services will continue as normal if the PDC crashes.

Each domain has only one PDC, but there is no effective limit to the number of BDCs. All account modifications are made to the master copy of the Security Account Manager (SAM) database on the PDC. The BDCs provide read-only access to the SAM database. These controllers can satisfy validation requests and account query requests, but they cannot update or modify information in the SAM.

## Trust Relationships

Trust relationships allow different domains to interact with one another. This allowance creates additional connections to an existing network environment, effectively a single sign-on connection for users so they can access data across domains without requiring additional accounts. Windows NT provides the control of resources so unauthorized users from foreign domains cannot access resources.

A computer cannot be a member of two domains at the same time, and two separate domains cannot access each other's resources by default. However, by setting up a trust relationship, a computer can belong to one domain and be trusted by another domain, thereby allowing a user to be authenticated and to access resources on both domains.

A trust relationship is a one-way administrative and communicative link between two domains, allowing one domain (the trusting domain) to honor authentication requests from users of another domain (the trusted domain). For example, when a user's attempts to access a resource in the trusting domain, that trusting domain is presented the user's credentials for authentication. At this point, the trusting domain passes the users credentials to the trusted domain, where the trusted domain authenticates the user. Of course, this allowance is only useful if the user has been granted appropriate rights and permissions to access that resource. The trusting domain will accept a list of global groups and access controls for authenticated users from the trusted domain.

Trusts simplify user experience and provide single sign-on by combining two or more domains into a single administrative unit. For example, in a network consisting of four domains, the standard administrative approach requires four separate databases, one for each domain. That means if no trust relationships exist, a user who needs to access resources in all four domains needs four separate accounts. Implementing trust relationships between these domains makes it possible for one account to be used for accessing resources across all four domains and for administrators to manage the entire network through one database and a smaller number of groups.

## Types of Trust Relationships

Trust relationships are strictly one-way. However, they can be implemented in such a manner that two-way trusts exist. The term two-way trust is a misnomer because a two-way trust is really two, one-way trusts set up reciprocally. Windows NT does not have a two-way trust function; it must be created by manually initiating two, separate one-way trusts. Figure 6-1 illustrates one-way and two-way trusts.

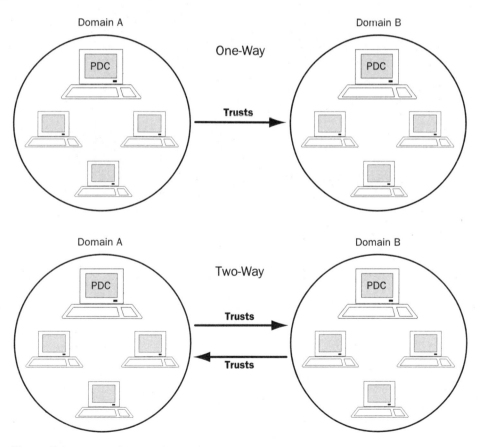

**Figure 6-1.** *Types of trust relationships*

The following example illustrates one-way trusts. Jeff is a user on the Marketing domain and Kelly is a user on the Accounting domain. If trusts are not established, they cannot access resources in each other's domains. However, Marketing can be configured as a trusted domain and Accounting can be configured as a trusting domain. This configuration change would allow Jeff to authenticate and access resources on Accounting, but Kelly would not be allowed to authenticate or access resources on Marketing.

A single domain can have trust relationships with any number of domains. Several domains can trust one domain so that the single trusted domain contains all the accounts. Conversely, one domain might trust several other domains so that the accounts can be spread among several account databases. Each of these trust relationships can be set up as either a single one-way or two-way trust.

Trust relationships are not transitive; that is, a trusted domain cannot take advantage of any trusts that exist between the trusting domain and any other domains. If Domain A trusts Domain B and Domain B trusts Domain C, then Domain A does not automatically trust Domain C. Figure 6-2 illustrates this concept.

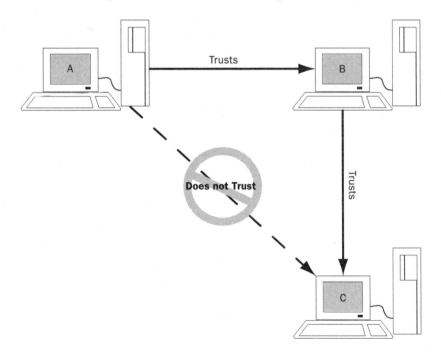

**Figure 6-2.** *Non-transitive trust*

## Pass-Through Authentication

*Pass-through authentication* allows a user who has an account defined in one domain to access resources in another domain where they do not have an account. By default, a domain controller of that user's domain will try to authenticate that user when they either log on to a trusted domain or access a resource in a trusting domain. If it cannot, because the user account is located in a different domain, then pass-through authentication occurs. The username and password are forwarded to a Windows NT server that can authenticate the user and then the user's information is returned to the requesting computer. This means a user can have an account on only one domain and still access the entire network's resources.

For example, user Kelly is a member of Domain B. She enters an office whose computers are in Domain A. Domain A trusts Domain B. The following scenario occurs:

1. Kelly attempts to log on the system by entering her user information in the Authentication dialog box. Because she is a member of Domain B, her authentication must occur in Domain B.

2. The PDC in Domain A cannot authenticate Kelly because she is a member of Domain B.

3. The PDC in Domain A passes the authentication request through to Domain B.

4. The PDC in Domain B authenticates Kelly's request.

5. The PDC in Domain B returns the authentication response back to the PDC in Domain A to let Kelly know she is allowed access to the network.

This process is illustrated in Figure 6-3.

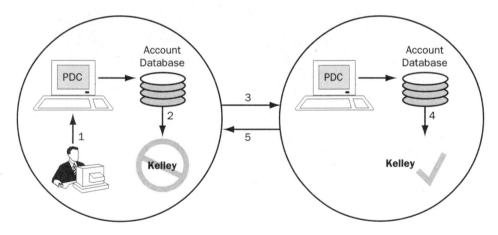

**Figure 6-3.** *Pass-through authentication*

When Kelly's logon request is completed, she will have access to the resources in Domain B and to the shared resources in Domain A.

## Creating Trust Relationships

Trust relationships are primarily an administration tool for managing user accounts, so the initial step in setting up a trust is to identify the domain where the accounts will reside. To create and maintain a trust, open the User Manager for Domains application, and choose Policies ➪ Trust Relationships.

The Trust Relationships dialog box displays the current domain on top and consists of two fields: Trusted Domains and Trusting Domains. In addition, there are buttons for adding and removing these domains.

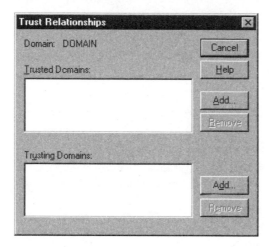

## Creating One-Way Trusts

For a trust relationship to exist, it must be configured on both domains. The preferred sequence for implementing a trust is for the administrator in a trusted domain to initiate the relationship by clicking the lower Add button. The Add Trusting Domain dialog box appears.

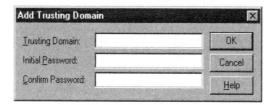

The administrator from the trusted domain specifies the name of the trusting domain in the Trusting Domain field and specifies the password in the Initial Password field. The password permits the trust relationship and is required to be entered by the trusting domain's administrator later. These passwords are unrelated to existing user passwords and are used to secure the trust relationship. A hidden account is created for the trust relationship.

The administrator from the trusting domain completes the trust relationship from his or her domain. The administrator launches the User Manager for Domains application, choosing Policies ⇨ Trust Relationships. The trusted domain's name is added to the trust relationship by clicking the upper Add button. The Add Trusted Domain dialog box appears.

The administrator specifies the name of the trusted domain in the Domain field and the trusted domain's password in the Password field. The trusted domain administrator receives a message indicating that the trust relationship has been successfully established.

---

**Note**   After the trust relationship is completed, the password is changed and managed by the system. Every seven days the password is changed by the trusting domain and remotely updated on the trusted domain.

---

**Note**   Trusts are not affected if a PDC is shutdown. When one side of a trust is deleted, however, both sides of the trust must be removed and re-created before the trust can be reestablished.

### Creating Two-Way Trusts

A two-way trust is simply two, one-way trusts, where both domains trust each other. Each domain can have both accounts and resources. Users may log on from either domain and can be granted rights or permissions to use any resource in either domain.

Creating a two-way trust can be easily understood through the following example. There are two domains, Accounting and Marketing. The first step is to create a one-way trust with Accounting as the trusting domain and Marketing as the trusted domain. The second step is to create a one-way trust with Marketing as the trusting domain and Accounting as the trusted domain. The two trust relationships are independent and, therefore, do not require both pairs of passwords to be the same.

### Deleting Trust Relationships

Trust relationships cannot exist unless they are configured on both domains. Therefore, to delete a trust, both domains must be modified. The preferred sequence is for the administrator in the trusted domain to remove the name of the trusting domain from the Trusting Domain field. The trust is now severed, but the process is not finished. The administrator in the trusting domain completes the revocation by removing the name of the trusted domain from the Trusted Domain field. Passwords are not necessary to remove a trust relationship.

## Considerations and Recommendations for Securing Trusts

Trust relationships create more points of entry for a possible attack because not only can an intruder attempt to compromise a user account in a given domain, but also all of the trusted domains. Therefore, it is critical for administrators to keep security controls in mind when creating trusts, especially because in a large corporation trusts can become complex and hard to manage. Each trust relationship should be created for a valid business purpose, and security controls need to be in place on all resources in all domains to ensure that users do not have unauthorized access. Users with accounts in the trusted domain should have the proper security controls such as rights and permission in the trusting domain to limit their access.

A good Windows NT security control for granting permissions to users across domains is to grant users, from the trusted domain, membership to global groups and allow those global groups to be members of local groups in trusting domains that have been given permissions to various resources within that domain. It is critical that all users of a global group be known and identified as authorized users. Do not grant a global group membership to a local group unless all users are known and accounted for. This process of granting local group membership is more preferred than simply granting global groups access permissions to files. If global groups become members of existing local groups, ensure that all access permissions granted to the local group are appropriate for these new members.

## Protocols

Windows NT supports many networking protocols. Because we are focusing on security in this book, we will look at those protocols that have security implications, regardless of the Windows NT implementation. The three principally supported protocols, NetBEUI, NWLink, and TCP/IP (Transmission Control Protocol / Internet Protocol) all play an important role in the networking of the Windows NT environment.

To examine which protocols are installed, or to install protocols, choose Start ⇨ Settings ⇨ Control Panel. Then click the Network applet and switch to the Protocols tab. The installed protocols are displayed and new ones can be added by clicking the Add button.

### Protocol Selection

Windows NT works with all of the above-listed networking protocols and is compliant with other standard networking and communication protocols. One of the top considerations for configuring a Windows NT server is deciding what protocols to install, how to use them, and how to configure their security controls.

A major challenge faced by Microsoft is creating a robust secure networking operating system while relying on old, insecure protocols. This has been an ongoing issue. Essentially, Windows NT does not attempt to fix weaknesses in any protocol. Compensating controls, such as the use of encryption for applications or data as it traverses the network, may be a necessary addition for security-conscious corporations. We will describe the protocols and their security implications so that systems administrators may make informed security decisions when it is their time to choose which protocol to implement.

### NWLink, NetBIOS, and NetBEUI

NWLink, Microsoft's implementation of the Internetwork Packet Exchange (IPX) protocol, allows connectivity between the Windows NT and the Novell NetWare environments. Unless a corporation's network is a mix of Windows NT and NetWare environment, it is recommended that this protocol not be used or installed.

NetBEUI, a Microsoft networking protocol, supports communication in a Microsoft environment when the network is small and composed of a single network segment. NetBEUI is a nonroutable protocol—that is, its packets contain no routing information and cannot pass through routers into other network segments. However, NetBEUI is routable—that is, it uses source routing—when used in a Token Ring network.

Microsoft networking requires the use of the NetBIOS protocol in conjunction with a standard transport protocol for complete addressing of a packet. NetBIOS can be routed into other network segments when combined with either the TCP/IP or NWLink protocols in a form known as an *encapsulated protocol*. All Windows NT file and print sharing services use NetBIOS to carry their information. This usage may create potential security implications, which are described in the proceeding section, "SMB Services (NetBIOS over TCP/IP)."

Fecha Manufacturing Corporation has determined that because it has a pure Windows NT network it will not implement NWLink. However, as previously described, Fecha's Windows NT environment is rather large and complex, as most corporations' are. Therefore, Fecha has also determined that implementing NetBEUI will not meet its business needs. In addition, because it does not support a WAN environment and because Fecha has plans to expand its business onto the Internet, NetBEUI would not meet its future business needs.

### TCP/IP

TCP/IP brings Windows NT, and Fecha, into the world of open networking, allowing communication with any other computer system running TCP/IP and, more importantly, allowing Windows NT to communicate over the Internet. This capability has made Windows NT networking more robust and powerful; however, it has also brought about some potential security implications that are discussed in the following section. Because Fecha is growing and expanding its business to include communication with clients through direct connections and through the Internet, Fecha will be using TCP/IP as its main networking protocol. Fecha has recognized the inherent security risks within TCP/IP that are described in the following sections and has accepted those risks.

### TCP/IP Packet Filtering

Windows NT allows the TCP/IP protocol to be filtered and restricted. This filtering can be used to enhance the security of the Windows NT system in any configuration. The filtering can be managed at both the port and protocol level, for each network interface card installed on the system. You can access the packet filtering applet from the Start ⇨ Settings ⇨ Control Panel ⇨ Network applet. Then highlight the Protocols tab, go to TCP/IP properties, click the Advanced button, check the Enable Security check box, and then click the Configure button.

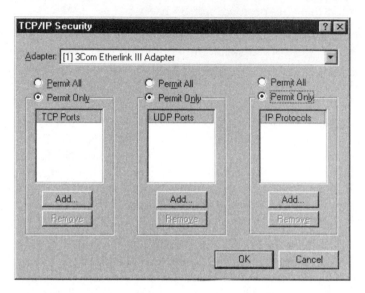

Packet filtering is not enabled by default, thus allowing all protocols and ports to be open and receive data. The Permit All radio button is selected when the menu is entered. By selecting the Permit Only button for the TCP or UDP ports or for the protocol definition, and by entering the appropriate port numbers, packet filtering is enabled. A listing of the well-known ports and the defined protocols available within the Windows NT system environment may be found in *services* and *protocols* files in the %systemroot%\system32\drivers\etc directory.

Packet filtering in the Windows NT system is not a strong enough security control when implemented by itself. This control should be implemented in conjunction with the packet filtering on the network routers and on the firewall, if the Windows NT system is going to be exposed to the Internet.

Fecha Manufacturing Corporation may find it beneficial to implement packet filtering on its internal web server so employees can only access certain ports. They will only allow ports 80, which is usually for the HyperText Transfer Protocol or HyperText Transport Protocol (HTTP), and 21, which is usually for the File Transfer Protocol (FTP). These protocols allow all employees to connect to web pages and FTP files. In addition, the only allowed protocol will be TCP (6).

## SMB Services (NetBIOS over TCP/IP)

*Server Message Block (SMB) services* form the backbone of Microsoft networking in the Windows NT environment. The SMB services present themselves on Windows NT servers and workstations as the *Server and Workstation Services.* When operating in the TCP/IP environment these services are found on ports 135–139. These access ports that are required for file sharing may present an access path, especially when exposed to the Internet or when used in conjunction with a UNIX server running the Samba service, which is a UNIX implementation of SMB. If TCP/IP is not running, then the SMB services are offered under the NetBEUI protocol. All file and printer sharing in Windows NT functions use the SMB services. There is an enhanced version of SMB services that is available for use over the Internet. This version is known as the *Common Internet File Sharing (CIFS)* protocol, and it was introduced under Service Pack 3.

The SMB Signing protocol was updated under Service Pack 3. A digital security signature is implemented into each SMB, which is then verified by both user parties to provide the authentication. To use SMB signing, it must be enabled on both the client and the server. If SMB signing is enabled on a server, then clients that are also enabled for SMB signing will use the new protocol during all subsequent sessions. Clients who are not enabled for SMB signing will use the older SMB protocol.

To implement SMB signing, Service Pack 3 must be installed. There are two ways to configure SMB signing: enabling SMB signing and requiring SMB signing. If it is enabled, then clients with SMB signing enabled will use this new SMB protocol and clients without SMB signing enabled will use the old SMB protocol. If SMB signing is required, then only clients with SMB signing enabled will be allowed to establish a connection to the server. It should be noted that only Windows NT clients with Service Pack 3 installed support SMB signing, and other operating systems such as Windows 95 do not.

The following must be set to configure SMB signing—Windows NT Server Registry Key: HKEY_LOCAL_MACHINE\SYSTEM\CurrentControlSet\Services\LanmanServer\Parameters

To enable SMB signing—Value Name: EnableSecuritySignature

To require SMB signing—Value Name: RequireSecuritySignature

Both values are Data Type: REG_DWORD.

An entry of 1 enables the value; an entry of 0 disables the value.

Windows NT Workstation Registry Key:

HKEY_LOCAL_MACHINE\SYSTEM\CurrentControlSet\Services\Rdr\Parameters

To enable SMB signing—Value Name: EnableSecuritySignature

To require SMB signing—Value Name: RequireSecuritySignature

Both values are Data Type: REG_DWORD.

An entry of 1 enables the value; an entry of 0 disables the value.

All Windows NT servers and workstations support SMB services by default, and you will probably not turn them off except in certain cases. In a workstation implementation, the server service should be disabled to prevent sharing of the workstation's local hard drive. In a web server implementation, all the SMB services should be disabled.

## PPTP

Windows NT further supports the confidentiality objective natively by offering the *Point-to-Point Tunneling Protocol (PPTP)*. Microsoft PPTP is a transport mechanism under which remote users can connect to corporate networks through secure channels creating connections commonly referred to as *Virtual Private Networks (VPNs)*. This VPN allows remote users to access internal network resources, including multiple protocols and applications, through virtual connectivity to the internal network.

A typical implementation of Microsoft PPTP provides remote users with the ability to connect to their Internet Service Provider (ISP) and then create a PPTP (VPN) connection. This connection would be from their workstation, over the Internet, to the corporate network. Once inside the corporate network, a Windows NT 4.0 Server authenticates the remote users through encrypted authentication. After successful authentication, both the client and the server generate RC4 encryption keys for encrypting subsequent communications, including IP, IPX/SPX, and NetBEUI protocols destined for the internal network. After every 256 packets are exchanged between the client and the server, new RC4 encryption keys are generated.

There are two implementations of PPTP today, one is a North American version featuring 128-bit encryption and the other is an exportable version with 40-bit encryption. PPTP uses the RC4 encryption engine from RSA, Inc., with keys generated using the Secure Hashing Algorithm (SHA-1) with input from the Microsoft encrypted authentication process.

When Fecha implements an Internet connection to its supplier Widget Pieces to purchase its widget supplies directly from them, it will use a PPTP connection to ensure its transactions are secure.

## Simple TCP/IP Services

Simple TCP/IP services in Windows NT provide many TCP/IP client and diagnostic utilities that can be used on the NT server and workstation. Some of the tools provided in the set may have some security implications because they allow information about the network or other systems to be discovered. These include the following tools:

- Nbtstat—Displays the contents of the remote computer's NetBIOS name table. The information listed in the NetBIOS name table can be used to determine the Domain name or workgroup the machine is in and the currently connected users. The information may also be used to uncover the Administrator's account, due to the fact that account SIDs are displayed in the name cache.
- Tracert—Traces the path that a packet follows to its destination server.

- Netstat—Displays the status of the TCP/IP stack, including what ports are open and what connections are active.
- Finger—Gathers information about users on any machine running a Finger server.
- TFTP—Allows unauthenticated file transfer to any TFTP server.

## Simple Network Management Protocol (SNMP)

SNMP is a service that is used in network management systems. It operates by sending traps (messages) to the defined network management console when predefined alerts or events occur. SNMP operates on the concept of communities for defining systems that are grouped together for data gathering or reporting. The security implication for SNMP in a Windows NT environment is that the default-defined community is known as *public*, which is the common name for the default community in all SNMP implementations.

**Note**   If SNMP is used in the Windows NT environment, care should be taken to define a unique community name for your particular environment.

## Remote Procedure Calls (RPCs)

Windows NT Server supports a distributed processing methodology known as *Remote Procedure Calls (or RPCs)*. RPCs allow commands to be sent from one system to execute programs on another system. Windows NT networking supports RPCs from several protocols, including TCP/IP and IPX (NWLink). In addition, Windows NT supports RPC execution in a NetBEUI environment using the named pipes interface. *Named pipes* provide a continuous data connection between the communicating systems. RPCs may be used on both Windows NT servers and workstations.

RPCs security implications include a denial of service attack against the RPC port of TCP/IP. RPC operates on port 135 and a telnet to this port in a Windows NT system that is not patched to Service Pack 3 could be susceptible to this.

## Denial of Service Attacks

As previously mentioned, most protocols have inherent security risks, and Windows NT is susceptible to hacker attacks due to the fact that it supports all these protocols. The following are common security threats against the protocols that systems administrators should be aware of when implementing the protocol. Following the list of attacks is a description of how Windows NT can be protected and how it can defend itself against attacks.

One of the most common security attacks on Windows NT systems are *denial of service attacks*, which attempt to prevent the use of a system either by using all available processor resources, memory resources, network resources, or by shutting down the system. Many general types of denial of service attacks can be used against machines running many operating systems. In this section, the attacks that Windows NT is susceptible to are discussed.

*Ping-of-Death (large Ping packet)* is an attack involving Ping. *Ping (Packet Internet Groper)* is a standard TCP/IP network utility that sends packets from one machine to another in order to determine if there is a valid network route between them. Windows NT Ping packets are sent out with a default of 32 bytes of data. Issuing a Ping packet of larger than normal size set at 64K causes the Ping-of-Death attack. If the Ping command is issued, specifying a larger than normal packet size, the TCP/IP stack on the receiving machine could cease to function correctly. This Ping-of-Death attack effectively takes the system off line until it is rebooted. Most implementations of Ping will not allow a packet size greater than the default to be sent; however, Windows 95 and Windows NT do allow this exception and can, therefore, cause or be vulnerable to such a system denial.

*Ping-of-Death 2* is a variation of the original Ping-of–Death attack, whereby either multiple packets greater than 64K in length or multiple 64K fragmented packets are sent, crashing the receiving system.

The *SYN Flood* attack is a flood of TCP connection requests (SYN) that can be sent to a server. The connection requests contain "spoofed" source IP addresses. Upon receiving the connection request, the server allocates resources to handle and track the new connections. A response (SYN-ACK) is sent to the "spoofed" nonexistent IP address. Because no acknowledgment is received, the server will continue to retransmit and eventually release the resources that were set aside earlier for the connection 189 seconds later. This process effectively ties up the server, and multiple requests can cause the server to respond with a reset to all further connection requests.

*Out-of-Band* attacks are attacks where data is sent outside the normal expected band that has been shown to affect Windows NT. This attack causes unpredictable results and sometimes causes Windows NT to have trouble handling any network operations. This attack most likely operates against a Windows NT machine listening on port 139 (NetBIOS listener), but it may also affect port 53 (DNS) as well.

Telneting to various unknown ports can lead to increased CPU usage or a system crash. Telnet expects connections to be made to port 23 only and connections to other ports can cause Windows NT to behave erratically. Affected ports include port 135 (RPC), port 53 (DNS), or port 1031 (inetinfo). Connections to these ports may either stop services or force the system CPU to 100-percent utilization.

The *Land* attack is a denial of service attack in which the source and destination SYN packets have the same address and the same port. This attack forces the computer to operate more slowly while trying to respond to packets sent to itself.

*Teardrop and Teardrop 2* attacks are attacks that can cause a system to halt by using up all available memory in the kernel. This attack is accomplished by sending fragmented UDP datagram packets to a Windows NT server.

*Bonk* and *Boink* are modified versions of the Teardrop attack. Like the Teardrop attack, they occur due to fragmented UDP packets and may cause the operating system to crash.

## Defenses to Denial of Service Attacks

The security controls needed to protect Windows NT against the attacks include installing the latest service pack and hotfixes for each type of attack. As new attacks become public, new fixes are released. Table 6-1 lists the various denial of service attacks and the specific solutions to them.

**Table 6-1.  Denial of Service Attack Fixes**

| Denial of Service | Defense |
| --- | --- |
| Telnet to unknown ports | Apply Service Pack 2. |
| Ping-of-Death (large Ping packet) | Apply Service Pack 2. |
| Ping-of-Death 2 | Apply Service Pack 3. Apply icmp-fix. |
| 'SYN' Flood | Apply Service Pack 2. |
| Out-of-Band | Apply Service Pack 3. Apply the OOB-fix. Apply the Post SP3 tcp fix. |
| Land | Apply Service Pack 3. Apply Land-fix. |
| Teardrop, Teardrop2, Bonk, and Boink | Apply Service Pack 3. Apply Teardrop-2 fix. |

# External Networking

External networking creates additional connection points where security controls need to be in place. All information passed through external connections need to be protected from unauthorized disclosure, especially data that is traversing the Internet. Information also needs to be accurate and complete. All connections need to be for a valid business purpose and if they do not fall in line with corporate objectives, they should not be used. All external network connections should be secured so that data is secure when it resides on the system and as it crosses the network.

Most corporations consider local area networking  (LAN) and wide area networking (WAN) as business requirements. For corporations whose employees are constantly on the road with laptops, such as salespersons and consultants, these features provide a great benefit. If configured appropriately, Windows NT allows clients to dial in the network and be authenticated as if they were sitting in an office on a workstation. However, remote access also provides another point of entry to a system, thereby giving an attacker a way of avoiding other security access controls.

There are two variations of external networking: remote control and remote node. Both methods allow users to log in a network and access resources granted to them. For the purposes of this book, we will concentrate on remote node because that is

Windows NT's native support; however, both are discussed briefly in the text that follows.

*Remote control* programs grant users remote control of a server so they can administer that server. Remote control applications place the server in host mode so clients can dial in and take full control over the machine remotely. The client actually takes control of the machine; all input devices, such as the keyboard and mouse, are routed to the remote client. All computer processes take place on the host server and output is displayed on the client machine. Users of this type of application should be very cautious, because if a server is currently logged in as the administrator, the client that takes control of the server now has administrator access. A server should never be left logged in as the administrator, but if this is the case, remote control hosts should be configured with an extremely difficult access password.

*Remote node* is the method employed by Windows NT Remote Access Service (RAS). The remote node method allows a remote client machine to dial in to a server and attach itself to the network using various protocols. It allows a network to be extended beyond the actual wires that connect computers together, to a dynamic location for people who travel. Remote node systems run the application on the remote user's computer and treat the connection line as an extension of the local area network, sending LAN-style traffic, such as requests for file and print services, over the line. This connectivity allows for greater flexibility and security.

RAS allows all types of Windows, DOS, and OS/2 users to dial in and authenticate to the server and access resources on the network according to their privileges. After they have logged in, the users can do anything they normally would from an office computer that is connected to the server. RAS allows dial-in users to access Windows NT servers across standard phone lines (standard telephone systems, frame relay, or Asynchronous Transfer Mode [ATM] or other asynchronous connections, X.25 packet switched networks, or Integrated Services Digital Network [ISDN] lines). RAS uses remote node systems to provide this capability. Because RAS treats the connection line as an extension of the LAN, it is designed to support Windows NT's security controls, complete with trust relationships and centralized domain administration.

## RAS Authentication

To configure RAS authentication settings, open the Control Panel and the Network applet. Choose the Services tab and double-click the Remote Access Service entry. After the Remote Access Setup dialog box appears, click the Network button. If you have dial out and receive calls enabled, the following dialog box will appear and allow you to configure RAS authentication settings.

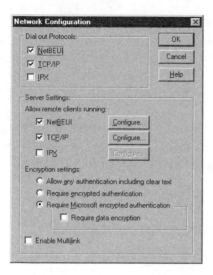

To ensure the confidentiality of authentication, Windows NT supports encryption. There are three settings for remote client authentication: Allow Any Authentication Including Clear Text, Require Encrypted Authentication, and Require Microsoft Encrypted Authentication.

If the *Allow Any Authentication* setting is enabled, the server will negotiate the highest level of encryption possible. Although Allow Any Authentication is effective if the server is communicating with another client that supports encrypted authentication, it is ineffective if the client does not. For example, *Password Authentication Protocol (PAP)* uses clear text password authentication. Remote clients that may be using PAP are those that use Winsock. It is strongly recommended that this option never be selected.

*Require Encrypted Authentication* is a setting that requires *Shiva Password Authentication Protocol (SPAP), Challenge Handshake Authentication Protocol (CHAP)*, or *Data Encryption Standard (DES)*. This setting is more secure than clear text. The *Require Microsoft Encrypted Authentication* setting requires MS-CHAP to be used, and no others are acceptable. This authentication protocol is considered the most secure of the three settings because it uses RSA's MD4 standard to encrypt authentication.

If you are using MS-CHAP, all data transmitted during the session can also be encrypted, even after authentication, thus providing another security control for securing data as it traverses the phone line. This encryption can be accomplished through the Require Data Encryption check box, which is located below the Require Microsoft Encrypted Authentication check box.  The default encryption is RSA Data Security's RC4 algorithm.

There are ways to implement better security controls for authentication, known as strong authentication. This method involves using a third-party device either instead of or in addition to Windows NT's authentication procedure. The most common device is a Single Use Password (SUP) card, which displays a different pass code every minute that must be entered with a fixed user password. Other forms of strong authentication are tokens or biometrics devices, although they only work across standard telephone systems. Biometrics devices can replace the standard Windows NT authentication dialog box with an external fingerprint scanner.

## Secure Remote Access Services

The Windows NT RAS is administered through the Remote Access Admin application. To launch Remote Access Admin choose Start ⇨ Programs ⇨ Administrative Tools ⇨ Remote Access Admin. The Remote Access Admin dialog box appears.

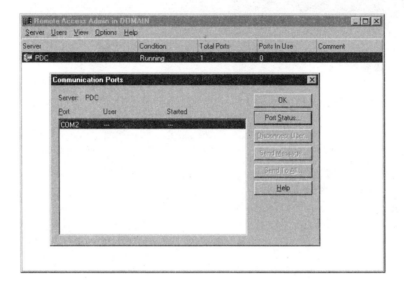

Administrators can use Remote Access Admin to view either an entire domain of machines with RAS installed or simply one server. Table 6-2 presents and describes the screen layout.

**Table 6-2.  Remote Access Admin Dialog Box**

| Column | Description |
|---|---|
| Server | The name of the active server |
| Condition | Whether or not the Remote Access Service has started |
| Total Ports | The number of ports available for users to simultaneously dial in |
| Ports in Use | The number of ports currently in use |
| Comment | Description for the server |

## Communication Ports

It is possible to view the communication ports of a particular server by either double-clicking on its name or choosing Server ⇨ Communication Ports, which opens the Communication Ports dialog box. Table 6-3 presents and discusses the Communication Ports dialog box.

**Table 6-3. Communication Ports Dialog Box**

| Column | Description |
| --- | --- |
| Port | Displays each serial communication port configured for RAS. |
| User | Displays the user connected to the specified port. |
| Started | Shows the start date and time of each connection. |

| Button | Description |
| --- | --- |
| Port Status | Displays the Port Status dialog box where information about the modem, connection, and port statistics can be found. |
| Disconnect User | Disconnects user from selected port. |
| Send Message | Sends a user on the selected port a message. |
| Send To All | Sends all users on a server or domain a message. |

Administrators can use this dialog box to disconnect users who should not be online or are suspected of committing malicious acts. To avoid data corruption, warn users with a message that they are being disconnected before you terminate their connection, unless the user is an intruder.

## Start / Stop / Pause / Continue Remote Access Service

Administrators have the ability to start, stop, pause, and continue the remote access service on any of the servers in the domain by choosing the appropriate menu item from the Server menu.

# Administering Users

One way to control a remote access service is to deny as many users as possible the privilege to dial in. Do not have only one account with a shared password, because if nonauthorized people find out the password, they will be able to dial in. It is never good to have shared passwords for an account, especially with dial in.

Administrators can use User Manager for Domains to manage user dial-in permissions as described in chapter 7, "Implementing Security Through User Management." User Manager is only appropriate when administering a few users because there is no way to get a summary of all users that have the dial-in capability. If administrators want to see all users and quickly manage dial-in permissions, Remote Access Admin is more appropriate. From within the main view, choose Users ⇨ Permissions to open the Remote Access Permissions dialog box.

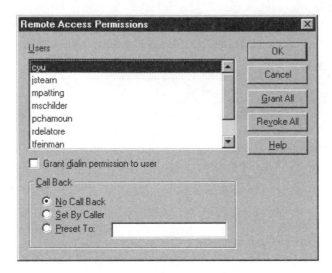

Table 6-4 presents and describes the Remote Access Permissions dialog box's sections and buttons.

**Table 6-4. Remote Access Permissions Dialog Box**

| Section | Description |
|---|---|
| Users | Lists all the users for the selected server. |

| **Check Box** | **Description** |
|---|---|
| Grant Dial-in Permission to User | Shows whether or not the selected user is granted dial-in capabilities. |

| **Call Back Radio Buttons** | **Description** |
|---|---|
| No Call Back | Disables Call Back for the selected user. |
| Set By Caller | Prompts the user for a number to call back when they log in. |
| Preset To | Calls a user back at the specified number when they dial in. |

| **Button** | **Description** |
|---|---|
| Grant All | Grants every user dial-in capabilities. |
| Revoke All | Revokes every user's dial-in capabilities. |

## Call Back

The Call Back feature can be a very useful security control. However, it is not always possible to implement for all users. When the Call Back feature is disabled, users can dial from anywhere. Disabling Call Back also means hackers have the ability to call from the privacy of their own home, or more likely from a phone booth in the middle of a crowded city. Hackers could then attempt to penetrate the system with little chance of being traced.

The Set By Caller option offers more security than not using Call Back at all. Forcing a user to have the server call them back to establish an RAS connection gives an additional degree of logging, because the phone number called back is recorded. When individuals dial in, they must give a phone number where they can be called back. Administrators can view the phone numbers that were called back because they appear in the audit logs. For corporations that have sales representatives on the road dialing in from hotels, this option is not very useful.

The last option, Preset To, is the most secure RAS dial-in control; however, it is infeasible for most average users, unless they only call in from a single location such as their home. This option allows administrators to have the server call a user back at a fixed number so that a hacker would first have to break into the user's home before trying to penetrate the server. The chances of a security breach diminish if physical location requirements are placed on a dial-up connection. Many corporations use a dial-in method for employees who travel, which disqualifies the Preset To option.

However, because a combination of these options can be used for different users, you can apply them as appropriate for individual users. For example, accounts used by people who do not regularly travel as part of their job may only be permitted to call in from a specified location, while individuals who regularly travel as part of their job may be permitted to call in from any location.

**Note**   It's good security control to not grant administrators or other sensitive accounts dial-in permissions because if such an account is compromised, the consequences can be detrimental.

## Monitoring Users

Administrators can monitor the users currently connected to a server via the Remote Access Users dialog box. To open this dialog box, choose Users ⇨ Active Users. Table 6.5 presents and describes the Remote Access Users dialog box.

**Table 6-5. Remote Access Users**

| Column | Description |
| --- | --- |
| User | Displays the username of users currently connected to the server. |
| Server | Shows the name of the server to which each user is connected. |
| Started | Displays the time each connection was initiated. |

| Button | Description |
| --- | --- |
| User Account | Shows the details of the selected user account. |
| Disconnect User | Terminates a user's session. |
| Send Message | Sends a message to the user. |
| Send To All | Sends a message to all connected users. |

The Remote Access Users dialog box is a fast way for administrators to see a list of all active users. An administrator can quickly browse the list for people that should not be dialed in or to see how long they have been online; perhaps someone forgot to log off.

### Configuring and Securing RAS

RAS is a service that can be configured in the Network applet of the Control Panel. The Services tab lists all the services installed on the system. To configure RAS, you can either double-click on Remote Access Service or highlight it and click the Properties button. The Remote Access Setup dialog box appears.

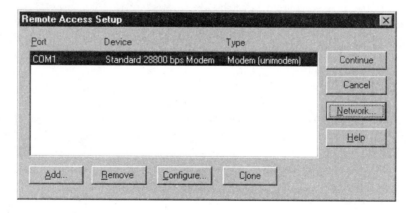

Table 6-6 presents and describes the columns and buttons in the Remote Access Setup dialog box:

**Table 6-6. Remote Access Setup**

| Column | Description |
| --- | --- |
| Port | Displays each serial communication port configured for RAS. |
| Device | Displays the device name. |
| Type | Shows the type of device, be it modem or other. |

| Button | Description |
| --- | --- |
| Add | Makes a port available to RAS. Modems can be installed through here or the Modem applet in Control Panel. |
| Remove | Makes a port unavailable. Modems cannot be deinstalled here, only through the Modem applet in Control Panel. |
| Configure | Configures how the selected port is to be used. |
| Clone | Copies the same modem setup from one port to another. |
| Network | Configures RAS network options and features. |

It is from this dialog box that administrators can restrict what types of network traffic remote users can access.

### Configuring Port Usage

To restrict whether a port can be used for dialing in or dialing out, click the Configure button. The Configure Port Usage dialog box appears.

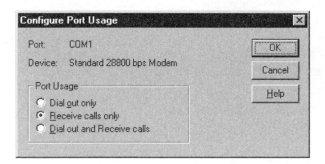

The top of this box displays the port and device being configured. The bottom contains a section called Port Usage. There are three radio buttons: Dial out only, Receive calls only, and Dial out and Receive calls.

There are typically two classifications of RAS servers—those administered and run by proper network authorities, and those installed by users on their own desktop systems. Because a Windows NT Workstation provides RAS server functionality, users that have a Windows NT Workstation can attach a modem to their machine, turn on RAS with Receive calls, and dial in from home to access the network. In some corporations, even systems administrators sometimes attach modems to their workstations or servers because they want to be able to dial in and administer a network from home.

**Caution** RAS dial-in servers should be closely monitored and users should not be permitted to run RAS servers on their own systems.

One common tool employed by hackers is a so-called "war dialer." *War dialers* are programs that rapidly dial a range of phone numbers defined by a hacker to determine which numbers have modems connected. After the hacker determines which numbers have modems, he or she attempts to log in the system that is connected to that modem. In the case of RAS receiving phone calls, if a hacker used a war dialer, he or she could discover the server running RAS and attempt to log in. Using this technique provides an opportunity for the hacker to break into accounts or, at the very least, to lock out many accounts trying.

To prevent this attack, administrators can set RAS to be a Dial out only service on systems that should not allow incoming phone calls, such as user desktops and laptop systems. However, it is possible administrators and users (with permission) will change this option to also receive calls so they can log in from home. One way to avoid users from setting their workstations to allow dial-in is to have the telephone corporation configure the telephone lines that are connected to computer modems as dial-out only, where appropriate.

### Configuring the Network

Administrators must exert caution when configuring the network protocols available through RAS. As more of the network is made accessible through RAS, the scope of damage that can be caused by a hacker that breaks into an RAS server increases. To open the Network Configuration dialog box, click the Network button.

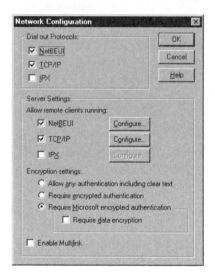

Table 6-7 presents and describes the Network Configuration dialog box.

**Table 6-7. Network Configuration Dialog Box**

| Dial-Out Protocols | Description |
| --- | --- |
| NetBEUI | Makes the NetBEUI protocol available for dial-out networking. If disabled, NetBEUI will not be available in phone book entries. |
| TCP/IP | Makes the TCP/IP protocol available for dial-out networking. If disabled, TCP/IP will not be available in phone book entries. |
| IPX | Makes the IPX protocol available for dial-out networking. If disabled, IPX will not be available in phone book entries. |

| Server Settings | Description |
| --- | --- |
| *Allow remote clients running* | |
| NetBEUI | Makes the NetBEUI protocol available for users who dial in. |
| TCP/IP | Makes the TCP/IP protocol available for users who dial in. |
| IPX | Makes the IPX protocol available for users who dial in. |
| *Encryption Settings* | |
| Allow Any Authentication Including Clear Text | Permits connections using any authentication including MS-CHAP, SPAP, and PAP. |
| Require Encrypted Authentication | Permits connections using any authentication except PAP. |
| Require Microsoft Encrypted Authentication | Requires connections to use MS-CHAP. |
| Require Data Encryption | Requires all data sent over the network to be encrypted using RC4. |

**Note**   If Dial out or Receive calls is not enabled in the Configure Port Usage dialog box, those respective sections will not be available in the Network Configuration dialog box.

## Dial-out Protocols

The dial-out protocols available here are a list of the protocols that must be configured for dialing out through Dial-Up Networking, which is Microsoft's dial-up solution for connecting to the Internet or other servers. The protocols selected here will be available in the phone book entries that can be configured through Dial-Up Networking.

## Server Settings

There are three protocols available for the Receiving Calls option. Users will have access to any enabled protocols if they successfully log in to the Windows NT server. A description of each protocol and the security control provided by each is listed in the "Protocols" section earlier in this chapter. Clicking the Configure button can configure each protocol.

## Recommendations and Considerations for Securing External Networking

If a corporation requires RAS because its employees need to dial in for network access, then extreme caution should be taken in securing the RAS server, and proper security controls should be used. Users need to be properly authenticated and the data they transmit must be protected to ensure integrity and confidentiality. If the source cannot be trusted, the data cannot be trusted. All remote access connections must be for a valid business reason and controls should be in place to prevent an individual from undermining system security.

Depending on the business environment and the level of security needed, we present the following three scenarios, with varying degrees of controls, to demonstrate different RAS security configurations that can be implemented. We created three new fictitious corporations (based on our experience) that have different business reasons for implementing RAS and different security control requirements. Describing the RAS security features in these three different ways helps systems administrators identify with the corporations that most closely match their own corporation, and to understand the RAS security configurations.

The highest level of security for external networking would be to disallow usage of remote access. However, because this is usually impossible for most corporations, this option will not be considered for purposes of the following scenarios. We will assume that all users need to be dialing in the network; therefore, the port usage in all scenarios will be set to Dial out and Receive calls.

### Scenario 1: Feinmerica Inc.—Very High Security

Feinmerica Inc. is in the business of designing widgets using Computer Aided Design (CAD). After a design is complete, Feinmerica sells the widget to manufacturing companies. All employees of Feinmerica log in the Corporate domain while on premises with their office workstations. However, for those employees that have home computers running Windows NT and CAD, they can dial in from home and work on their designs, as long as all data files are stored in the corporate file server, CADATA. CADATA is set up as a stand-alone server in its own workgroup, outside the corporate domain, and it runs RAS.

Each employee has an account in the domain and an account on CADATA. Because employees dial in from home and do not need access from dynamic locations, such as a hotel or client facility, RAS is configured to call back a preset number, which is the user's home telephone number. Users need only upload and download their designs to CADATA, so the protocol used to dial in has been configured to allow access to *This Computer Only*. In addition, only users have been granted dial-in capabilities. Members of other groups (such as administrators) have been denied because the Administrator account is too powerful to take the risk of allowing someone to guess its password, although highly unlikely. Individuals who dial in must authenticate with their own unique password; therefore, anonymous or guest access has not been set up or allowed.

Users log in with Microsoft Encrypted Authentication, which is Microsoft Challenge Handshake Authentication Protocol (MS-CHAP). It uses RSA's MD4 standard to encrypt authentication. After users have successfully logged in, they are given TCP/IP network access and assigned an IP address from a dedicated pool. All data is controlled and encrypted with RSA's RC4 algorithm throughout the entire session.

### Scenario 2: The Chamoun Company—High Security

The Chamoun Company is another widget-designing company. Employees use CAD in the office or from home on their Windows NT machines and store their data on a file server, CADATA, which is a domain member server within the Corporate domain. Employees also access an analytic marketing software program and a research and development program, which are located within the domain. These two software programs are actually stored on member servers and are huge databases for which users have a small front end. When employees access these programs from home, they are required to authenticate on the domain. There is an RAS server in the domain that allows users to dial in and authenticate with their domain user accounts.

The RAS server allows users to access all computers on the Entire Network because employees may need to access the database products from home or a client facility. In addition, when employees are visiting a client site, promoting their widget design, they sometimes dial in and demonstrate some of the market analysis that has been completed on their future widget releases, using the analytic marketing software product. For this reason, employees need to be able to dial in from any location. RAS is set to call back a number set by each caller. Auditing is turned on and any telephone number that is called back is recorded in the log. Administrator and guest access is not allowed for the same reasons as Feinmerica.

Users log in with Microsoft Encrypted Authentication, which is Microsoft Challenge Handshake Authentication Protocol (MS-CHAP). This setting uses RSA's MD4 standard to encrypt authentication. After users have successfully logged in, they are given TCP/IP network access and assigned an IP address from a dedicated pool. In addition, they are given IPX network access so users can access a NetWare server.

### Scenario 3: JJ's Widget Inc.—Secure

JJ's Widget Inc. is a third competitor in the widget industry. JJ's network is identical to The Chamoun Company's network in almost every aspect, except for a few configuration settings on the RAS server.

JJ's Widget realizes that it will never check the audit logs, so it does not enable Call Back. This decision is common in many companies, although not a good practice to follow. In addition, RAS is configured to the Allow Any Authentication setting, including clear text, because users do not always dial in from Windows NT machines; they sometimes dial in using Winsock or some other method that does not support encryption. This method, in itself, is secure because RAS always tries the most secure authentication methods first. Even if clear text is used, JJ's Widget has implemented compensating controls such as placing restrictive file and directory permissions on the RAS server so that a network monitor cannot be installed to capture the passwords. All other settings match that of The Chamoun Company.

Table 6-8 summarizes the various levels of RAS security configurations.

**Table 6-8. RAS Security Configurations**

| Settings | Very High Security | High Security | Secure |
|---|---|---|---|
| | *Feinmerica Inc.* | *The Chamoun Company* | *JJ's Widget Inc.* |
| Domain Member Server | No | Yes | Yes |
| Port Usage | Dial Out and Receive Calls | Dial Out and Receive Calls | Dial Out and Receive Calls |
| Administrator Access | Denied | Denied | Denied |
| Guest or Anonymous Access | Denied | Denied | Denied |
| Call Back | Preset | Set By Caller | None |
| Network Access | This Computer Only | Entire Network | Entire Network |
| Network Protocols NetBEUI | TCP/IP | TCP/IP IPX | TCP/IP IPX |
| TCP/IP | Assign IP Addresses | Assign IP Addresses | Assign IP Addresses |
| Encryption | Require Microsoft Encrypted Authentication and Data Encryption | Require Microsoft Encrypted Authentication | Allow Any Authentication Including Clear Text |

These three scenarios were intended to demonstrate different RAS security configurations that can be implemented. Your corporation will certainly differ from them and you should create a secure policy that only allows a level of access that is absolutely necessary for business purposes. Always grant users the least amount of privileges possible, in order for them to complete their job responsibilities.

# Chapter 7
# Implementing Security Through User Management

This chapter is designed to give administrators an understanding of how users are identified within the Windows NT environment; it also explains how to control users and groups. In addition, this chapter is used to understand the security risks surrounding user management and how to implement security controls in a manner that is appropriate for your corporation. Each topic is explained and then the implementation is shown, all of which is followed by security considerations and recommendations.

Accounts are an important piece of the Windows NT Security structure; they control access to a computer system. They are the keys that grant authorized users appropriate access to components within the Windows NT environment. If implemented correctly, accounts provide a safe and secure way to allow users to access resources on a network or local system, an accurate audit trail for tracking users' actions, and a means of monitoring users.

Security through user management is the most fundamental component of Windows NT. User management comes in two variations:

- User Manager—Manages security on workstations and member server or server stand-alones (*non-domain controllers*)
- User Manager for Domains—Manages security on Primary or Backup Domain Controllers (*domain controllers*)

---

**Note**  While many aspects of Windows NT's Security architecture are common between the domain controllers and non-domain controllers, this book focuses primarily on a domain controller except when otherwise noted.

The security features provided by User Manager consist of creating and managing user and group accounts, creating and editing account and audit policies, designating user rights, and establishing trust relationships.Group and User Accounts

Group and user accounts are the means by which administrators assign permissions, privileges, and rights to people who use Windows NT. A person is assigned a unique user account and that account is granted membership to various group accounts depending on their job functions. A user account can be a part of a group account; however, a group account cannot be a member or a user account.

## Groups

A *group account* contains other accounts, known as *members*. Job assignment, specific access requirements, or any other criteria can determine membership of groups. Administrators use groups to facilitate the management of rights and permissions for users who perform similar tasks within the Windows NT environment.

Groups are good security controls that allow an administrator to treat large numbers of users as a single entity for the purposes of assigning privileges. Without group accounts, each individual user would have to be provided abilities and restrictions. Users with similar job functions would be given similar abilities and restrictions. Although it is recommended that users belong to groups and groups are assigned permissions to access resources, users are commonly granted explicit access to resources, making it more difficult to manage and maintain access controls. Some administrators feel that creating a group for a limited number of users is a waste of time; however, managing one group is easier than a number of individual user accounts. All the users in a group have the abilities and restrictions of the group, in addition to those of any other groups to which the users belong. To change the permissions or rights that users are granted due to their group membership, only that group account needs to be modified.

For example, if Alice, Bob, and Carl need access to the c:\marketing directory, the administrator could create a group called *Finance* and grant the group rights to the c:\marketing directory rather than granting the users individual permissions to c:\marketing. Underlying the administrative reasoning for creating groups are the security controls that groups provide. Groups are considered a more secure way of maintaining users because there is less chance of neglecting a user's restrictions. If 1,000 users are independently granted access to a resource and an administrator needs to revoke their access, there is a chance an administrator will neglect a user. However, by using groups, an administrator needs only to remove access to one group of users, rather than the 1,000 potential members.

Windows NT provides two classifications of groups for controlling user membership: local groups and global groups. *Local groups* are defined on each machine and may have both user accounts and global groups as members. Depending on how Windows NT is installed, there are a number of built-in local group accounts. Non-domain controllers produce a different group list than domain controllers. Domain controller installations also produce three built-in global group accounts. *Global groups* are defined at the domain level (only applicable to a machine connected to a domain) and may only contain users as members.

## Local Groups

On a stand-alone Windows NT system that is not on a domain, only local groups are created and maintained. They set group-wide access permissions to resources on the local machine where it is located. If the system is part of a domain, a local group can contain user accounts from the domain where it is located and from any trusted domain.

In multiple domain configurations, local groups are useful for assembling global groups into one manageable unit. Instead of assigning permissions to each global group separately, the administrator simply assigns permissions to a local group and then makes global groups members of the local group. Through membership in a local group, users from other domains are allowed access to resources in the current domain.

Figure 7-1 depicts local group memberships, depending on whether or not the computer is a domain member.

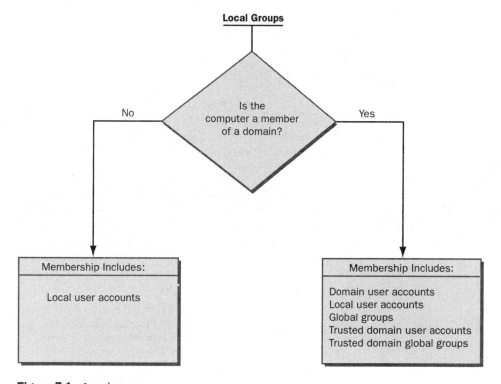

**Figure 7-1.** *Local groups*

Local groups can only be used where their specific accounts exist; that is, they are only used on the machine in which they are created. A local group can contain both individual user accounts and global groups but it cannot contain other local groups.

### Built-in Domain Controller Local Groups

A domain local group can contain user accounts and global groups from the local domain or any domain trusted by that domain. However, the local group can only be granted permissions to resources in the domain where the local group is defined.

The eight built-in local groups for a Windows NT server functioning as a domain controller are as follows:

- *Account Operators*: Members of the Account Operators group can use User Manager for Domains to create and manage user and group accounts for the domain and to modify or delete most user and group accounts in the domain. These members may not modify or delete accounts with security privileges higher than their own. For example, account operators cannot delete administrators. They are allowed to log on locally and shut down the system, as well as keep a local profile.

  Although we often see systems administrators performing these functions, a good security control is to have the security officer be part of this group and perform these functions.

- *Administrators*: Accounts in the Administrators local group on a Windows NT server have control over the local machine. Because they can do anything, administrators are the most powerful types of system users. They can create and manage user and group accounts for the machine, assign user rights, lock and override the lock on the local machine, format hard disks, create common groups, maintain a local profile, and share and stop sharing directories and printers.

  Because it is such a powerful group, membership to the Administrators group should be limited to as few accounts as possible. Only the person or persons responsible for the server should be granted administrator privileges, and they should be held accountable for that machine. Granting users membership to the Administrators group is very common among corporations, although it may not be required. For example, an individual may be required to manage other user and group accounts (and therefore given membership to Administrators) when all they needed was membership to the Account Operators group. Always grant the least amount of privileges as necessary and be cautious when granting membership to the Administrators groups, because they will be in full control of the system. All administrators must be fully and completely trusted, accountable, and responsible.

**Note**   The domain administrator cannot override the workstation lock of another machine, only the lock on its local machine, unless they are members of the local Administrators group.

- *Backup Operator*: The Backup Operators group allows the user to back up and restore files on a system. Any user can back up and restore those files for which he or she has the appropriate file permissions. The Backup Operators group can back up any disk file, regardless of file permissions. They also can override the access control lists on files for backup operations only. They can read or write to all files on the system without explicit permissions. Backup Operators can also log on locally and shut down the system, as well as maintain a local profile.

  Personnel responsible for creating and restoring backups should be granted membership to the Backup Operators group. Granting membership to the Backup Operators group should also be controlled and monitored, as it is a powerful group.

- *Guests*: The Guests group is the most restricted group within Windows NT, because it provides its members with the least amount of functionality. Guests can log on locally to a workstation; however, they cannot log on locally to a domain controller. By default, there is one member of this group, the Guest account. Guests cannot keep a local profile.

  Individuals should not be granted membership to this group unless they are temporary employees who need minimal access to the system resources.

- *Print Operators*: Members of the Print Operators group can create, delete, and manage printer shares for a Windows NT server. They can log on the system locally, shut it down, and keep a local profile. Only employees who are responsible for printer configurations and security of the printers should be granted membership to the Print Operators group.

- *Replicator*: The Replicator group allows users to replicate files and directories with other authorized systems. To do this, members would need the Log On as a Service right. This right is very powerful, as discussed in the "Advanced User Rights" section in Chapter 8, "Securing Accounts with Account Policies." Therefore, members of this group should be limited to the account created for the Replicator services. No other users should be members of this group.

- *Server Operators*: Excluding administrators, the Server Operators group is granted the most rights. Members of this group can manage a domain's servers, which include, but are not limited to, creating, deleting, and managing printer and network shares. They can also log on locally to the server, change the system time, shut down the machine, and back up and restore files and directories.

  Employees that perform system maintenance and need authority to manage file sharing are usually placed in the Administrators group. However, a better security control would be to place them in the Server Operators group, where they would have only the privileges needed to perform their responsibilities.

- *Users*: Anyone who uses a computer on a routine basis should have an account in the Users group. Membership to the Users group provides the user with the necessary rights to operate the system as an end user, such as running applications and managing files. By default, new accounts in a domain are placed into the Domain Users group, and the Domain Users group is a member of the local Users group on all domain member machines.

### Built-in, Non-Domain Controller Local Groups

Windows NT provides six built-in local groups for machines that are not set up as domain controllers. Groups that are common to both non-domain and domain controllers have the same function and description. The built-in, non-domain controller local groups are listed as follows:

- Administrators
- Backup Operators
- Guests
- Power Users
- Replicator
- Users

Notice that only the Power Users group is not in the domain controller set of groups.

Members of the Power Users group can perform system administrative functions without having control over the system. A member of the Power Users group can do anything a user can in addition to the following:

- Access the computer from the network
- Change the system time
- Force the shutdown of a remote system
- Create and manage user accounts
- Lock the machine
- Create common groups
- Maintain a local profile
- Share as well as stop the sharing of directories

Most employees should not be placed in the Power Users group, because they do not need the privileges this group provides. This group is analogous to a combination of the Server Operators, Account Operators, and Print Operators groups on domain controllers.

## Global Groups

A *global group* is a domain-level administrative tool for organizing users. These groups facilitate securing a system across a collection of computers. The sole purpose of a global group is to gather users together at the domain level so they can be placed in the appropriate local groups. Global groups set group-wide access permissions across multiple domains.

Users in a global group are assigned rights and permissions to resources by including the global group in a local group that has the desired permissions. Through membership in a local group, the users in a global group can access resources on a Windows NT client, such as a local or trusted domain.

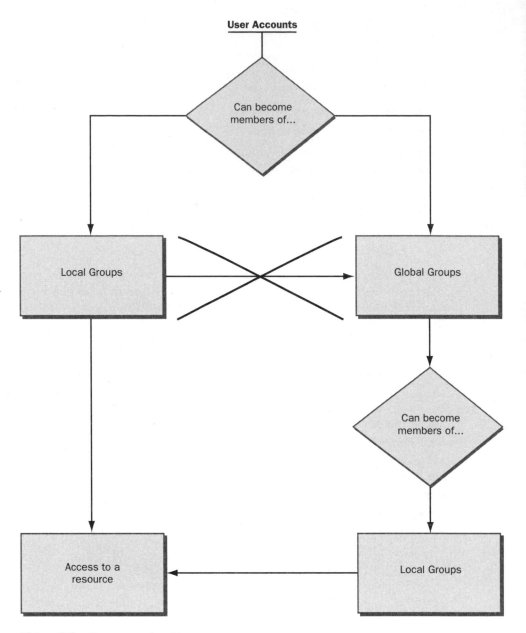

**Figure 7-2.** *Group memberships*

Although global groups can become members of local groups, local groups (or other global groups) cannot become members of global groups. Only user accounts located in the domain where the global group exists can be assigned to that global group.

Through trust relationships, accounts in a global group can be given access to resources anywhere in the network, regardless of where the resources are physically located. Trust relationships were previously discussed in Chapter 6, "Securing All External and Internal Network Connections."

---

**Note**  A user's credentials are made up of three items: domain name, username, and password. Within her own domain, a user appears as her username only, without a domain prefix. However, in other domains, a user appears with the prefix of the domain of origin. Because the prefix classifies from which domain a group originates, a global group in one domain can have the same name as a local group in another.

### Built-in Global Groups

Windows NT Server provides the following three built-in global groups:

- *Domain Admins*: The Domain Admins global group is the most powerful group in a domain and should be limited to only certain high-level administrators. The Domain Admins group is a member of the Administrators local group on the PDC and all domain member machines. By default, only the Administrator account from the PDC is a member of the Domain Admins group.

- *Domain Guests*: The Domain Guests global group is the equivalent of the local Guest group. Only users with temporary IDs that need to access domain resources should be placed in this group.

- *Domain Users*: By default, the Domain Users group contains all the users in the domain, including the built-in user accounts and any new accounts that are created. This group provides a minimal amount of access to the system and is not a high risk.

### Special Groups

In addition to local and global groups, there is a third type of group available in the Windows NT environment, the *special groups*. These special groups are more behind the scenes, because they are not visible in the Groups section of the User Manager. Special groups may appear when assigning rights or permissions to directories, files, or shared resources.

Special groups dynamically organize users based on how they access various resources. Special group membership is not granted by the administrator but is granted by default, or automatically granted by the system to the user according to the users network activity. The six special groups are listed as follows:

- *Authenticated Users:* The Authenticated Users group is similar to the Everyone group described in the following text, except individuals connecting via the null credentials logon (or null session connections) are not members of the Authenticated Users group.

**Note**   Windows NT contains a type of logon known as the null credentials logon. This logon cannot be controlled as if it were a user account nor may it be disabled. However, it can be forced to require authentication, as explained in Chapter 11, "System Security Management." The rights of this type of logon are derived from the rights assigned to the Everyone group.

The threat with the null credentials logon is a NULL session connection over the Named Pipes share (IPC$) that allows a potential intruder to obtain a listing of user account names, group memberships, password properties, user Security Identifiers, account policy details, and share names and permissions.

- *Creator Owner*: The Creator Owner group typically has only one member for any object on the Windows NT system. Membership in the Creator Owner group is granted dynamically when you attempt to interact with a resource. For example, the default printer permissions grants the Everyone group the *Print* permission and the Creator Owner group the *Manage Documents* permission. When you access one of someone else's documents, you are only a member of Everyone and, therefore, are only granted the permissions of the Everyone group. However, when you access one of your own documents, you are granted the permissions of the Creator Owner group.  Therefore, you can manage your own documents in a print queue, but no one else's.

- *Everyone*: All accounts with access to the Windows NT environment are members of the Everyone group. This group includes guests and users from trusted domains, as well as interactive and network users. Administrators should be cognizant of the default permissions that are created on new objects and remove the Everyone group from access control lists where appropriate. For instance, by default, the Everyone group has Full Control of a newly shared directory. Administrators would be wise to secure this share by limiting the Everyone group's access.

- *Interactive Group*: The Interactive group is another system or implicit group that exists by default in every Windows NT system. Membership is granted to this group if the log-on process occurs on the local machine. Any user whose account has been granted the Log on Locally right could potentially become a member of this group. In most cases, at any given time, there is only one member of this group. That particular user would be the one who has logged on the server or workstation at the console. The other case where the interactive group could have more than one member at any given time is in the Microsoft Internet Information Server (IIS). In this environment, the IIS anonymous account, usually IUSR_machinename, requires the Log on Locally right. This requirement means that any user connecting to the web server anonymously becomes a member of the Interactive group as part of the log-on process.

- *Network*: The Network group is another system default implicit group. This group could potentially include any users who have been granted the Access This Computer from the Network user right and who have successfully logged on using a network log-on process. The Network groupmay also include connections made from the network anonymously, using the null credentials logon or accounts that authenticate using the regular Windows NT log-on process.

- *System*: The sole member of this group is the operating system.

---

**Note**  The group Authenticated Users exists only within Windows NT after Service Pack 3 has been installed.

### Considerations and Recommendations for Securing Group Accounts

Windows NT installs groups with preexisting access rights and files and directories with permissions. These groups are not tailored for any specific organizational structure and will probably not meet your corporation's confidentiality objectives without some fine-tuning. It is safer to create customized groups to fit specific needs and job functions. The tighter a group is with respect to its restrictions, the more effective and secure a system will be. If a user only needs access to directories A and B, they should not be part of a group that also has access to directory C. The tighter the restrictions, the less risk. The built-in groups created by Windows NT are a baseline; as groups are needed, they should be created and propagated with users.

One way the administrator can implement groups is to create a global group in each first-tier domain that contains all the senior managers of a particular division. The administrator must make sure that all senior managers have equal access to the files accessible by the group before creating such schemes.

This group of senior managers can be assigned permissions and rights in other domains, so the global group is a means of making these user credentials available for authentication to other domains within the network. If the group name is preceded by a domain name, the administrator knows both the type of user accounts that the group represents (by the group name) and the origin or location of that group (by the domain name).

Depending on the size of the installation, the administrator may find it necessary, and in some cases desirable, to delegate some administrative tasks to other people in the corporation. Certain administrative tasks require users to have special privileges in order to perform these tasks. Some common tasks are backup and restoration of files, adding new user accounts to the system, and starting and stopping resource sharing. Individuals performing these functions will be granted membership to the Backup Operators, Account Operators, and Server Operators groups respectively.

You can use Table 7-1 to match administrative functional needs with group types.

**Table 7-1. Local and Global Group Scenarios**

| Type of Need | Group Membership | Explanation |
|---|---|---|
| A group of individuals whose main function is to back up the entire domain | Create a Domain Backup Operator group (a global group) and grant them membership in local Backup Operator groups. | The global group can be a member of local groups within multiple domains and have those local groups' permissions and rights. |
| A group of users who need permissions and rights only on the local machine | Grant users membership to the Users group (a local group). | The local group can contain users from the local system and global groups from other domains. |
| A group of users who need access to resources on domain member servers or workstations | Grant users membership to the Domain Users group (a global group) and grant Domain Users groups access to the local Users groups of servers they need to access. | A domain's global group can be granted access to a member server or workstation, but a domain's local groups cannot. |
| A group that will contain global groups from the local or trusted domains whose main function is to manage the check printer on the local machine only | Use the local Print Operators group and grant the Domain Check Print Operators group (a global group that was created to manage the domain's check printer) membership. | Local groups can contain global groups as members. However, global groups cannot contain any other type of group within itself. Although a local group can only be used on the domain it was created, the members can come from the local domain and global groups from other domains. If it is necessary to grant this local group access to another domain, the local group must be manually created on the other domain. |

## Users

A user account contains all the information that defines that particular user in the Windows NT environment. Everything needed to secure a user is associated with that user's Security Identifier (SID). User account security may include a unique user name, password, and the rights and permissions the user has for using the system and accessing its resources. Each user of the system has a user account and associated password for their individual use. These users' accounts and associated passwords are Windows NT authentication controls. In addition, all the rights and permissions that can be assigned to users are Windows NT's security controls for securing the system. By correctly configuring these controls so that user rights are commensurate with their job responsibilities, a corporation can be assured of securing their data. Chapter 8, "Securing Accounts with Account Policies," describes these controls and the recommended implementations for securing the system.

User accounts may be defined on the local machine or on a domain. Accounts defined on the local machine may only be utilized on that machine, while accounts defined on the domain may be used on any machine in that domain or trusting domains.

### Built-in Accounts

Windows NT provides two built-in user accounts: Administrator and Guest. These accounts were created for specific functions and are, by default, members of certain built-in groups.

These accounts are common targets for attack because by default they exist on every system. Therefore, they should have strong security controls protecting them.

### Administrator

The *Administrator* account has complete control over the entire system's operation and security. It even has control over the files owned by other users. Anyone who can log in as an administrator has complete control over the administration of the entire system. This is a very important point because the Administrator account and its equivalents should be fully trusted.

#### Administrator Defaults

By default, the PDC's Administrator account is a member of the built-in Administrators, Domain Admins, and Domain Users groups and, therefore, receives the rights and permissions granted to those groups.

The Administrator account is intended for the individual who manages the configuration of the domain. The Administrator account should be kept secure with a system of checks and balances. Misuse of the account could be disastrous because of its associated rights and permissions. Therefore, strong security controls (such as monitoring and auditing the Administrator's use by the security officer) are extremely important. For example, if the administrator deletes the Audit Log, an entry is automatically created in the new log that states the administrator deleted the old one. The security officer should review the log for these types of entries and follow up with the administrator.

Administrators should only use their account for administrative activities. For example, do not use the Administrator account for word processing or to access the Internet. The administrator should have an individual account for such activities. Finally, the Administrator account should be available only to the administrator and never be shared with other users. If other users need particular administrator rights or permissions, they should be placed in appropriate groups with those rights and permissions.

For example, when an administrator, Todd, is not in the office, user Dawn manages user accounts. As a security control, when Todd created Dawn's account, he provided Dawn with membership in the Account Operators group. This account and its group membership allows Dawn to perform account administration duties when Todd is out of the office, but prevents Dawn from performing other administrator duties, such as taking ownership of files.

By default, the Administrator account is set with a password that never expires. The major concern with this account is that it is very powerful and everyone knows it exists. Since it is common to every system and everyone knows it is, the account is a very susceptible target for attacking. Therefore, security controls protecting it should be stringent.

A good security control is renaming the Administrator account to an obscure value to disguise its function. Although there are ways of identifying the current name of the Administrator account via its Security Identifier (SID), renaming the account could potentially thwart an attacker.

---

**Note**   Security through obscurity does provide an additional layer of protection but should not be relied upon as the sole security control. Multiple-layered security controls are the best method.

Although there is no technological way to force the Administrators account password to expire, a security policy stating that the Administrator's account password should be very strong and changed every 30 days needs to be documented and enforced. Lastly, a decoy account named *Administrator* should be created with a complex password (possibly randomly inputted), with no access, and disabled. This decoy account might slow an attacker down if they spent time thinking it was the real Administrator. Audit logs of failed login attempts would be generated and the real Administrator could be alerted to the attack.

### Guest

Windows NT provides the Guest account for the one-time or occasional user. However, we recommend that the Guest account never be used; rather, temporary accounts that provide better individual accountability and auditing controls should be created for temporary employees or contractors. By default, the account is disabled and configured as a member of the local Guests group. It has a blank password and its profile cannot be changed from the default user profile.

The Guest account can be a source of concern. Although the account is disabled by default, if it were inadvertently enabled, it would create security vulnerability. When it is enabled, its default password is blank. A good security control is to assign a complex password to the Guest account, in order to mitigate this vulnerability. Because it is an account on the system, any time a user grants permissions to Everyone members, the Guest group and Guest account are implicitly granted permissions.

Rename *Guest* to an obscure name and set a complex password (possibly random). Guest access should be avoided at all cost because it circumvents individual accountability and auditability.

## Creating and Modifying Accounts

User Manager for Domains is the vehicle for local and global groups, and user account administration. It controls user rights, password policies, and memberships. Both user and group accounts can be created, modified, and deleted. To launch User Manager for Domains, choose Start ⇨ Programs ⇨ Administrative Tools ⇨ User Manager for Domains.

**Note**   Do not delete user accounts until it is certain they will never be needed again. Even if a new user account with the same name is created, permissions and rights will have to be reassigned because a new SID is created.

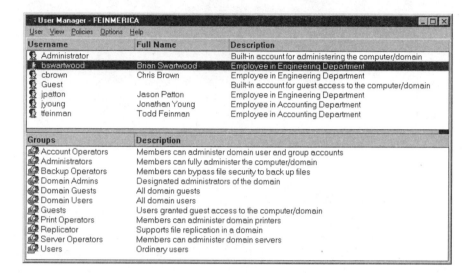

## Group Accounts

After group accounts are created, group membership needs to be managed by adding and removing members. In addition, membership in built-in groups must be managed.

### Creating a Local Group

To create a new local group, choose User ➪ New Local Group from the menu bar. The New Local Group dialog box appears and prompts for a new Group Name, Description, and Members.

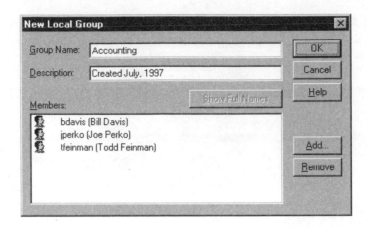

Table 7-2 presents and describes the New Local Group dialog box.

**Table 7-2. New Local Group**

| Fields | Function |
| --- | --- |
| Group Name | Specifies the name of the group to be created. |
| Description | Specifies the description of the group. This description should be as detailed as possible. |
| Members | Displays all the members of the group. |

| Button | Function |
| --- | --- |
| Show Full Names | Displays the full name of all users next to the username. |
| Add | Opens the Add Users and Groups dialog box. |
| Remove | Removes highlighted members from the group. |

### Adding Users and Groups to a Local Group

When the Add button in the New Local Group dialog box is selected, the Add Users and Groups dialog box appears and allows members to be added.

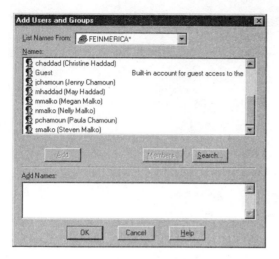

Table 7-3 presents and describes the Add Users and Groups dialog box.

### Table 7-3.  Add Users and Groups

| Fields | Function |
| --- | --- |
| List Names From | Drop-down menu that lists all domains. It is used to select from which domain names will be listed. |
| Names | Shows all users and global groups in the selected domain. |
| Add Names | Displays all the names selected to add to the new group. It is also possible to manually type in any user names to add to the group from this field. |

| Button | Function |
| --- | --- |
| Add | Adds names from the Names section to the Add Names section. Double-clicking on names will also perform the same function as selecting the Add button. |
| Members | Displays the Global Group Membership dialog box, which lists the members of the selected global group. This field allows members of a global group to be individually added to the local group. |
| Search | Opens the Find Account dialog box, which can be used to search the current domain (or other domains) for a specific name. |

When the Search button in the Add Users and Groups dialog box is selected, the Find Account dialog box appears. It allows administrators to search through domains for a specific user or group account name.

### Creating a Global Group

You can only create a new global group from within User Manager for Domains. If the computer is not in a domain, either User Manager for Domains will not be installed or the New Global Group options will be grayed out.

To create a new global group, choose User ⇨ New Global Group from the menu bar.

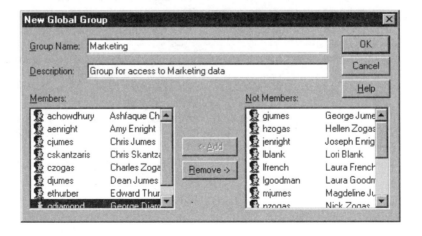

The New Global Group dialog box appears and will look similar to the New Local Group dialog box with one major exception. The Add button does not display the Add Users and Groups dialog box, because global groups cannot contain other groups or users from other domains.

Table 7-4 presents and describes the New Global Group dialog box.

**Table 7-4. New Global Group**

| Fields | Function |
| --- | --- |
| Group Name | Specifies the name of the group |
| Description | Specifies the description of the group |
| Members | Displays all the members of the group |
| Not Members | Displays all the members in the current domain, not in the group |

| Button | Function |
| --- | --- |
| Add | Adds highlighted members to the group |
| Remove | Removes highlighted members from the group |

## Managing Local and Global Groups

After groups have been created, it may be necessary to modify an attribute, such as permissions or rights, if the employee's job function changes. It is an important security control to periodically review user properties and permissions to ensure employees can access resources according to their job responsibilities.

To manage groups, use either the Group Properties or User Properties dialog box. If you are using the Group Properties method, select a group name and add or delete members from its member list. When using the User Properties method, select a user and add or delete groups (both local and global) to which the user belongs.

You can institute modifications to existing groups, whether local or global, from the User Manager for Domains dialog box by one of two ways: either double-click on the group name or highlight the group name and choose User ⇨ Properties from the menu bar. If you are modifying a local group, the Local Group Properties dialog box appears.

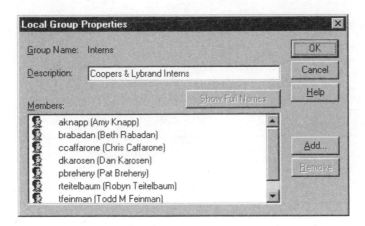

If you are modifying a global group, the Global Group Properties dialog box appears.

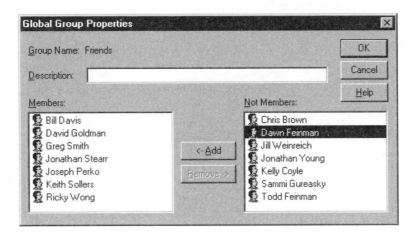

The Local Group Properties and Global Group Properties dialog boxes have the exact same functionality of the New Local Group Properties and New Global Group Properties dialog boxes, respectively, except that it is impossible to change the group name from here.

## User Accounts

After user accounts are created, users should be granted membership into the proper groups and allowed to access appropriate system resources. Upon account creation, many settings can be configured to limit a user's access to system resources. All settings for a user can always be modified later through procedures identical to the account creation.

## Creating a User Account

You can create a new user account with User Manager for Domains, which can be launched by choosing Start ⇨ Programs ⇨ Administrative Tools ⇨ User Manager for Domains. To open the New User dialog box, choose User ⇨ New User.

**Note**   By default, User Manager for Domains focuses on the User Account Database for the domain, not the local machine.

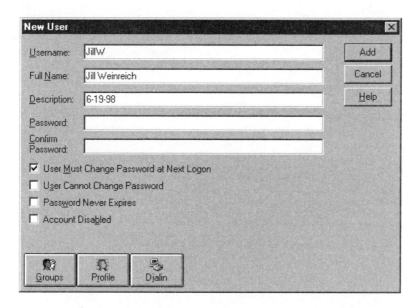

Table 7-5 presents and describes the New User dialog box.

**Table 7-5. The New User Dialog Box**

| Field | Function |
|-------|----------|
| Username | Specifies the name of the user. This is the name the user will have to enter upon logon. |
| Full Name | Specifies the full name of the user. |
| Description | Specifies the description of the user. |
| Password | Sets the password for the new user. |
| Confirm Password | Same as the Password field but is used for verifying whether the Password field was correctly entered. |

| Check box | Function |
|-----------|----------|
| User Must Change Password at Next Logon | Forces users to change their password the next time they log in. The administrator uses this to make sure users |

*(continued)*

**Table 7-5** *(continued)*

| | change their password from the original one assigned. Changing original passwords assures users that the administrator cannot access their resources without their knowledge. |
|---|---|
| User Cannot Change Password | Restricts users from changing their password. |
| Password Never Expires | Overrides the setting for Maximum Password Age in the account policy. |
| Account Disabled | Suspends the account's access to the system for an indefinite period of time. This feature should be used instead of deleting accounts, because even if you create a new account with the same privileges as the original, it will not automatically be able to access the original user's files. |

| Button | Function |
|---|---|
| Groups | Used to add and remove the groups that the user is a member of. |
| Profile | Specifies the User Profile, Logon Script, and Home Directory. |
| Hours | Restricts the hours that the user is allowed to connect to a server. |
| Logon To | Specifies whether the user can log on to all workstations or is limited to a predefined number. |
| Account | Indicates the account expiration date and whether this is a global or local account. |
| Dialin | Sets a user's permission for access to dial in the server from a remote location via a modem. |

 **Note** Employees who go on vacation and will not be accessing the network for an extended time should have their accounts disabled.

### Securing a New User Account

Administrators should always think in terms of security; therefore, it is important to secure an account upon its creation. For better administration, all user accounts should be created on a domain rather than on a workstation. Workstations should only contain the Local Guest and Administrator accounts. Some of the options described in this section, if configured incorrectly, may not provide sufficient security controls on the user account, allowing a hacker to take advantage of that account.

### User Must Change Password at Next Logon

By default, the User Must Change Password at Next Logon option is enabled for new users so when the administrator assigns the user a password, the user is forced to change it to one unknown to the administrator. If an administrator did know a user's password, the administrator could access the system under the user's account, thereby creating a false audit trail. When a user changes the password, the only way an administrator could gain access to the account would be to change the password, which would alert the user because his original password would no longer be valid.

### User Cannot Change Password

The User Cannot Change Password option is used on accounts where more than one person has access to the account (for example, the Guest account). These accounts should have very limited access to the system, if any at all. One problem with Guest accounts that are used by multiple people is that there is no individual accountability.

### Password Never Expires

The Password Never Expires option should never be selected for user accounts. Over time, it is possible a password could be compromised and, if it never expires, a malicious individual could gain access to a system. However, for accounts created for services, this option may be checked.

### Account Disabled

When an employee is on vacation, suspended from work, or terminated, that employee's account should be disabled. When an employee is terminated, that employee's account can be renamed, and his or her password can be changed and used by a replacement employee. The Account Disabled option ensures that the replacement employee will have the same access privileges because the SID did not change. If an account was deleted and a replacement employee with the same user account name is created, a new SID is also created, even if every other attribute is the same as the original account. Therefore, the replacement employee will not be able to automatically access the same files.

---

**Note**   When you disable an account, it is a good idea to give the account a complex random password until it is reenabled. This password will add an extra layer of protection in case the account is inadvertently enabled.

### Groups

The Groups button launches the Group Memberships dialog box where users can be assigned to different groups. This dialog box is similar in functionality to the Global Group Properties dialog box. The right list box shows all the groups in the domain that the user is not a member of, and the left list box displays all the groups that the user is a member of. The less access granted to a user, the less risk he can compromise a system. The user should only be a member of the groups necessary to support his job function.

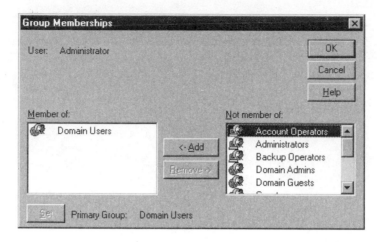

### Profile

The Profile button launches the User Environment Profile dialog box, where the user's profile path, logon script, and home directory location are configured. A user's profile is made up of an NTUSER.DAT file in addition to an entire directory structure that contains information about a user's desktop operating environment. The directory structure begins with a parent directory named after the individual's username and is located in the %systemroot%\profiles.

Profiles are good controls for administrators to secure the Windows NT environment and restrict what a user can do. The System Policy Editor is a comprehensive tool for accomplishing this task.

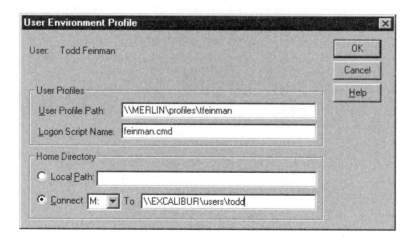

## Logon Scripts

*Logon scripts* are used for automating certain tasks when a user logs in. Logon scripts can be executable (.EXE) or batch files (.CMD and BAT). A logon script can initiate a network connection, configure a user environment, or start an application. Because these scripts run after a user logs in, it is important that scripts are properly secured. Therefore, you should store all scripts in a directory that is only readable by administrators and individuals responsible for creating and maintaining scripts. After a user logs in, only his script is downloaded to his machine.

Logon scripts are not as powerful as user profiles. There are certain advantages to using logon scripts. To begin with, clients logging in with workstations that do not support profiles, such as MS-DOS, can use logon scripts. Logon scripts can be used to manage only part of the user's environment, and they can create common network connections for multiple users. Logon scripts are easy to create and maintain, and they can be replicated on any server; therefore, any server can validate accounts with logon scripts. Lastly, scripts are read-only, while profiles are generally writable.

To implement strong security controls, scripts should be stored on an NTFS partition with restricted access permissions. Otherwise, an individual could edit a script and possibly promote his or her own access or possibly attack part of the system. For example, if an administrator's script was stored in an insecure directory that was accessible by some user named Joe, Joe could edit the script. Joe could have the script execute a dump of the password hash, against which he could run a password-cracking program. If the password hash were dumped to a directory on the network accessible by Joe, he would then eventually figure out the administrator's password and take control of the system, either granting his own account administrator privileges or reading data files. Security controls on the replication directory mitigate these security risks.

To ensure that logon scripts always work for all user accounts in a domain, the administrator must make sure that all logon scripts are kept up-to-date through the Directory Replicator service. The Replicator service can be used to synchronize script files among multiple servers. In addition, logon scripts for all user accounts in a domain must exist on every Windows NT server in the domain. The administrator must use the Replicator service for this because it maintains identical copies of a directory tree on multiple computers.

## Home Directories

A home directory should be assigned to each user for storage of individual files. This directory becomes the user's default directory for the File ⇨ Open and File ⇨ Save As dialog boxes, as well as the command prompt, and all applications with an unspecified working directory. Users should be granted Full Control permissions over their own home directory. The home directory should be specified for each user in the user policy or in the logon script. The home directory should be created and accessed on a file server within the domain.

Home directories have no specific security significance by default, they are just a methodology for providing each system user some space on the server to store corporate data that they use in their normal job performance.

Home directories on a file server should be accessed through a hidden ($) share that is identified in the appropriate login script. These share points should have permissions set explicitly for the individual user's access as *Username*: Full Control. This should be the only ACL entry for the directory.

### Hours

The Hours button launches the Logon Hours dialog box, which allows the administrator to specify what hours the user is allowed to log on. To use the Hours option as a security control, an administrator should only designate the hours a user needs to be online. If this is followed, the risk that this account will be used in a hacking attempt after hours is mitigated.

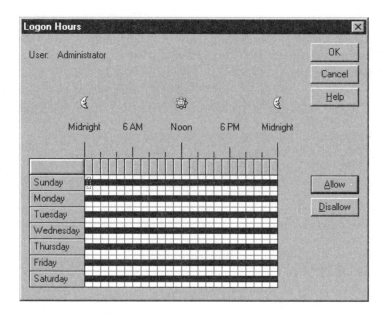

### Logon To

When you press the Logon To button, the Logon To dialog box appears. This dialog box enables administrators to designate which workstations the users are allowed to log on. Users can be set up for connecting to up to eight workstations specified by the administrator or all workstations. Depending on the environment, administrators may have only several specific workstations that they want employees to have access to. In those particular cases, this feature is very beneficial.

Logon To is not a reliable method for preventing a user's access to other workstations because only the names of accessible workstations are specified here. Although users could rename a workstation and gain access to it, Windows NT prevents a typical user from renaming her machine by requiring her to have two privileges: administrator rights to that workstation and access to an account on the domain with the Add Workstations to the Domain user right.

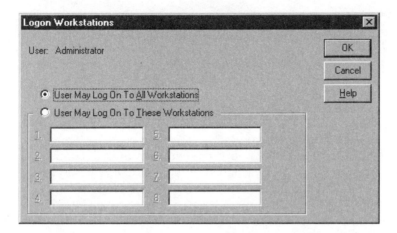

## Account

Choosing the Account button brings you to the Account dialog box. The Account dialog box enables an administrator to set the account expiration date. This feature can be used for temporary employees. In corporations where temporary employees or contractors are common, it would be prudent to input an expiration date as a security control. The expiration date should coincide with the date the contractor is expected to complete his or her job. The administrative hassle of manually disabling the many user accounts of temporary employees may be overwhelming and an administrator may forget to disable one. It is unwise to have an account active if no one will be using it.

By using the Account button, an administrator can also select whether an account is local or global. Local accounts cannot be used to log in a Windows NT domain, and they cannot be used within other trusting domains. A global account is the default for a new account on a domain.

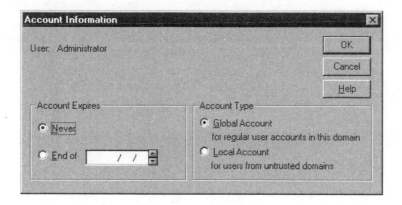

### Dialin

The Dialin button opens the Dialin dialog box. The Dialin dialog box enables an administrator to set Dialin permissions and callback options for Remote Access Services. When the Grant Dialin Permission to User check box is enabled, the user can connect to the Windows NT domain via a modem. If it is disabled, the user will not have permission to dial in and will not be able to authenticate when he tries to connect. Limiting Dialin permissions is an important security control that should be limited to only those users that require remote access because of the exposure. This is discussed in detail in the "Network Security Management" section in Chapter 6.

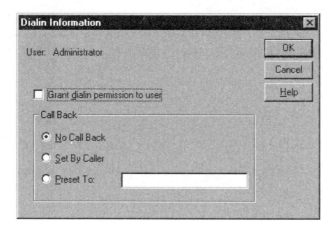

There are a lot of settings for creating and modifying users and groups, but it is very important that users and groups are secured from the early stages of implementing Windows NT. All settings should be carefully thought out and a corporate security policy should be developed for implementing those settings.

The bulk of securing a Windows NT system involves making sure users and groups are appropriately configured. It is critical that you spend time understanding user and group account management in order to achieve a high level of security.

# Chapter 8
# Securing Accounts with Account Policies

Windows NT provides a number of functions that allow administrators to secure and control user accounts. The types of passwords that users select can be controlled, as well as the rights and privileges users have on a system. Users that are not educated on strong password selection will typically choose the easiest one to remember, which could turn out to be the easiest one for an intruder to guess. There are ways for you to force a stronger password selection based on the options provided by Windows NT and the Service Pack 3 enhancements, discussed throughout this chapter. You also need to restrict what users can do on a system so that they do not have the power to override system controls. Limiting their user rights will provide a control for preventing their misuse of the system.

The User Manager for Domains program contains three policies that can be customized for different security needs: Account Policies, User Rights, and Auditing Policies. The first two are discussed in this chapter, and auditing is discussed in Chapter 4, "Monitoring and Auditing."

## Account Policy

The Account Policy dialog box enables the administrator to force users to adhere to password procedures and to safeguard accounts against possible attacks using an account lockout. The policies set forth affect all users across the entire domain or on a given stand-alone server within a workgroup. They take affect for each user at their next logon.

To open the Account Policies dialog box, launch User Manager for Domains by choosing Start ⇨ Programs ⇨ Administrative Tools ⇨ User Manager for Domains. Then choose Policies ⇨ Account from the menu bar.

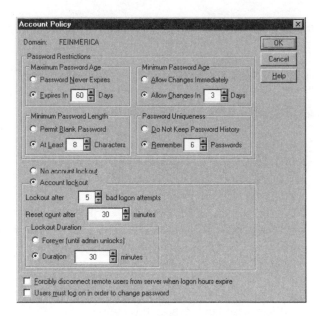

The fields that can be set are split up into two sections: Password Restrictions and Account Lockout. The Password Restrictions section, which forces users' passwords to meet certain guidelines, is divided into four subsections: Maximum Password Age, Minimum Password Age, Minimum Password Length, and Password Uniqueness. The Account Lockout section, which is used to set the parameters that decide when an account is locked out, and for how long, is divided into three subsections: Bad Logon Attempts, Reset Counter, and Lockout Duration. In addition, there are two check boxes for added control: Forcibly Disconnect Remote Users, which is only available for domains, and Logon to Change Password.

Strong password controls and account lockouts make it more difficult for hackers to attack the system, thus safeguarding the data. However, many corporations are lax in implementing or enforcing these controls. In the following text, each feature is described with its appropriate level of security controls.

## Password Restrictions

The Password Restrictions section of the account policy contains four fields that allow an administrator to set certain parameters users must abide by when changing their passwords. It is vital that password restrictions are configured because the default settings are not restrictive. Often, users will have a complex password and will not want to change it because they do not want the hassle of memorizing a new one.

**Note**   In addition to the four settings listed below, Service Packs 2 and 3 come with a filter that can enforce stronger passwords. The password filter forces users to use a six-character, minimum-length password and to include at least three of the four following alphanumeric groups: lowercase letters, uppercase letters, symbols, and digits.

The filter is called passfilt.dll and is copied into the %systemroot%\system32 directory. It can be enabled by adding passfilt to the Notification Packages (Data Type: REG_Multi_SZ) registry entry at HKLM\System\CurrentControlSet\Control\Lsa

It should be used on the primary domain controller and on any backup domain controllers that might ever be promoted to primary.

## Maximum Password Age

The *Maximum Password Age* option limits the maximum amount of time the system will allow a user to keep the same password. If the Password Never Expires radio button is selected, the user can keep the same password indefinitely. As a security control, it is strongly recommended that this option never be enabled because the older a password is, the more time a hacker has to try to guess it. Usually, users will never change their passwords on their own, so it is a good idea to implement this feature. By default, this feature is set to never expire.

## Minimum Password Age

With the *Minimum Password Age* option, an administrator can set the minimum amount of time before the system will allow users to change their password. If the Allow Changes Immediately radio button is selected, users can change their password as often as they want. If this radio button is enabled users who were forced to change their password could immediately change it back, thus bypassing the Password Aging security control. Users who are comfortable with an old password, which must be changed, may not want the hassle of memorizing a new password. However, if they are forced to use a new password for a few days, they may decide to stick with it. Therefore, to deter users from using the same password continuously, implement this feature.

By default, the Minimum Password Age option allows changes immediately; however, when turned on, the minimum age is set to allow changes in one day. This option should be increased so that users who do not want to change their password, will not be able to cycle through passwords in a short period of time until their original password is removed from the history list, which can be configured in the Password Uniqueness option.

## Minimum Password Length

The *Minimum Password Length* option sets the minimum number of characters a password must contain. If Permit Blank Password is selected, the user does not need to have a password. Setting this option, which allows users to have blank passwords, would be like leaving a pile of cash in the middle of the street with a note asking people not to take it. It should also be noted that the maximum password length that a user can have in Windows NT is 14 characters.

Regardless of the account policy, the administrator can set up new users with blank password or passwords that do not comply with the password restrictions. These initial passwords are valid; however, when the administrator or the user attempts to change this original password, the Minimum Password Length restriction is applied.

For example, assume the Minimum Password Length is set to six characters. The administrator creates an account for user Jenny without setting the password. Essentially, the password is blank. Jenny can log on with no password unless the User Must Change Password at Next Logon is set or her password expires, at which time she must follow the Minimum Password Length restriction.

This circumstance provides reason for concern. If a user can maintain a blank password for even a short time, the exposure is as wide as the user's individual and group rights and permissions. Even if the administrator selects User Must Change Password at Next Logon, the exposure is present until Jenny logs on the system.

This concern can be resolved by implementing a security policy to which the administrator must assign a password. This password must contain at least six characters (the default minimum length when this option is enabled), and it must be assigned to the account at the time of creation.

## Password Uniqueness

The *Password Uniqueness* option controls the amount of passwords that Windows NT remembers before a user can reuse a password. The maximum setting for this field is 24 passwords in history.

The Do Not Keep Password History option creates a situation that allows users to resort back to the password they had before being forced to change it, as soon as the minimum password age is met. Even with a password history, if the Allow Changes Immediately option is selected in the Minimum Password Age section, users can change their password enough times within a few seconds, thereby cycling through their password history until it is reset using the original one.

The Password Uniqueness option, set to remember a number of previous passwords, in conjunction with an appropriate minimum age, will truly force a user to keep a fresh password and will provide the appropriate controls. When enabled, this feature has a default value of 5 passwords. To be sure that at least 6 different passwords are used within a year, a password uniqueness of 6 should be set with a maximum password age of 60 days. On the more extreme side, to make sure that at least 24 different passwords are used within a 2-year period, a password uniqueness of 24 should bet set with a maximum password age of 30 days.

## Account Lockout

Windows NT provides the ability to automatically lock an account out of the system if it appears as though it is being tampered with. The administrator can set what constitutes tampering through the Bad Logon Attempts field. For example, it is possible to set the account to be locked out if there are five bad logon attempts, which could be an indication of a brute force or dictionary attack on an account. With the number of bad logon attempts at five, Windows NT automatically locks the account, which keeps the attacker from using that account. The options for configuring Account Lockout and the recommended settings based on the security needs of different corporations are described in detail in the text that follows.

Although it is possible to select No Account Lockout, it is unwise. No Account Lockout provides no security control and exposes all accounts to the possibility of the attacks previously mentioned. By default, there is no account lockout; therefore, it is strongly recommended to turn on the Account Lockout feature.

Regardless of the settings, the Administrator account can never be locked out locally. This is a special case that applies only to the Administrator account. If this account could be locked out, the potential would exist to lock out every account on the system, thereby restricting all access to the system. However, because the Administrator account cannot be locked out, this account is a favorite target for attacks, subject to unlimited logon attempts. By implementing the compensating control of changing the name of the Administrator account to a name known only by the administrator, this risk can be mitigated.

---

**Note**  Passprop is a utility included with Resource Kit that is used to lock out the Administrator account over the network. After it is invoked, the Administrator can be locked out if too many bad logon attempts occur. However, the Administrator account will never be locked out locally.

The goal of account lockouts should be to detect intruders, not to punish users for inputting the wrong password. If a password were complex, it would take an extremely long time to guess what it is by simply attempting values at an authentication box. Therefore, it is likely that if a hacker will not guess a password in the first 25 attempts, he or she probably will not guess it in a short time period. Locking accounts out forever after only three attempts might be too extreme in a corporation; however, many corporations do just that.

The entire discussion of password strength and password length as it relates to account lockout can be stated differently based on the security culture of each corporation. Unfortunately, in most corporations, strong hard-to-guess passwords are rarely the case, making password guessing more of a reality.

## Bad Logon Attempts

The *Bad Logon Attempts* option specifies how many times a password can be entered incorrectly before an account is locked out. A locked out account cannot be used to log on until the predetermined time duration passes or it is reset by the administrator. This is a beneficial security control because it is one activity that the administrator does not have to monitor in real time. It is important for administrators to review the event log periodically for failed attempts to make sure a brute force attack was not being used on the account's password. However, by implementing this feature, the administrator can be performing other network maintenance and when users realize their account has been locked out, they can wait for the lockout duration time to expire or, more likely, get the administrator to reinstate it.

## Reset Counter

The *Reset Counter* option is used to reset the counter that counts the amount of times a bad logon was attempted. The counter can be reset after a certain number of minutes specified by the administrator. When the Reset Counter time limit is met, no matter how many bad logon attempts have taken place, Windows NT sets the count back to zero.

The counter should be set to a high enough number of minutes so that a hacker would not be able to spend ten hours, after business hours, brute force attacking a user account. For example, an account policy may be set to lockout after five bad logons and the Reset Counter set to ten minutes. After 5:00 P.M., a hacker could try four passwords, wait ten minutes so the counter is reset, and try four passwords again, repeating this process all night or until he or she guesses the password.

## Lockout Duration

With the *Lockout Duration* feature, the administrator can set how long an account is locked out before being automatically reinstated. A hacker who knows the lockout duration is 30 minutes could do a brute force attack on a password until the account is locked out and then try again after the lockout duration has cycled. However, if the Forever radio button is selected, the administrator must manually unlock the account. This is a very strong security control, but infeasible in most corporations because of the administrative task it entails.

One caveat to be aware of is that although locking out an account forever eliminates the brute force attack possibility, it creates a new problem known as *denial of service*. A hacker could deliberately generate multiple failed logon attempts in a short time period for hundreds of users. All those accounts would require an administrator to manually unlock each one.

## Forcibly Disconnect Remote Users

The *Forcibly Disconnect Remote Users* option disconnects remote users who remain logged on beyond their allowed times (as prescribed in the Hours section of User properties). If the Forcibly Disconnect Remote Users from Server When Logon Hours

Expire check box is selected, the system gives the user a visual warning five minutes prior to being disconnected. If the user does not save his or her work and shuts down, the system automatically terminates the user's session. If the Forcibly Disconnect Remote Users from Server When Logon Hours Expire check box is not selected, the user is still given a prior warning, and then a new warning every ten minutes upon hour expiration, but the user is not disconnected. During this time, no new remote connections can be established.

It is recommended that this feature be enabled. If users do not lock their workstation, which is located in a cubicle with no doors, and forget to log off before leaving the workstation unattended, an intruder could walk up to the system and possibly gain access. The forced disconnection could prevent this scenario.

The only obvious disadvantage to engaging this function is: If a user initiates a process that runs past the authorized hours of logon, the process will terminate. This termination can be avoided if the administrator grants the user access to the system for an expanded range of logon hours when requested.

### Log On to Change Password

The *Log On to Change Password* option requires users who have an expired password to ask the administrator to change their password. If the Users Must Log On In Order To Change Password check box is disabled, users can change their expired passwords without informing the administrator. In addition, users who have exceeded the number of days in the Minimum Password Age option but not exceeded the Maximum Password Age, can change their password while logged on if the Log On to Change Password option is selected.

## Recommendations for Account Policy

User accounts are common ways for hackers to attempt to attack systems. The controls protecting user accounts should be stringent to ensure confidentiality of data and integrity of the system. Because of the many Windows NT security features available to do this and because every corporation's security needs are different, securing the system effectively sometimes may be a daunting task.

We present the following two scenarios, with varying degrees of security controls, to demonstrate the different user account security configurations that can be implemented, based on different security control requirements. Describing the user account security features in this way will help systems administrators identify with the corporation that most closely matches their own and to understand the user account security configurations.

### Scenario 1: Feinmerica, Inc.—Very High Security

Feinmerica is running Windows NT as its network platform. It is very concerned about security because it is developing a brand new widget design concept that will revolutionize widget production. This will make it a leader in the market of widget design. For this reason, senior management has decided that confidentiality of data is the number one priority. Strong user security controls and a help desk are implemented to help achieve this IT security objective.

Feinmerica has done a security assessment on its users' password strength and found that users always choose weak passwords. Therefore, Feinmerica has implemented a strong password policy in hopes that users will start choosing passwords that are harder to guess. To enforce this control, Feinmerica will implement the password filter (*passfilt*), which will ensure that users do not choose easily guessed passwords. It has also set the password length to be a minimum of eight characters.

Administrators believe that if a hacker does not guess a password within the first five to ten attempts, then he probably will not in a reasonable amount of time. Therefore, protecting against the first few attempts is critical.

All passwords must be changed within 60 days but cannot be changed for at least 7 days. The administrators believe that if users cannot change their password for 7 days, they will have sufficient time to get comfortable with remembering it. Although password changing of 60 days seems to be a weak control, when used in conjunction with the password filter and the password length of 8 characters, it becomes an effective security control. In addition, employees do not become disgruntled that they have to change their passwords so often. Also, they have set password uniqueness to 6, which means a user must cycle through 6 passwords before being able to use the same one again. If users do not change their password until they are forced to in the 60-day period, they will then have passed through 1 year before being able to use the same password again.

Because there is a help desk, Account Lockout is set to a lockout duration of forever. A user who is locked out can always call the help desk to be unlocked. Lockouts occur after 3 bad attempts and the counter does not reset until after 1440 minutes (24 hours). This length of time encompasses an entire day because this ensures only 3 attempts will be made on the account in one particular day, unless of course the help desk or administrators unlock the account.

### Scenario 2: The Chamoun Company—High Security

Although security is important to the Chamoun Company, senior management has determined that, because its data is not highly sensitive and the likelihood of someone wanting to break in is low, the cost of highly securing its systems is not beneficial. It has decided to implement some security controls and live with the risk. Although IT security is not the most important objective in its environment, it is taken into consideration. The company has not implemented a help desk.

Users must change their passwords at least every 30 days, but no sooner than every 3 days. Passwords must be at least 6 characters. In addition, there is a password history of 12 passwords so that if users wait 30 days to change their password, they will not repeat a password for 1 year.

Accounts are set to lockout after 10 bad attempts; however, after an account is locked out, it is locked out for only 30 minutes or until an administrator unlocks it. This situation occurs because the administrators do not want to deal with the extra administrative hassle of resetting the accounts. In addition, the lockout counter is reset every 30 minutes.

If a hacker attempted to randomly guess a password over the network or locally, he or she would get no more than 480 attempts a day (that is, 10 attempts every 30 minutes in a 24-hour period). In the period of 30 days, only 14,400 password guess attempts can occur. If a password is 6 characters long, consisting of characters from the lowercase alphabet set (26 letters), then there are a total of 308,915,776 password possibilities. If a hacker is unable to guess a password within the first 25 attempts, these statistics will usually deter a hacker from attempting any more. It is also unlikely that such a large number of attempts would go undetected if proper auditing controls were enabled.

### Security Settings for Scenarios 1 and 2

Table 8-1 summarizes the security configurations for the two corporations in Scenarios 1 and 2. The table illustrates how each corporation's security configuration is translated into Windows NT Account Policy.

**Table 8-1. Security Configurations**

| Account Policy Setting | Feinmerica, Inc.—Very Secure, With Help Desk | Chamoun Company—Secure Without Help Desk |
|---|---|---|
| **Password Restrictions** | | |
| Maximum Password Age (days) | 60 | 30 |
| Minimum Password Age (days) | 7 | 3 |
| Minimum Password Length (characters) | 8 | 6 |
| Password Uniqueness (passwords) | 12 | 6 |
| **Account Lockout** | | |
| Account Lockout | Yes | Yes |
| Account Lockout (bad attempts) | 3 | 10 |
| Account Lockout (reset count in minutes) | 1440 | 30 |
| Lockout Duration (minutes) | Forever | 30 |

# User Rights

Rights authorize a user to perform certain actions on the system and affect specific resources. They are broken down into two classifications: standard rights and advanced rights. There are 10 standard rights that are normally assigned to users and 17 advanced user rights that are not commonly assigned to a user.

## Rights vs. Permissions

To use the policy correctly, rights and permissions need to be understood. Both are forms of security control. A *right* is an authorization for a user to perform actions on the system. Rights apply to the system as a whole. *Permissions* are rules associated with a particular object (such as a file, directory, or printer); these regulate which users can access the object and in what manner.

Rights can override permissions on an object. For example, when user Chris is assigned the right to restore files and directories, Chris needs to be able to read all files on the system, including files for which the owners have set permissions that deny access to all users. The Restore Files and Directories right overrides permissions set by users, and Chris is able to perform his task.

The rights described in this section should be assigned to local groups and not directly to individual users for easy administration. Users who need any of these rights can be placed in the groups that have been assigned the rights.

To open the User Rights Policy dialog box, launch User Manager for Domains by choosing Start ⇨ Programs ⇨ Administrative Tools ⇨ User Manager for Domains. Then choose Policies ⇨ User Rights from the menu bar.

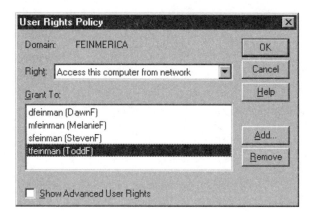

By default, the User Rights Policy dialog box lists all the standard rights in the drop-down list and in each account that is granted this right. Both user accounts and group accounts can be granted rights, although it is better to only grant rights to groups. If the Show Advanced User Rights check box is selected, then all the advanced user rights are presented with the standard rights in the drop-down list.

## Standard Rights

Each of the ten standard user rights is discussed in the following text. These rights are most commonly given to users who access the system in some manner. Recommended settings for each right are summarized later in this section.

## Add Workstations to the Domain

The *Add Workstations to the Domain* right allows users to add machines to the current domain such as with Server Manager. To ensure that they have the responsibility to add workstations to a domain, domain administrators are the only ones who should get this right. If any other users were to add workstations to the domain, they could add a domain controller, which would allow them to obtain the domain Security Account Manager (SAM) database.

## Access Computer from the Network

The *Access Computer from the Network* right allows users of the system to connect to the server and access resources over a network. To keep an environment secure from outside threats, it is best to grant this right to users with an absolute need. Everyone does not need access to the server via a network connection. Because the Administrator account is such a sensitive account, the person who owns the Administrator account should have to be physically at the server and not on a network link. This control protects that Administrator account from hackers.

## Back Up Files and Directories

The *Back Up Files and Directories* right gives designated groups the ability to back up files and directories regardless of the file permissions. Users with this right can bypass the Access Control Lists (ACLs) on objects within Windows NT. To create a secure environment with a segregation of duties, it is better to have a separate group, such as Backup Operators, for backing up files, rather than granting the Administrators group this right, which is the default. Although Backup Operators cannot read the data they back up, they can restore the data onto another file system and read anything and everything from there. For this reason, this right is an extremely high security risk.

## Change the System Time

The *Change the System Time* right allows a group member to set the internal clock on a Windows NT system. Accuracy of the system time is a prerequisite for an audit trail, because knowing who was accessing resources at a specified time could implicate a user. The entire audit, event monitoring, and logging system is based on time and, therefore, requires that time not be tampered with. Security policies, such as those for account lockout and expiration, are based on the system time. Normal users should not be granted this right.

## Force Shutdown from a Remote System

The *Force Shutdown from a Remote System* right allows group members to shut down a Windows NT system from over a network connection. This right is currently not implemented.

### Log on Locally

Users who use the *Log on Locally* right can interact with the system while being physically at the console. Without this right, a network connection is necessary. Users who need access to resources must be allowed to *Log on Locally* or *Access This Computer from the Network*, as described earlier. Users should not be able to log on locally to the domain controllers as a security control.

For example, there is security bug in Service Pack 3 that a rogue program called *GetAdmin* exploits. This bug allows a user who has logged on locally to the primary domain controller to run GetAdmin, which adds their account to the local Administrator group. Not allowing users the Log on Locally right would keep a user from being able to run the GetAdmin program locally on the PDC in the first place.

### Manage Auditing and Security Log

The *Manage Auditing and Security Log* right allows users to configure auditing on objects such as files, directories, and printers. However, this right does not grant users the ability to configure the audit policy for the entire domain. In addition, the Security Log can be viewed and cleared. Because users with this right can clear a Security Log, they have the ability to attempt an attack on the system and then delete the log. Although, the first entry in the new log states that the old log was cleared and by whom, only authorized individuals, such as the security officer or the internal auditor, should be given this right. One method is to create an Auditors group and grant it this user right.

### Restore Files and Directories

The *Restore Files and Directories* right is the complement of the Back Up Files and Directories right. Individuals with this right can restore files by bypassing ACLs. This right is considered more powerful than the Back Up right because it gives users the ability to add and replace files. It is better to only grant Backup Operators this right because administrators should not be restoring files.

### Shut Down the System

With the *Shut Down the System* right, users can shut down the Windows NT system. It could be very dangerous if a malicious user decided to shut down a server in the middle of the day while jobs were running and employees were online. For this reason, this right should only be given to select individuals such as the Administrator and Server operators. Users should never have the ability to walk up to the server's console and shut down the system. Although denying them this right will not stop them from pulling the plug on the server if they have physical access.

### Take Ownership of Files or Other Objects

The *Take Ownership of Files or Other Objects* right is one of the most powerful rights in the standard rights classification. It allows users to take control of any file, directory, printer, or process, regardless of the current owner. This action can be audited in the

Security Log. For example, Melanie is the current owner of the document, c:\parents.doc. Steven wants to edit it, but does not have permissions to change it. However, Steven does have the right to take ownership of files or other objects. So Steven takes owner-ship, grants himself Full Control permission to the file, edits the document, and deletes most of its contents. Normally, Melanie would take the blame for this, but because Steven is now the owner, there is an audit trail pointing toward him. He cannot give owner-ship back to Melanie; only Melanie can take ownership of the file herself, if she has the right. To avoid scenarios such as this, only give administrators this right.

## Recommendations for Securing Standard User Rights

For security to be maintained on a domain, all user rights should be restricted to only those individuals who require such access. Although administrators are powerful and are granted more rights than any other group, they should not be granted all rights.

It is difficult to give recommendations regarding the proper security configuration of user rights because of the wide variety of scenarios. Table 8-2 lists basic recommendations that systems administrators should use as a guideline when planning out their user right security controls.

**Table 8-2. Recommendations for Securing Standard User Rights**

| Feature | Domain Controller | File and Print Server | Data-base Server | Web Server | RAS Server | Work-station |
|---|---|---|---|---|---|---|
| Add Workstations to the Domain | Adminis-trators | None | None | None | None | None |
| Access this Comput-er from Network | Domain Users | Domain Users | Domain Users | Domain Users | None | None |
| | Server Operators | | | | | |
| | Account Operators | | | | | |
| | Print Operators | | | | | |
| | Backup Operators | | | | | |
| | Domain Users | | | | | |
| Back Up Files and Directories | Backup Operators | Backup Operators | Backup Operators | Backup Operators | Backup Operators | Backup Operators |
| Change the System Time | Admin-istrators | Admin-istrators | Admin-istrators | Admin-istrators | Admin-istrators | Admin-istrators |
| | Server Operators | | | | | Power Users |

*(continued)*

**Table 8-2.** *(continued)*

| Feature | Domain Controller | File and Print Server | Data-base Server | Web Server | RAS Server | Work-station |
|---------|-------------------|----------------------|------------------|------------|------------|--------------|
| Force Shutdown from a Remote System | N/A | N/A | N/A | N/A | N/A | N/A |
| Log on Locally | Administrators Server Operators Backup Operators | Administrators | Administrators | Administrators | Administrators | Administrators Users |
| Manage Auditing and Security Log | Administrators Auditors (must be created) | Administrators Auditors (must be created) | Administrators Auditors (must be created) | Administrators Auditors (must be created) | Administrators Auditors (must be created) | Administrators Auditors (must be created) |
| Restore Files and Directories | Backup Operators | Backup Operators | Backup Operators | Backup Operators | Backup Operators | Backup Operators |
| Shut Down the System | Administrators Server Operators | Administrators | Administrators | Administrators | Administrators | Administrators Users |
| Take Ownership of Files or Other Objects | Administrators | Administrators | Administrators | Administrators | Administrators | Administrators |

## Advanced User Rights

The Advanced User Rights, like the Standard User Rights, can be found in the User Rights Policy dialog box. You can view the advanced rights by enabling the *Show Advanced User Rights* check box.

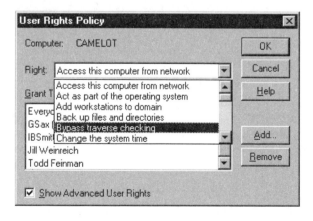

Each of the 17 advanced user rights is discussed here. These rights are most commonly given to services or accounts that need an extremely high-level access to the system. As a good security control, normal users should never be granted any of these rights. The recommended settings for each right are described later in this section.

## Act as Part of the Operating System

The *Act as Part of the Operating System* right is one of the most powerful rights within Windows NT. It allows the designated accounts to act as a trusted part of the operating system and can, therefore, do anything regardless of other rights. By default, only certain portions of the Windows NT subsystem are granted this right. No users should be granted this right.

## Bypass Traverse Checking

The *Bypass Traverse Checking* right allows Windows NT to be configured in a POSIX-compliant manner. It allows users to traverse subdirectories regardless of parent permissions. This right operates based on the Execute permission at the directory level. The Execute permission on a directory indicates that the permission holder can change to subdirectories within the parent.

Normally, if a directory has access restrictions, then all subdirectories inherit those permissions. For example, if Christine does not have the Read permission on c:\tools, then she normally would not have Read permission on c:\tools\hammer. However, if Christine has the right to bypass traverse checking, she can read c:\tools\hammer, despite the permissions of c:\tools.

If everyone is removed from this user right, POSIX-compliant applications could cause a denial of access when they try to traverse subdirectories.

## Create a Page File

With the *Create a Page File* right, users are permitted to create page files on the local system. Page files are used for virtual memory within the Windows NT environment.

## Create a Token Object

The *Create a Token Object* right permits users to create a security access token. This right should only be used by the system, processes, and threads, never a user.

## Create Permanent Shared Objects

The *Create Permanent Shared Objects* right enables the creation of special permanent shares that are used by Windows NT regularly. An example is a system device represented by \\Device.

### Debug Programs

The *Debug Programs* right allows users to debug low-level objects such as processes and threads. Due to the power this right grants, it should only be given to developers on development machines.

### Generate Security Audits

The *Generate Security Audits* right grants the right to generate security audit log messages.

### Increase Quotas

The *Increase Quotas* right gives an individual the privilege to increase the object quotas.

### Increase Scheduling Priority

Given the *Increase Scheduling Priority* right, an individual can increase the priority of a process within Windows NT. Setting processes' priorities to high will deny system time for other processes to run, which could potentially cause a denial of service.

### Load and Unload Device Drivers

Using the *Load and Unload Device Drivers* right, memory-resident device drivers can be loaded and unloaded. If a Trojan Horse device driver were developed, it could be used to exploit the system because device drivers have no security restrictions placed on them.

### Lock Pages in Memory

The *Lock Pages in Memory* right allows users to make their allocated RAM static, which means that whatever is in memory cannot be swapped to the page file. There is a potential to crash the system because available memory can get filled up and resources can get extremely low. No one needs to be granted this right.

### Log On as a Batch Job

With the *Log On as a Batch Job* right, users are able to log on using a batch queue facility. It is currently not implemented.

### Log On as a Service

The *Log On as a Service* right allows a user to log on as a service, similar to those required by virus scanners and faxing software. These services run in the background without any interaction from any additional users. Some services have full control over the system and could be very powerful if configured in that manner. Therefore, only select accounts should be granted this right. No users should ever be allowed to log on as a service, and all accounts logged on as a service (such as an account that is used for a virus scanner's auto protect) should be monitored closely because they have such high-level control.

## Modify Firmware Environment Variables

The *Modify Firmware Environment Variables* right allows users to modify the system environment variables that affect certain programs. For example, in the System Properties dialog box (you can open this by opening the System applet in Control Panel), the Environment tab's *ComSpec* variable should point to CMD.EXE. However, if modified, it could be set to point to a batch program that first creates a new user account with administrator privileges and then runs CMD.EXE. Every time an administrator tries to access the command line, a new account is created and the administrator would not know. This is extremely dangerous, and for that reason, only administrators should be granted this right.

## Profile Single Process

The *Profile Single Process* right is another performance tuning right that allows the user to monitor Windows NT's performance of a single process.

## Profile System Performance

The *Profile System Performance* right is a performance tuning right that allows users to utilize performance monitoring tools.

## Replace a Process Level Token

The *Replace a Process Level Token* right allows individuals to replace the security access token of a process with another token. If users had the ability to do this, they could breach the system's security because Windows NT is supposed to control this process. No users should be given this privilege.

# Recommendations for Securing Advanced User Rights

It is difficult to give recommendations regarding the proper security configuration of user rights because of the variety of scenarios. The following table lists basic recommendations that systems administrators should use as a guideline when planning out their advanced user right security controls.

**Table 8-3. Recommendations for Securing Advanced User Rights**

| Feature | Domain Controller | File and Print Server | Data-base Server | Web Server | RAS Server | Work-station |
|---|---|---|---|---|---|---|
| Act as Part of the Operating System | None | None | None | None | None | None |
| Bypass Traverse Checking | Admin-istrators<br><br>Server Operators<br><br>Backup Operators | Admin-istrators | Admin-istrators | Admin-istrators | Admin-istrators | Admin-istrators |

*(continued)*

**Table 8-3.** *(continued)*

| Feature | Domain Controller | File and Print Server | Data-base Server | Web Server | RAS Server | Work-station |
|---|---|---|---|---|---|---|
| Create a Page File | Administrators | Administrators | Administrators | Administrators | Administrators | Administrators |
| Create a Token Object | None | None | None | None | None | None |
| Create Permanent Shared Objects | None | None | None | None | None | None |
| Debug Programs | Administrators | Administrators | Administrators | Administrators | Administrators | Administrators |
| Generate Security Audits | None | None | None | None | None | None |
| Increase Quotas | Administrators | Administrators | Administrators | Administrators | Administrators | Administrators |
| Increase Scheduling Priority | Administrators | Administrators | Administrators | Administrators | Administrators | Administrators |
| Load and Unload Device Drivers | Administrators | Administrators | Administrators | Administrators | Administrators | Administrators |
| Lock Pages in Memory | None | None | None | None | None | None |
| Log On as a Batch Job | None | None | None | None | None | None |
| Log On as a Service | Replicators | None | None | None | None | None |
| Modify Firmware Environment Variables | Administrators<br><br>Server Operators<br><br>Backup Operators | Administrators | Administrators | Administrators | Administrators | Administrators |
| Profile Single Process | Administrators | Administrators | Administrators | Administrators | Administrators | Administrators |
| Profile System Performance | Administrators | Administrators | Administrators | Administrators | Administrators | Administrators |
| Replace a Process Level Token | None | None | None | None | None | None |

# Chapter 9
# Managing Resource Security

Controlling user access to files and directories is critical for securing your system. Configuring objects with the appropriate permissions ensures confidentiality of data by denying users access to objects that are not commensurate with their job responsibilities. The following section describes how to implement Windows NT permissions as security controls on the system.

## File Systems

Windows NT supports two file systems, but the two are not equal in security and auditability. The choice to use either one of these file systems or a combination thereof is guided by the corporation's IT security objectives. Windows NT 4.0 supports the following disk-based file systems:

- File Allocation Table (FAT)—common to MS-DOS
- NT File System (NTFS)—exclusive to Windows NT

**Note**  Windows NT 4.0 does not support the FAT32 file system in Windows 95 Original Equipment Manufacturer Service Release 2 or Windows 98. Nor does Windows 95 or Windows 98 support NTFS. In addition, Windows NT 4.0, unlike Windows NT 3.5x, does not support the high-performance file system (HPFS), which is common to OS/2.

The decision as to which file system will be used for the operating system is an important security control consideration and should be made prior to installation. The FAT file system does not support object permissions, which are the security controls for securing the system, whereas NTFS does. For this reason, we recommend the implementation of the NTFS file system to take advantage of these security controls. Table 9-1 lists some of the differences between FAT and NTFS.

**Table 9-1. NTFS vs. FAT**

| Consideration | NTFS | FAT |
|---|---|---|
| Security | Supports Windows NT security, which allows for protection of files and directories. | The local security features of Windows NT do not protect files and directories under FAT. However, shared permissions can be placed on shared FAT files and directories. |
| Recoverability | Maintains a log of activities to restore the disk in the event of power failures or other problems. | No log is maintained. |
| Maximum File and Partition Size Support | $2^{64}$ bytes or 16 Exabytes | $2^{32}$ bytes or 4 GB |
| Filename Support | 255 Unicode characters [multiple periods (delimiters) allowed] | 255 Unicode characters [multiple periods (delimiters) allowed] |
| Compression | Native support | No support |
| Operating System Compatibility | Recognizes only the Windows NT operating system. Other operating systems (such as MS-DOS) cannot access files on an NTFS partition when running on the same computer. Network users can access files on an NTFS file system when using MS-DOS, UNIX, or Macintosh operating systems. Windows NT presents the files in a form that the other systems can accept. | Allows access to files when your computer is running another operating system. |

# NTFS

NTFS is the more secure of the two file systems. NTFS does not provide encryption, but it is the only file system to utilize Windows NT file and directory security features. This system also offers recoverability in the event of a disk fault or system failure. The recoverability feature utilizes a log file service to record redo and undo information during file updates. The redo information allows NTFS to re-create the file change, while the undo information allows it to delete incomplete or erroneous transactions. NTFS is also supported on both fixed and removable hard disks; however, security is only maintained if the disk is used on the machines that are connected to the same domain.

# FAT

Files using the FAT system can be accessed with the Windows NT and Windows 95 operating systems. However, the FAT system does not support Windows NT security features and does not offer any of the robust NTFS features. RISC-based systems, such as MIPS and ALPHA, must contain a small FAT partition to enable the firmware to load the first system files. These files are required for the boot process and only understand the FAT file system. The first partition should be 1MB to hold the HAL.DLL and OSLOADER.EXE. The rest of the system and data files should be on NTFS partitions.

If the FAT file system is used, shared files or directories can use the share permissions of Windows NT. However, the FAT file system cannot utilize the local file and directory security of Windows NT, which leaves a machine and its content vulnerable to attack when accessed locally.

## Converting between File Systems

After Windows NT has been installed and drives have been formatted, you can convert from FAT to NTFS. However, this conversion is one-way. When a volume is NTFS, it is impossible to convert it to FAT. Administrators may format a volume to FAT, however all data will be lost. If the 1MB partition used for the first system files on an RISC-based system is inadvertently converted to NTFS, the system will not boot. Administrators can remedy this problem by booting to the Windows NT CD-ROM and formatting the 1MB partition back to FAT, and then reinstalling the HAL.DLL and OSLOADER.EXE system files.

## Recommendations for Choosing a File System

FAT should never be used. The NTFS file system is the more secure of the two file systems. Network servers should use NTFS to utilize the inherent security features of Windows NT. NTFS also provides extensive logging capabilities and allows for long filenames of up to 255 characters, short file names of eight-plus-three characters (eight characters for the filename and three for the extension) for other operating system compatibility, multiple extended attributes, and compression.

It should be noted that some programs allow other operating systems to read, not write, to an NTFS volume. For example, if you have physical access to a server, you can boot to a DOS system disk and invoke NTFSDOS, which is a well-known program. This program will mount the NTFS volume and make it readable. To prevent against anyone booting from a DOS system disk, all critical servers and data servers should be physically secured.

RISC-based Windows NT systems should be set up such that the operating system is installed on an NTFS secondary partition and the first system files are installed on a 1MB primary partition. The installation process knows to automatically place the first system files in this 1MB partition.

# File and Directory Permissions

File and directory permissions, the basis of most object-control security in Windows NT, are set from the Security menu in the Windows NT Explorer. This command is only available for files stored on NTFS volumes.

File and directory permissions and ownership for files apply exclusively to NTFS partitions. However, shared directory permissions can be established for FAT or NTFS file structures. File and directory permissions are the security controls that determine if and how a user or group can access a file or directory. File and directory ownership allows the user to change permissions. The user who creates the file or directory is typically the owner. An administrator can take ownership of files or other objects of a file or directory without permission from the owner.

## Implementing Permissions

Actions users can perform are dependent on the rights and permissions that they have been assigned. Rights apply to users and permissions apply to specific objects, such as printers, directories, and files. Examples of rights include managing auditing and security logs, shutting down the system, loading and unloading device drivers, and logging on as a service. Permissions allow for the fine-tuning of access and security over an object. The types of permissions available are dependent upon whether the file or directory is accessed on the local machine or across a network connection. A file accessed on a local machine uses only NTFS file or directory permissions, while a file that is accessed over a network connection uses shared-level permissions as well as NTFS permissions.

### NTFS File Permissions

File permissions and ownership for files that are accessed at a local machine apply exclusively to NTFS partitions. NTFS file permissions are set through Windows NT Explorer. Select a file, choose File ⇨ Properties from the menu bar, switch to the Security tab, and click the Permissions button. The File Permissions dialog box appears.

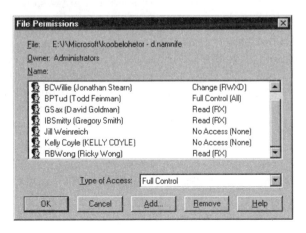

Table 9-2 presents and describes the File Permissions dialog box.

**Table 9-2. File Permissions Dialog Box**

| Fields | Description |
| --- | --- |
| File | Displays the logical drive, the NTFS directory, and the file to which security is to be applied. This selection cannot be changed from this dialog box; it must be selected through Windows NT Explorer. Multiple files can be simultaneously selected. |
| Owner | Displays the owner of the file. The owner cannot be changed from this dialog box; it must be changed through the Owner dialog box from the Security tab. Initially, only the owner can change permissions of a file. |

| Section | Description |
| --- | --- |
| Name | Displays the name of the user or group accounts and the type of permissions granted. If multiple files are selected, the permissions displayed will be common to the selected files. |

| Drop-down List | Description |
| --- | --- |
| Type of Access | Displays the permissions that can be granted. |

| Button | Description |
| --- | --- |
| Add | Opens the Add Users and Groups dialog box. |
| Remove | Deletes the selected account from the Names list. |

## Types of File Permissions

File permissions can be applied via predefined groups called *Standard File Access* permissions or separately by choosing individual *Special Access permissions*. By choosing Special Access as the type of access for file permissions, the Special Access dialog box opens.

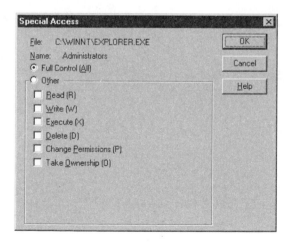

Special Access permissions can be set for any file. Table 9-3 presents the Special Access permissions and the associated actions they allow.

**Table 9-3. Special Permissions and the Associated Actions They Allow**

| Special Permissions | Display the File's Data | Display the File's Attributes | Run the File If it Is a Program | Display the File's Owner and Permissions | Change the File's Attributes | Change the Data In and Append Data to the File | Delete the File | Change the File's Permissions | Take Ownership of the File |
|---|---|---|---|---|---|---|---|---|---|
| Read (R) | X | X | | X | | X | | | |
| Write (W) | | | | X | X | X | | | |
| Execute (X) | | X | X | X | | | | | |
| Delete (D) | | | | | | | X | | |
| Change Permissions (P) | | | | | | | | X | |
| Take Ownership (O) | | | | | | | | | X |
| Full Control (RWXDPO) | X | X | X | X | X | X | X | X | X |

The Standard File Access permissions have certain associated actions that are relevant to files. Table 9-4 presents these permissions and the associated actions they allow.

**Table 9-4. Standard File Permissions and the Associated Actions They Allow**

| Standard File Permissions | Display the File's Data | Display the File's Attributes | Run the File If It Is a Program | Display the File's Owner and Permissions | Change the File's Attributes | Change the Data In and Append Data to the File | Delete the File | Change the File's Owner and Permissions |
|---|---|---|---|---|---|---|---|---|
| No Access (None) | | | | | | | | |
| Read (RX) | X | X | X | X | | | | |
| Change (RXWD) | X | X | X | X | X | X | X | |
| Full Control (RWXDPO) | X | X | X | X | X | X | X | X |

## NTFS Directory Permissions

Directory permissions that are accessed at a local machine apply exclusively to NTFS partitions. NTFS directory permissions are set through Windows NT Explorer. Select a directory, choose File ⇨ Properties, switch to the Security tab, and click the Permissions button. The Directory Permissions dialog box appears.

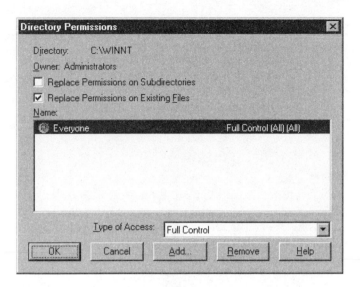

Table 9-5 presents and describes the Directory Permissions dialog box.

**Table 9-5. Directory Permissions Dialog Box**

| Fields | Description |
| --- | --- |
| Directory | Displays the logical drive and NTFS directory to which security is to be applied. This selection cannot be changed from this dialog box; it must be selected through Windows NT Explorer. Multiple directories can be simultaneously selected. |
| Owner | Displays the owner of the directory. The owner cannot be changed from this dialog box; it must be changed through the Owner dialog box from the Security tab. Initially, only the owner can change permissions of a directory. |

| Check Box | Description |
| --- | --- |
| Replace Permissions on Subdirectories | Allows the user to make changes and apply them to all subdirectories exclusively. By default, this option is not selected. |
| Replace Permissions on Existing Files | Allows the user to make changes and apply them to the files in the directory. This option is enabled by default because permissions applied to the directory affect the files in that specific directory. |

| Section | Description |
| --- | --- |
| Name | Displays the name of the user or group accounts and the type of permissions granted. If multiple directories are selected, the permissions displayed will be common to the selected files. Two sets of permissions are displayed for each user: the permissions set in the directory and the permissions set on the files in the directory. |

*(continued)*

**Table 9-5.** *(continued)*

| Drop-down List | Description |
| --- | --- |
| Type of Access | Displays the permissions that can be granted. |
| Button | Description. |
| Add | Opens the Add Users and Groups dialog box. |
| Remove | Deletes the selected account from the Names list. |

## Types of Directory Permissions

Directory permissions can be applied via predefined groups called *Standard Access Directory permissions* or separately by choosing *Special Directory Access permissions* individually. By choosing Special Directory Access as the type of access, the Special Directory Access dialog box opens.

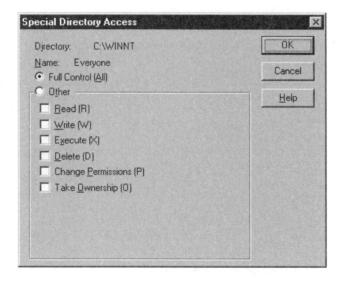

The Special Directory Access permissions are identical to those for files. In addition, Special File Access permissions can be enabled for all the existing files in the directory. Choosing Special File Access from the Type of Access drop-down list opens the Special Access dialog box. In effect, it is possible to set different file permissions on the files within a directory than those permissions set on the directory itself.

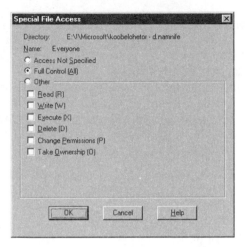

The Special File Access permissions are identical to those for files as described earlier. However, an additional radio button allows Access to Not be Specified. If this is enabled, files will not inherit permissions from the directory.

Special Directory Access permissions can be set for any directory. The following table presents Special Directory Access permissions and the associated actions they allow on directories.

**Table 9-6. Special Directory Access Permissions and the Associate Actions They Allow**

| Special Directory Access and Permissions | Display the File Names In the Directory | Display the Directory's Attributes | Add Files and Subdirectories | Change the Directory's Attributes | Go to the Directory's Subdirectories | Display Directory Owner and Permissions | Delete the Directory | Change the Directory's Permissions | Take Ownership of the Directory |
|---|---|---|---|---|---|---|---|---|---|
| Read (R) | X | X | | | | X | | | |
| Write (W) | | | X | X | | X | | | |
| Execute (X) | | X | | | X | X | | | |
| Delete (D) | | | | | | | X | | |
| Change Permissions (P) | | | | | | | | X | |
| Take Ownership (O) | | | | | | | | | X |
| Full Control (RWXDPO) | X | X | X | X | X | X | X | X | X |

**Note**  Full Control is different from assigning (RWXDPO) special permissions, due to POSIX-compliance.

The Standard Directory Access permissions, or predefined groups of Special Directory Access permissions, are presented as the standard permission followed by two sets of parentheses for individual Special Directory Access permissions. The first set of parentheses is for the directory itself, and the second set is for the files in the directory that will inherit permissions from the directory when created. For example, a directory permission of (RWXDPO) (RWXD) means that the directory permission is (RWXDPO) and newly created files within that directory have the permission of (RWXD). All newly created files in a directory inherit the permissions defined in the second set of parentheses, by default.

It should be noted that Full Control includes a "hidden" special permission called *File Delete Child (FDC)*, which may create a security vulnerability if the file owners are not aware of FDC. All user accounts with Full Control permissions on a directory can delete files within the root level of a directory. One way to avoid FDC issues is to use Special Directory Access permissions instead of the standard permission, Full Control, to grant access to directories.

FDC permission was necessary for POSIX compliance. The POSIX specification states that a user who has Write permissions to directory must be able to delete all files in that directory, regardless of the permissions on the files. This permission only applies to files within a directory and not to subdirectories below it.

An asterisk (*) following the set of directory permissions indicates that subdirectories do not inherit the permissions granted to that group or user account. This can occur when a group or user has been granted permissions through the Creator Owner special group.

Some directory permissions set file permissions to Not Specified. When access to files for a user or group is not specified, that group or user cannot access files in the directory unless access is granted by another means, such as by setting permissions that grant access on individual files.

When setting permissions on a directory, the Creator Owner special group can be used to allow users to control only those subdirectories and files that they create within the directory. Permissions set in the Creator Owner are transferred to the user who creates a directory or file within the directory. For example, the Everyone group has Add & Read permission to the directory and Creator Owner has Change permission. When user Dawn adds files to the directory, she can read and delete the files she creates, while other users will only be able to read her files. However, although Dawn is the owner, she will not be able to change permissions on the file, because Creator Owner does not have Full Control, which includes the Special Access, Change Permission.

Standard Directory permissions can also be set on directories. These are groups of special directory permissions and special file permissions that are commonly used together. Table 9-7 presents and describes the Standard Directory Access permission.

**Table 9-7. Standard Directory Permissions**

| Standard Directory Access Permissions | Description |
|---|---|
| No Access (None) (None) | Users cannot access the directory or files within, regardless of which group they belong to. |
| List (RX) (Not Specified) | Users can view file and subdirectory names. Users cannot access files from within, unless granted by other directory or file permissions. |
| Read (RX) (RX) | Users can view files and subdirectory names, traverse subdirectories, read data files and execute program files. |
| Add (WX) (Not Specified) | Users can add files and subdirectories to the directory. Users cannot access files within, unless granted by other directory or file permissions. |
| Add & Read (RWX) (RX) | Users can view file and subdirectory names, traverse subdirectories, read and execute files, and create files and subdirectories. |
| Change (RWXD) (RWXD) | Users can view file and subdirectory names, traverse subdirectories, read, write, and execute files, create files and subdirectories, and delete files, subdirectories, and the current directory. |
| Full Control (All) (All) | Users can read, write, execute, delete, change permissions, and take ownership of the files, subdirectories, and the current directory. |

The Standard Directory Access permissions have certain associated actions that are relevant to directories. Table 9-8 presents these permissions and the actions they allow on directories.

**Table 9-8. Standard Directory Access Permissions and Associated Actions on Directories**

| Standard Directory Access Permissions | Display Directory File Names | Display the Directory's Attributes | Go to the Directory's Subdirectories | Change the Directory's Attributes | Create Subdirectories and Add Files | Display the Directory's Owner and Permissions | Delete the Directory | Delete Any File or Empty Subdirectory | Change Directory Permissions | Take Ownership of the Directory |
|---|---|---|---|---|---|---|---|---|---|---|
| No Access | | | | | | | | | | |
| List | X | X | X | | | X | | | | |
| Read | X | X | X | | | X | | | | |
| Add | | X | X | X | X | X | | | | |
| Add & Read | X | X | X | X | X | X | | | | |
| Change | X | X | X | X | X | X | X | | | |
| Full Control | X | X | X | X | X | X | X | X | X | X |

The Standard Directory Access permissions have certain associated actions that are relevant to files. Table 9-9 presents these permissions and the actions they allow on files.

**Table 9-9. Standard Directory Access Permissions and Associated Actions on Files**

| Special Directory Access Permissions | Display the File's Data | Display the File's Attributes | Run the File If It Is a Program | Display the File's Owner and Permissions | Change the File's Attributes | Change the Data In and Append Data to the File | Delete the File | Change the File's Permissions | Take Ownership of the File |
|---|---|---|---|---|---|---|---|---|---|
| No Access | | | | | | | | | |
| List | | | | | | | | | |
| Read | X | X | X | X | | | | | |
| Add | | | | | | | | | |
| Add & Read | X | X | X | X | | | | | |
| Change | X | X | X | X | X | X | X | | |
| Full Control | X | X | X | X | X | X | X | X | X |

## Ownership

In Windows NT, every file and directory on an NTFS partition has an owner who controls how permissions are set on the file or directory and can grant permissions to others.

By default, the creator of a file or directory is the owner of that file or directory. It is not possible to give someone ownership of a file or directory, but the owner can grant permission to someone else to take ownership. Administrators can always take ownership of a file or other objects. To open the Owner dialog box, select a file or directory, choose File ⇨ Properties, switch to the Security tab, and click the Ownership button.

The current directory or filename is displayed along with the current owner. The Take Ownership button grants the current user ownership of the object. To take ownership of a file or other object, the user must have the Take Ownership of Files or Other Objects user right, or the Special Access file or directory permission that includes Take Ownership.

## Recommendations

Permissions should be granted only to groups, not individual users, whenever possible. Granting permissions to groups simplifies server maintenance. If several users need access to a certain set of files, they can be placed into a group, and then permissions can be given just to the group. Then, if another user needs the same type of access, just add the user to the group, instead of giving the user access to each file individually.

When Windows NT is installed, certain system directories are assigned default permissions. When a new subdirectory is created, it will automatically inherit the permissions from its parent directory. In addition, when applications are installed, default file and directory permissions are created. For example, Microsoft SQL Server 6.5 installs its system directories with Everyone having the Full Control permission set. Because these permissions may create security control weaknesses, administrators should be cognizant of this possibility and substitute a set of permissions that are appropriate.

Setting the appropriate permissions is a critical security control for securing the system that is usually not implemented because it takes much planning. Recommending appropriate permissions for one specific corporation is difficult due to the wide variety of Windows NT implementations and the applications installed. The best policy would be to restrict individuals wherever possible and add permissions when needed. This procedure should be done in a test environment and then implemented in production when complete. However, as we have seen with most of our clients, this procedure is not usually done because of the level of frustration created and the time expended. As a guideline, we recommend some baseline directory permissions for the Windows NT Server default directories. Table 9-10 breaks down the permissions we recommend administrators use to begin building a secure system.

**Table 9-10.  Recommended Permissions**

| File and Directory Permissions | Recommendations | |
| --- | --- | --- |
| \ (Root on an NTFS volume) | Administrators | Full Control |
| | Server Operators | Change |
| | Everyone | Read |
| | CREATOR OWNER | Full Control |
| | SYSTEM | Full Control |
| \winnt\ | Administrators | Full Control |
| | Server Operators | Change |
| | Everyone | Read |
| | CREATOR OWNER | Full Control |
| | SYSTEM | Full Control |
| \winnt\system32 | Administrators | Full Control |
| | Server Operators | Change |
| | Everyone | Read |

*(continued)*

**Table 9-10.** *(continued)*

| File and Directory Permissions | Recommendations | |
| --- | --- | --- |
| creator owner | Full Control | |
| | SYSTEM | Full Control |
| \winnt\system32\config | Administrators | Full Control |
| | Everyone | List |
| | CREATOR OWNER | Full Control |
| | SYSTEM | Full Control |
| \winnt\system32\drivers | Administrators | Full Control |
| | Server Operators | Full Control |
| | Everyone | Read |
| | CREATOR OWNER | Full Control |
| | SYSTEM | Full Control |
| \winnt\system32\spool | Administrators | Full Control |
| | Server Operators | Full Control |
| | Print Operators | Full Control |
| | Everyone | Read |
| | CREATOR OWNER | Full Control |
| | SYSTEM | Full Control |
| \winnt\system32\repl | Administrators | Full Control |
| | Server Operators | Full Control |
| | Everyone | Read |
| | CREATOR OWNER | Full Control |
| | SYSTEM | Full Control |
| \winnt\system32\repl\import | Administrators | Full Control |
| | Server Operators | Change |
| | Everyone | Read |
| | CREATOR OWNER | Full Control |
| | Replicator | Change |
| | NETWORK | No Access |
| | SYSTEM | Full Control |
| \winnt\system32\repl\import | Administrators | Full Control |
| | Server Operators | Change |
| | CREATOR OWNER | Full Control |
| | Replicator | Read |
| | SYSTEM | Full Control |
| \winnt\repair | Administrators | Full Control |

Normally, the Everyone group has the Full Control permission for the root directory. All other directories created under the root directory will inherit the Change permission for the Everyone group. Because all users are members of the Everyone group, everyone will have this permission. Everyone having the Change permission is excessive and should be modified to only grant Everyone Read access.

### The No Access Permission

If a user assigns the No Access permission to a group, all members of that group are explicitly denied access to that directory, even if a user is an administrator. No Access is the most restrictive permission and should be used cautiously. By assigning the Everyone group the No Access permission, an object will be configured so that it cannot be accessed at all. However, an individual with the Take Ownership of Files or Other Objects user right can circumvent the No Access permission by exercising the Take Ownership option for the object. After ownership has been established, the user can change permissions.

### Moving and Copying Secured Files and Directories

When moving files or directories within a single volume, permissions are retained. The moving of files or directories could potentially be a security risk if the user moving the file or directory does not understand this behavior. When files with weak security permissions are moved into a secure directory, the files retain their weak security permissions, thus creating a security risk. Users should be cognizant of this fact because they might move insecure files into their secured home directory and not realize those files do not take on the permissions of the directory. Even if the Replace Permissions on Existing Files check box is enabled on the directory, the file will still retain its permissions. This is because the Replace Permissions on Existing Files check box is not a state; it is an option that can be executed at a specific time. If it is checked, all files within the directory inherit permissions at that moment and not again until this box is checked again.

When copying files or directories, permissions take on those of the directory to which they are moved. Potential security risks arise when users copy files from a secured directory (such as their private home directory) to a public directory, and the files inherit the permissions of the public directory. However, it is possible to secure the permissions if the Scopy program, which comes with the Windows NT Resource Kit, is used for the copying (the Backup Files and Folders user right is required). Scopy can be run from the command prompt just like the Copy command.

### Executable Files

Administrators should set up a directory so that data files and executable program files are kept separate. When they are mixed together, users may be able to place a Trojan Horse or virus-infected file in with the program files. Authorized users should be granted Read permission on programs, not write permission. Granting only Read permission to a directory in which program files are located decreases the risk that malicious code will be placed in that directory. Some programs require users to have Write access to the directory in which they reside, so users should be granted access accordingly.

### Deleting Files

When a file is deleted from a local drive using Windows NT Explorer, it is actually moved to the Recycle Bin, where only the individual who deleted the file can undelete it. When restored, the security permissions of the file prior to it being deleted are retained.

### Sum of Permissions

The actions a user can take with an object are determined based upon the sum of the permissions a user acquires through group memberships and through direct assignment to the user. For example, several users and groups have permissions in a specific directory. Steven is a member of groups A, B, and C. The groups have the following permissions to this directory:

- Group A—Members have read permissions (R) (R).
- Group B—Members have update and add permissions (W) (W).
- Group C—Members have delete permissions (D) (D).

In addition, Steven has been granted the Take Ownership permission (O) (X) to administer the directory. Therefore, Steven's permissions are the sum of the following:

- (R) (R)    From Group A
- (W) (W)  From Group B
- (D) (D)   From Group C
- (O) (X)    From Steven's user account

Steven's permissions to the directory and its files are (RWDO) and (RWDX), respectively.

Because of its security implications, it is important to repeat that the No Access permission explicitly denies access. If Steven had been granted No Access, then regardless of any other permission, he would not be able to access the directory or files.

## Shared File and Directory Permissions

Shares allow the user to access resources (Files, Directories, and Printers) across the network. Shared directory permissions determine if and how a user or group can access a shared directory. Shared directory permissions and ownership can be set for the NTFS or FAT file system.

File and print sharing is possible because of the Server Message Block (SMB) protocol, which is supported in Windows NT Server and Workstation. The machines that run the SMB protocol communicate with redirector services that allow files to be located, opened, read, written to, and deleted.

## Creating and Managing Shares

You create a share by granting a particular resource a *share name*. This name is what other users or devices recognize as the entity with which they have permission to access. When the share is created, the shared name is independent of the actual resource that is shared—that is, a shared resource can have different share names for different users.

To create or modify a new share, a user must be logged on as Administrator, Server Operator, or Power User. In Windows NT Explorer, select the directory you want to share. Choose File ➪ Properties and then switch to the Sharing tab.

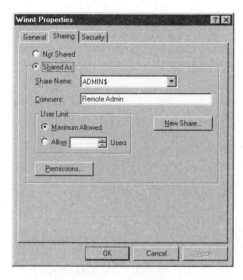

Table 9-11 presents and describes the Sharing tab of the Properties dialog box.

### Table 9-11.  The Sharing Tab of the Properties Dialog Box

| Radio Buttons | Description |
| --- | --- |
| Not Shared | Disables sharing on the directory |
| Shared As | Enables sharing on the directory |
| **Fields** | **Description** |
| Share Name | Specifies the name used to connect to the shared directory |
| Comment | Specifies a comment for the shared directory |
| **Radio Buttons** | **Description** |
| Maximum Allowed | Allows the maximum number of users that can connect to the shared directory at one time |

*(continued)*

**Table 9-11.** *(continued)*

| Radio Buttons | Description |
| --- | --- |
| Allow *XX* Users | Specifies the maximum number of users allowed that can connect to the shared directory at one time |

| Button | Description |
| --- | --- |
| Permissions | Opens the Access through Share Permissions dialog box, which is similar to the Directory Permissions dialog box |

### Deleting a Share

At any time after a share is created, if the Not Shared radio button is selected, the share will be deleted. The share can only be re-created by entering all the same preferences again. Even if the share is re-created with the same preferences and same name, its old permissions are still lost and must be reapplied. Only Administrators, Server Operators, and Power Users can delete shares.

### Share Permissions

When accessing a share, share permissions and the NTFS permissions must be taken into account. The permissions that determine user access are the most restrictive of the two. For example, Lillian (the user) attempts to access *Document1* on the share *Share1*. The permissions for *Share1* are Lillian, Change. The file permissions on the NTFS volume for *Document1* are Lillian, Read. Lillian's maximum permissions for *Document1* on a share would be Read.

Permissions set through a share apply to the directory, the subdirectories, and to any files in the shared directory. Clicking on the Permissions button on the Sharing tab will open the Access through Share Permissions dialog box, which allows you to place permissions on the share. Table 9-12 presents the share permissions available from the Type of Access drop-down list and their descriptions.

**Table 9-12. Share Permissions**

| Share Permissions | Description |
| --- | --- |
| No Access | Users cannot access the directory or files within, regardless of the group to which they belong. |
| Read | User can view files and subdirectory names, traverse subdirectories, and read and execute files if they are programs. |
| Change | Users can view file and subdirectory names, traverse subdirectories, read, write, and execute files if they are programs, create files and subdirectories, and delete files, subdirectories, and the current directory. |
| Full Control | Users can read, write, execute, delete, change permissions, and take ownership of the files, subdirectories, and the current directory. |

Table 9-13 presents the share permissions and the associated actions on directories and files that they allow.

**Table 9-13. Share Permissions and the Associated Actions on Directories and Files They Allow**

| Share permissions | Display Subdirectory and File Name | Display File Data and Attributes | Run Program Files | Go to the Directory's Subdirectories | Create Subdirectories and Add Files | Change and Append File Data | Change File Attributes | Delete Subdirectories and Files | Change Permissions (NTFS Files and Directories only) | Take Ownership (NTFS Files and Directories only) |
|---|---|---|---|---|---|---|---|---|---|---|
| No Access | | | | | | | | | | |
| Read | X | X | X | X | | | | | | |
| Change | X | X | X | X | X | X | X | X | | |
| Full Control | X | X | X | X | X | X | X | X | X | X |

## Hidden Shares

Windows NT Server automatically creates special shares for the administrative and system use. When Windows NT is installed, an administrative shared directory is created for the root directory of each drive on the computer and for the Windows NT Server system root; for example, *c:\winnt*. Administrative shares created for drives are named using the drive letter and dollar sign, *C$* for example. The shared directory created for the system root is called *ADMIN$*. Members of the Administrators, Server Operators, and Backup Operators groups can connect to these shared directories. Only members of the Administrators group can change their properties.

Administrative (Hidden) shares and default shares are listed as follows:

- C$, D$, E$,...      C:\, D:\, E:\,...
- ADMIN$             c:\winnt
- IPC$               InterProcess Communication Share
- PRINT$             c:\winnt\system32\spool\drivers
- REPL$              c:\winnt\system32\repl\export\
- NETLOGON           c:\winnt\system32\repl\import\scripts

Administrators and Server Operators can create their own hidden shares so that users cannot browse them over the network by adding a dollar sign ($) to the end of the share name.

**Note** To disable the administrative shares on Windows NT Server, set the following value to 0:

Registry Key:
HKEY_LOCAL_MACHINE\SYSTEM\CurrentControlSet\Services\LanmanServer\Parameters

Value Name: AutoShareServer

Data Type: REG_BINARY

### Recommendations for Securing Shares

Shares are defined points of entry to the system. As such, they can provide not only an entry for appropriate users but also an attractive target for hackers. The Windows NT system directories should not be shared to anyone but administrators, because users might be able to transfer malicious executable files into the Windows NT directory. This ability could lead to an administrator inadvertently executing malicious code.

As recommended in the "NTFS File Permissions" section, Share permissions should be thought out and tailored for each Windows NT implementation. Consideration should be given when creating shares because both NTFS permissions and share permissions apply. However, NTFS permissions provide more granular security controls, and, therefore, the system should be secured through strong NTFS permissions. If NTFS permissions are set appropriately, share permissions could be more lax.

# Managing Printers

Managing printers provides the means to add, configure, and delete local and network printers. It controls how printers are shared on the network; it controls the settings of the share permissions and the auditing of printer events; and it identifies who has printer ownership. Access to a printer should be restricted to authorized individuals; otherwise, sensitive documents could have their printer destinations rerouted to a less secure area where unauthorized users could access the output. Print Manager addresses security in three ways: permissions, auditing, and ownership. To view a printer's setting, choose Start ⇨ Setting ⇨ Printers. Double-click on a printer to open that Printer's dialog box (see following graphic). Choose Printer ⇨ Properties.

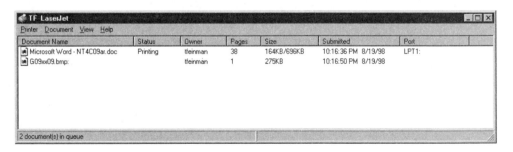

## Permissions

To view the Printer Permissions dialog box, double-click on a printer to open that Printer's dialog box. Choose Printer ⇨ Properties and then the Permissions Tab.

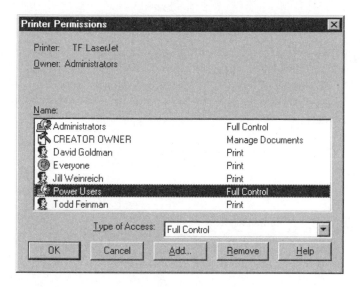

The owner of the printer or the users who have Full Control permissions set printer permissions. Four permissions can be assigned to printers, as shown in Table 9-14.

**Table 9-14. Printer Permissions**

| Standard Printer Permission | Printer |
|---|---|
| No Access | Users cannot access the printer. |
| Print | Users can print to printer. This permission is by default granted to the Everyone group. |
| Manage Documents | Users can print documents and pause, resume, start, and remove queued documents. This right is by default granted to the creator/owner. |
| Full Control | Users have full control over the printer. They can change printer properties and remove the printer, regardless of the group to which they belong. This right is by default granted to Administrators, Printer Operators, and Server Operators. |

The No Access permission is the strongest of all permissions, and should only be used when you want to ensure a user cannot gain access to a printer. It overrides all other group permissions, even those permissions made directly to the user's own account. The Manage Documents permissions allow users to control document settings and delete, pause, resume, and restart documents. Full Control permissions allow users to change logical printer permissions, delete logical printers, change logical printer properties, change document printing order, and purge, pause, and resume logical printers. Full Control permissions also include those actions of Manage Documents. The user who creates a document is the document's owner; all users can perform Manage Documents on documents they own.

## Ownership

The user who creates a printer is the printer's owner and can administer all the characteristics of the printer. The owner can grant others administration of the printer by giving them Manage Documents or Full Control permissions. Any user with the Full Control permissions can access the Ownership option and click the Take Ownership button. This action allows the user to assume ownership of the printer.

# Chapter 10
# Managing Server Security

Securing the server entails many controls, and the main objective is to secure the system configurations so that unauthorized users cannot change them in anyway. By doing so, you secure the computer and the data residing on it so that you are assured the objective of Confidentiality is met. Controls should be in place to ensure that all access to the computer system, programs, and data are appropriately restricted, meaning that you secure system configurations files so that individuals cannot simply change them.

Windows NT provides many security features for setting, organizing, and maintaining system configurations. For this reason, the security controls that can be implemented to protect these items are numerous. In the following section, we recommend the controls we believe are most important in reaching the objective of securing the system.

Server Manager is the application within Windows NT that allows an administrator to control most domain activity. Some of these activities include domain administration, setting up shares, configuring replication settings, modifying services, and monitoring user connections. These functions can all be performed remotely or locally by the administrators.

To launch the Server Manager application, choose Start ⇨ Programs ⇨ Administrative Tools ⇨ Server Manager.

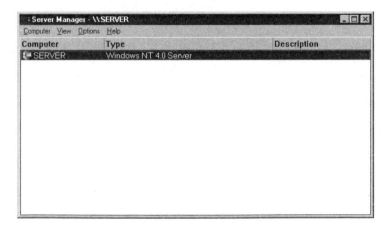

The Server Manager application appears and, in the title bar of the main window, the name of the domain currently being administered is displayed. The main viewing area displays the computer name in the Computer column, the Windows NT version and server type (if possible) in the Type column, and the description in the Description field. The icon to the left of each Computer name represents the server type.

You can view computers three ways: servers only, workstations only, and all. In addition, administrators can choose to view the domain members only. Depending on what needs to be managed, these views should facilitate finding a particular computer. Administrators should periodically review the current members of a domain and make sure all computers belong.

## Computer Properties

Both workstations and servers can be displayed in the view. To display the properties of a particular server either double-click on the computer name or choose Computer ð Properties from the menu bar. The Properties dialog box appears.

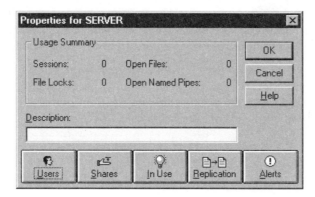

Administrators should use Server Manager as a tool for monitoring and controlling connections to a computer. Security can also be monitored and controlled through some of these features because an administrator can disconnect a user in real time if they are accessing certain resources incorrectly.

Table 10-1 presents and describes the Properties dialog box.

**Table 10-1.  Computer Properties**

| Usage Summary Section | Function |
| --- | --- |
| Sessions | The number of users remotely connected to the computer. |
| File Locks | The number of file locks by open resources on the computer. Another user cannot access a resource if it is locked. |
| Open Files | The number of shared resources opened on the computer. |
| Open Named Pipes | The number of named pipes opened on the computer. Named pipes are interprocess communication mechanisms that allow processes to communicate with each other locally and remotely. |
| Field | Function. |
| Description | Specifies the description of a computer—typically the computer's location, user, and function. |

| Button | Function |
| --- | --- |
| Users | Lists and allows the disconnection of connected users and their open resources. |
| Shares | Lists the shared resources and allows disconnection of users who are connected to them. |
| In Use | Lists opened resources and who is using them. |
| Replication | Allows management of directory replication. |
| Alerts | Lists and allows management of the users and computers that receive alerts. |

## Users

Administrators can monitor the users who are currently connected to the computer over the network and view the resources those users have open. This ability allows administrators to monitor how many users are connected at any given time, the shared resources that are being accessed, and the length of time a user has been connected to the open resource. To open the User Sessions dialog box, click the Users button.

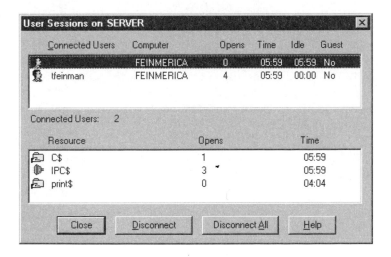

There are two fields: The top field is for viewing the users that are connected, and the bottom field is for viewing the resources that are in use by a specific user. Table 10-2 presents and describes the User Sessions dialog box.

**Table 10-2. User Sessions**

| Top Field Columns | Function |
| --- | --- |
| Connected Users | Lists the users or computers that are connected to the computer over the network |
| Computer | Displays the connected user's computer name |
| Opens | Displays the number of resources opened on this computer by the user |
| Time | Displays the hours and minutes that have elapsed since the session was established |
| Idle | Displays the hours and minutes that have elapsed since the user last initiated an action |
| Guest | Indicates whether or not this user connected to this computer as a guest |

| Bottom Field Columns | Function |
| --- | --- |
| Resource | Lists the shared resources to which the selected user is connected |
| Opens | Displays the number of times the listed resource is open for a selected user |
| Time | Displays the hours and minutes that have elapsed since the user first connected to a shared resource |

| Button | Function |
| --- | --- |
| Disconnect | Disconnects the highlighted user from the computer |
| Disconnect All | Disconnects all users from the computer |

Administrators can disconnect users from the network. This ability might be advantageous if the administrator wanted to terminate a connection immediately because a user was suspected of accessing resources in a manner they should not be. In addition, the fewer users connected, the better performance will be. To disconnect a user, highlight his name in the top field and click the Disconnect button. If you want to disconnect every user currently connected, click the Disconnect All button. Administrators should always warn legitimate users before disconnecting them to prevent data loss and corruption.

**Note**   Users who are disconnected via this method may reconnect at any time. This does not disallow future connection attempts.

## Shares

Administrators can monitor and control shares on a machine. For example, they can disconnect users from those shares by clicking the Shares button, which opens the Shared Resources dialog box.

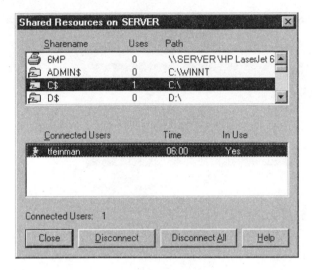

This box is divided into two sections: shares in the top field and connected users in the bottom field. Table 10-3 presents and describes the Shared Resources dialog box.

**Table 10-3. Shared Resources**

| Top Field Columns | Function |
| --- | --- |
| Sharename | Lists the shared resources available on the computer |
| Uses | Displays the number of connections to the shared resource |
| Path | Displays the path of the shared resource |

| Bottom Field Columns | Function |
| --- | --- |
| Connected Users | Lists the users who are connected to the selected-shared resource |
| Time | Displays the hours and minutes that have elapsed since the user first connected to the shared resource |
| In Use | Indicates whether the user currently has a file open from the selected resource |

| Button | Function |
| --- | --- |
| Disconnect | Disconnects the highlighted user from the computer |
| Disconnect All | Disconnects all users from the computer |

Similar to the functionality of the User Sessions dialog box, the Shared Resources dialog box is used to monitor what is in use and to terminate what is being used. Administrators should use this as a tool in controlling network usage of shared resources.

## In Use

To view or manage the shared resources open on a selected computer, click the In Use button. The Open Resources dialog box appears.

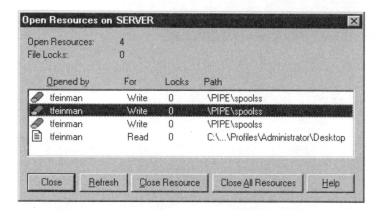

An administrator can close one or all the open resources that are being accessed by remote users. Reasons for doing this include if administrators suspect users of gaining unauthorized access to files and if administrators need to free up connections. Table 10-4 presents and describes the Open Resources dialog box.

**Table 10-4. Open Resources**

| Area | Function |
| --- | --- |
| Open Resources | Displays the total number of open resources on the computer |
| File Locks | Displays the total number of file locks by open resources |

| Column | Function |
| --- | --- |
| Opened By | Lists the type of opened resources on the computer and the user name who opened it |
| For | Lists the permissions granted when the resource was opened |
| Locks | Displays the number of locks on the resource |
| Path | Displays the path of the open resource |

| Button | Function |
| --- | --- |
| Close Resource | Disconnects the highlighted user from the computer |
| Close All Resources | Disconnects all users from the computer |

The functionality of the Open Resources dialog box is similar to the User Sessions dialog box because it is a tool administrators can use to view what is in use and it provides administrators the ability to terminate a connection of what is being used.

## Replication

Directory replication provides the ability to create and maintain identical directory trees and files on multiple servers and workstations. To open the Directory Replication dialog box, click the Replication button.

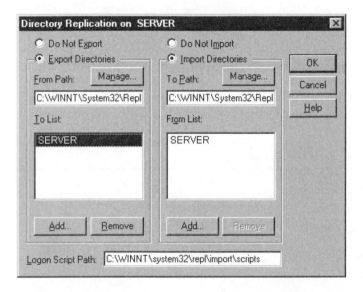

The screen is divided into two halves: the Exportation settings on the left and the Importation settings on the right. Administrators should not confuse the two because highly sensitive data will be passed from the export server to the import clients.

Replication is a powerful feature for load balancing, file maintenance, and distribution of logon scripts and policy files. The use of replication relieves the load placed on a single server because the files are available on more than one system. File maintenance is reduced because updates to files are derived from a single source. This reduction creates potential security vulnerabilities, because there are now two places hackers can try to access sensitive information. Windows NT Workstation can only import data, whereas Windows NT Server can both export and import data through replication.

The replication process contains two component systems: the export server and the import computer. The *export server* is the system that contains the files to be replicated to the import computer. The *import computer* receives the replicated directories and files from the export server.

## Configuring and Securing Replications

Configuring directory replication is a two-step process, because it involves configuring the export server and import computer(s). During both steps, it is important to stay focused on security; if configured incorrectly, a Windows NT server could be breached or data could be compromised.

### Step One: The Export Server

Three different applications need to be used to configure and secure the export server: User Manager for Domains, Server Manager, and the Services applet from the Control Panel, which can also be accessed from within Server Manager.

From the export server, launch User Manager for Domains and create a new user account called *Replicator*. (This is a common name, which is not recommended. You should use a name that is more obscure.) The new Replicator account should be created on the domain, which will allow the account to be used on both the export server and import client. Table 10-5 indicates what the settings should be in order for the Replicator account to be able to perform the replication functions and still be secure.

**Table 10-5. Replicator Account Settings**

| Option | Value |
| --- | --- |
| Password Never Expires | Select. |
| User Must Change Password At Next Logon | Do not select. |
| User Cannot Change Password | Do not select. |
| Account Disabled | Do not select. |
| Groups | Replicator. |
| Profile | Do not define a user profile. |
| Hours | Enable 24-hours a day, 7-days a week. |

Return to the Server Manager application and choose Computer ⇨ Services. Highlight the Directory Replicator Service and click the Startup button. The Service dialog box appears.

The Service dialog box allows the administrator to configure settings for the type of logon and account that logs on. The Replicator account just created should be the account that logs in to run the Directory Replicator service. By default, the LocalSystem account is used. The following is a list of options and their configurations:

- Startup Type—Automatic
- Log On As—Select the This Account radio button
- This Account—Input the user account (Replicator and password created for Directory Replicator)

After typing in the name of the Replicator account and clicking OK, the following Server Manager dialog box will appear, notifying the administrator that the Replicator account has been granted membership to the local Replicator group and the Log On As A Service user right. For administrative purposes, we recommend taking the Log On As A Service user right away from the Replicator account and granting it to the Replicator local group.

Return to the Directory Replication dialog box of Server Manager and select the Export Directories radio button. It is also possible to have the export server set up as an import client, but for the purposes of this configuration, the machine will be solely an export server. Type the path of the directories to be replicated in the To Path field. By default, the directory is %systemroot%\system32\repl\export.

To configure the directory and subdirectories to be replicated, click the Manage button, which opens the Manage Exported Directories dialog box.

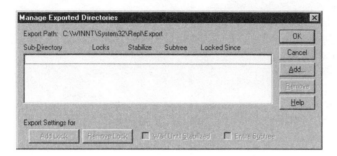

The directory being managed is displayed at the top, adjacent to Export Path. Table 10-6 describes the settings for managing directories.

**Table 10-6. Manage Export Directories**

| Column | Description |
| --- | --- |
| Sub-Directory | A list of the subdirectories that are exported from this computer—maximum amount is 32 |
| Locks | Displays the number of locks on the subdirectory and locks prevent exportation |
| Stabilize | Indicates whether specified subdirectory must be idle or stable—for two minutes before replication (see the note that follows this table) |
| Subtree | Indicates if the entire subtree will be exported or just the first-level subdirectory |
| Locked Since | Displays the date and time that the oldest lock was placed on the export path |
| **Button** | **Description** |
| Add | Adds subdirectories |
| Remove | Removes subdirectories |
| Add Lock | Adds one lock and multiple locks that can be placed on subdirectories |
| Remove Lock | Removes a lock |
| **Check Boxes** | **Description** |
| Wait Until Stabilized | Enables stability |
| Entire Subtree | Enables entire subtree exportation |

**Note**   Although the default is two minutes, you can set the number of minutes an export directory must be stable before it will be replicated. To modify the default, set the following Registry key:

HKEY_LOCAL_MACHINE\System\CurrentControlSet\Services\Replicator\Parameters

Insert the value name GuardTime (REG_DWORD) and its value will be equivalent to the number of minutes.

After management of the directory replication is complete, go back to the Directory Replication dialog box and click the left-most Add button. This action opens the Select Domain dialog box, where computers can be selected as import clients. All clients selected appear in the To List section.

The last field to be edited is the Logon Script Path field at the bottom of the Directory Replication dialog box. This field specifies the location of the local directory where logon scripts are stored.

### Step Two: Import Computers

If the import computer exists in a different domain than that of the export server, a Replicator account will have to be created that exactly matches the account created in the export server's domain. Next, at the import computer, open Server Manager and choose Computer ⇨ Services. Similar to what was done on the Windows NT export server, it is necessary to adjust the Directory Replicator Service's startup options to the following values:

| Option | Value |
| --- | --- |
| Startup Type | Automatic |
| Log On As | Select the This Account radio button |
| This Account | Input the Replicator account and password created for the Directory Replicator Service |

The Replicator account will automatically be granted membership to the local Replicator group and given the Log On As A Service user right.

Open the Directory Replicator dialog box by choosing Computer ⇨ Properties and then clicking the Replicator button. On the right side of the dialog box is the Import Directories options. Select the Import Directories radio button. Type the path of the directories to be replicated in the To Path field. By default, the directory is %systemroot%\system32\repl\import. Click the Add button and select the computer name of the export server. Click the Manage button if you want to edit the settings for the Export Path. If so, the Manage Imported Directories dialog box will appear, which is almost identical to the Manage Exported Directories dialog box with the following exceptions:  There are no Entire Subtree and Wait for Stability check boxes, nor is there a stabilize column. However, the Status column and the Last Update column  gives information about the import subdirectory's status (that is, whether or not updates are being received).

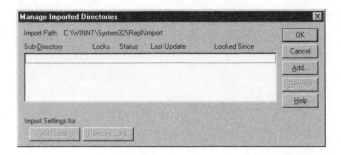

Lastly, if needed, edit the Logon Script Path field at the bottom of the Directory Replication dialog box to specify the location of the local directory where logon scripts are stored.

### Recommendations for Securing Directory Replication

Replication can cause a major security exposure if not administered properly. Administrators replicating directories and files onto a Windows NT machine in the network must be aware of the groups that have access to the directories and files on the importing client. It is very important for the administrator to assign a password to the Replicator account as a security control, because the account is a member of the Replicator group and has the Log On As A Service user right. If no password is assigned, the Replicator service can be a point of entry for unauthorized users.

Replication is better suited for read-only files because modifications to import data on the import client will be superseded by the newly replicated import data from the export server. Two examples of files well suited for replication are *logon scripts* and *user policies*.

Several features can further enhance the security and integrity of exported files and directories. On the export server, an administrator can lock directories from exportation, prevent subtree exportation within the export path, monitor the date and time that a lock was placed on a directory, and force directory replication after two minutes of directory stability.

On an import client, an administrator can determine the location of imported files, lock directories from importation, monitor the status and effect of updates, and monitor the date and time that an update was made to a file in the import directory.

## Alerts

Alerts that warn about security and access errors, user session problems, server shutdown, and printer problems are generated by the system and can be sent to a list of specified users and computers. To view and manage the list of users and computers that are notified, from the main viewing area of Server Manager, either double-click on the computer name or choose Computer ⇨ Properties from the menu bar. The Properties dialog box appears. Then click on the Alerts button.

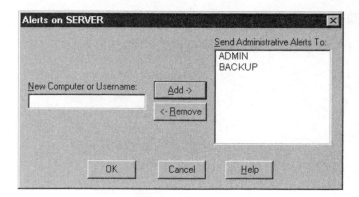

The Alerts dialog box appears. On the left is the New Computer or Username field, which allows an administrator to input the name of computers or users who should receive alerts. On the right is the Send Administrative Alerts To section, which lists all the current users and computers that are receiving alerts.

Both the Alerter and Messenger service need to be running on the originating machine for the alerts to be sent. Only the Messenger service needs to be running on the recipient machine.

Sending alerts to administrators is a good control to immediately notify them of potential security or system problems.

## Services

Services are processes that run in the background of a Windows NT environment. Services may be started automatically at boot time or they may be manually started and stopped by the administrator or server operators. Services typically run under the System account, but they may also run under a user-defined account. There are two types of services: those that operate as part of the system kernel and those that operate under the Win32 subsystem. The services that run under Win32 that may have user interaction are of most concern.

There are two sets of services: those installed as part of the default Windows NT installation and those installed as part of add-on software or as options within the operating system or third-party packages.

Services are critical to system security and must be managed appropriately to ensure that they do not present any security risks. Click Start ⇨ Programs ⇨ Administrator Tools ⇨ Server Manager. When you are inside Server Manager, highlight a server and then click Computer ⇨ Services. This function is helpful when you want to remotely manage a server's services. You must be part of the Administrators group or the Server Operators group to manage services.

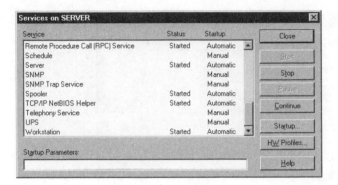

Services could present a security risk because many are installed by default and many are run under the local System account, which, by default, has full access to the entire system. In some cases, this may be inappropriate for certain services. In addition, running nonessential services may present another place for a hacker to attack.

At the Services dialog box, you can view all the services that are installed and running. Here you can stop or pause a service. Highlight the service you want to manage and then click Pause. This function will prevent users from accessing the specific service, but the service will still be accessible by the administrators and server operators. Clicking Stop will disconnect all users, and no one will be able to use the service until it is restarted. It is important to be very careful when stopping a service; other services may be dependent on it and stopping the service may have detrimental effects on the system. Be sure to test the effect of stopping a service on a test system before actually stopping a service in production.

## Changing Startup Accounts for Services

As previously mentioned, some services start under the local System account. This account has full access to an entire operating system. The potential security risk is that if security vulnerabilities are discovered in the service, a hacker might try attacking that service with the intent of gaining access as the local System account. For this reason, nonessential or nontrusted services should be run under accounts with the least amount of privileges possible. First, you must create an account with the appropriate rights. Then you must enable the services to run under this new account.

The Scheduler (AT) is an example of a service that uses the local System account. It is a scheduling service provided by Windows NT to schedule the execution of commands and programs. Because this service runs with the security account of local System and not a predefined user account, a command or program that is executed with the AT command will have access to all operating system resources. The local System account is the Windows NT operating system itself. This security level is the highest in the system.

From the list of services in the Service dialog box, highlight the service you want to change and then click the Startup button. The following dialog box appears.

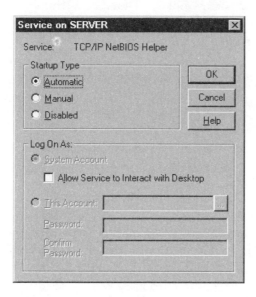

In the bottom half of the dialog box, you will see the Log On As option. Click the This Account radio button and specify the new user account name and password that you created for the service.

In the top half of the dialog box, you can choose whether to disable the service, have it startup automatically when Windows NT boots up, or have it startup manually. Disabling the service stops any user from accessing it. Automatically starting the service causes the service to run as soon as the server is turned on.

## Recommendations

The following services are installed by default. Your server may include additional services depending on how you installed your server or additional hardware and software. Carefully evaluate the following services and keep only the ones you need. Then evaluate and change the Startup account for the services that you want to keep. Table 10-7 can be used as a guideline in helping you determine which services should be installed based on your Windows NT environment.

- Alerter—Used by the server and other services. This service broadcasts the logged on user name in the NetBIOS name table, which can be considered a security breach. As well, the Alerter service notifies user and computers of the administrative alerts that occur on selected computers.

- Clipbook Viewer—Supports the Clipbook viewer application, allowing pages to be seen by remote Clipbooks.

- Computer Browser—Maintains an up-to-date list of computers and provides the list to applications when requested. Provides the computer list displayed in the Select Computer and Select Domain dialog boxes and in the main Server Manager window.
- Directory Replicator—Replicates directories and the files in the directories between computers.
- Event Log—Records system, security, and application events to be viewed in Event Viewer.
- FTP Publishing Service—In Windows NT 4.0, FTP is part of the Internet Information Server (IIS).
- Messenger—Sends and receives messages sent by administrators or by the Alerter service. This service stops when the Workstation service stops.
- Net Logon—Performs authentication of accounts on primary and backup domain controllers; it also keeps the domain directory database synchronized between the primary domain controller and the backup domain controllers. For other computers running Windows NT, supports pass-through authentication of account logons. This service is used when the workstation participates in a domain.
- Network DDE—Provides a network transport as well as security for DDE (Dynamic Data Exchange) conversations.
- Network DDEDSDM—Dynamic Data Exchange Share Database Manager manages the shared DDE conversations. This service is used by the Network DDE service.
- NT LM Security Support Provider—Provides Windows NT security to RPC (Remote Procedure Call) applications that use transports other than named pipes.
- Remote Procedure Call (RPC) Locator—Allows distributed applications to use the Microsoft RPC service and manages the RPC Name Service database. The server side of distributed applications registers its availability with this service. The client side of distributed applications queries this service to find available server applications.
- Remote Procedure Call (RPC ) Service—This is the RPC subsystem for Windows NT. It includes the endpoint mapper and other related services.
- Schedule—Must be running if the AT command is to be used. The AT command can be used to schedule commands and programs to run on a particular date and time.
- Server—Provides RPC support, and file, print, and named piping sharing by using SMB services.
- Spooler—Provides print spooler services.
- UPS—Manages an uninterruptable power supply connected to the computer.
- Workstation—Provides network connections and communications.

**Table 10-7. Windows NT Services Recommendations**

| Feature | Domain Controller | File and Print Server | Database Server | Web Server | RAS Server | Work-station |
|---|---|---|---|---|---|---|
| Alerter | None—Requires Messenger Service. | | | | | |
| Clipbook Viewer | Not required. | | | | | |
| Computer Browser | No change. | Disable. | No change. | Disable. | No change. | Disable. |
| Directory Replicator | Start automatically on PDC—Can be configured to start with another account. | Start automatically—Can be configured to start with another account. | Start automatically—Can be configured to start with another account. | Start manually when required—Can be configured to start with another account. | Do not start. | Do not start. |
| Event Log | No change. | No change. | No change. | No change. | No change. | No change. |
| FTP Publishing Service | Do not use. | Do not use. | Do not use. | No change. | Do not use. | Do not use. |
| Messenger | No change. | No change. | No change. | No change. | No change. | No change. |
| Net Logon | None—This service is required in most cases. | None—This service is required in most cases. | None—This service is required in most cases. | None—This service is required in most cases. | None—This service is required in most cases. | None—This service is required in most cases. |
| Network DDE | Not required. | Not required. | Not required. | Not required. | Not required. | Not required. |
| Network DDE DSDM | Not required. | Not required. | Not required. | Not required. | Not required. | Not required. |
| NT LM Security Support Provider | None—This service is required in most cases. | None—This service is required in most cases. | None—This service is required in most cases. | None—This service is required in most cases. | None—This service is required in most cases. | None—This service is required in most cases. |

*(continued)*

**Table 10-7.** *(continued)*

| Feature | Domain Controller | File and Print Server | Database Server | Web Server | RAS Server | Work-station |
|---|---|---|---|---|---|---|
| Remote Procedure Call (RPC) Locator | None—Can be configured to start with another account. | | | | | |
| Remote Procedure Call (RPC) Service | None—Pausing or stopping this service on network-connected servers will result in un-predictable results and lockups.<br><br>Can be con-figured to start with another account. | | | | | |
| Schedule | Create and use Sched-uler account if needed. | Create and use Sched-uler account if needed. | Create and use Sched-uler account if needed. | Create and use Sched-uler account if needed. | Do not use. | Do not use. |
| Server | No change. | No change. | Disable if not required for database use. | Disable. | No change. | Disable if sharing is not required. |
| Spooler | None—Can be configured to start with another account. | None—Can be configured to start with another account. | Not needed. | Not needed. | Not needed. | |
| UPS | Not required —Can be configured to start with another account. | Not required —Can be configured to start with another account. | Not required —Can be configured to start with another account. | Not required —Can be configured to start with another account. | Not required —Can be configured to start with another account. | Not required —Can be configured to start with another account. |
| Workstation | No change. | No change. | No change. | Disable. | No change. | No change. |

## Promote to Primary Domain Controller (PDC)

If the primary domain controller (PDC) fails, needs to be taken offline temporarily, or is being replaced, it is possible to promote a BDC (backup domain controller) to a PDC. This promotion is only required if the original PDC is expected to be down for an extended period because it will not automatically be demoted. To promote a BDC, within Server Manager, highlight a BDC and choose Computer ➪ Promote to Primary Domain Controller. If the original PDC is brought back online, it will have to be deliberately demoted to a Backup, where it will remain the Backup until this command is used to promote it back to its original status.

When demoting a PDC to a Backup, it is good to edit the descriptions of the computers so that an administrator does not forget which was the original.

## Considerations and Recommendations for Using Server Manager

Server Manager is a tool used in controlling a network. Server Manager, itself, does not need to be secured because in order to perform actions in Server Manager, you need certain privileges and without them you cannot do anything. However, Server Manager contains some features that are good security controls.

Make sure that all computer accounts for machines no longer connected to the domain are removed. The way to browse all machines that have accounts is to use Server Manager and view all computers. Reconcile the computer names that appear here with ones that may be connected to the domain.

Administrators should take advantage of the User Sessions, Shared Resources, and Open Resources dialog boxes. These three screens can display the current connections and allow an administrator to disconnect any users that are suspected of being unauthorized. For example, an administrator might use the Shared Resources dialog box to find out if someone has connected to the hidden C$ administrative share. If that share is in use, and the administrator is the sole authorized user of it, the administrator would know to terminate that session and find out who was using it. If an administrator was to disconnect users to increase performance, they should warn those authorized users before disconnecting them. Otherwise, data loss and corruption may occur. Regardless of the reason for terminating a connection, administrators should be wary that a user simply has to reconnect in order to gain access again, unless the administrator takes further actions, such as pausing or stopping a share. Disconnection does not remove authorization.

Detailed steps for securing directory replication, described earlier in this section, are summarized here as well. To use the Directory Replication service, you must create a separate replicator account in the domain. By taking the proper steps to secure this account, you are ensuring that the account cannot be used to compromise the domain. In addition, proper permissions must be set on the replication directories so that only the appropriate users have access to those directories. The export directory, which usually contains scripts and executables that are run on client machines, should be writable by an administrator only; this precaution prevents users from putting malicious executable code in the directory.

To ensure that they are promptly notified of system errors and, more importantly, security breaches, administrators should use alerts. Administrators can send alerts to their workstations so that they are alerted even when they are sitting in their office, away from the actual PDC.

# Chapter 11
# System Security Management

Securing the system also entails properly controlling system configuration files so the system cannot be compromised in any way. Even if all the proper security controls have been placed on files and directories, if the system files, such as the Registry Key settings, are not secured, unauthorized users may find a way to access the system.

In the following section, we recommend the controls we believe are most important in securing the Registry keys and other important configuration files such as user and computer policies. In addition, we recommend values for certain Registry keys that can be used as security controls.

## The Registry

The Windows NT Registry is a database containing the Security Account Manager database and configuration data for applications, hardware, and device drivers. The Registry also contains data on user-specific information, including settings from user-profiles, desktop settings, software configurations, and network settings. In previous versions of Windows, this type of information would be stored in .INI files (such as WIN.INI and SYSTEM.INI) except these files could not store executable code like the Registry can. The Registry keys are similar to the bracketed headings in an .INI file, and the key values are similar to the .INI entries under those brackets. Windows NT centralizes the storage of all this information and creates a single point of editing. Changes to the Registry can be made indirectly through the administrative tools or applets within the Control Panel, or directly within the Registry Editor. For example, when administrators use User Manager for Domains, the changes are updated in the Registry, even though the Registry Editor is never opened.

Two applications are commonly used to manually edit the Registry: REGEDT32.EXE and REGEDIT.EXE. Normal users should not be editing the Registry, and administrators should be very cautious when modifying values because no warning messages exist for incorrect values. The REGEDIT.EXE application is limited in functionality compared to REGEDT32.EXE, although it does support importing and exporting of the Registry keys and superior search capabilities, which REGEDT32.EXE does not. REGEDT32.EXE is where security management of the Registry is performed.

**Note**  When editing the Registry, administrators should use other applications (such as User Manager for Domains or the Control Panel) instead of the Registry Editor to prevent input of incorrect values. Any changes made to the Registry may have detrimental effects to the system and should be fully tested before implemented in a production environment.

Open the REGEDT32.EXE application by choosing Start ⇨ Run. Enter REGEDT32.EXE and then click OK. The Registry Editor window appears. If administrators want to simply view the Registry and not make any changes, they should choose Options ⇨ Read Only Mode from the menu bar to protect the Registry contents while it is being viewed.

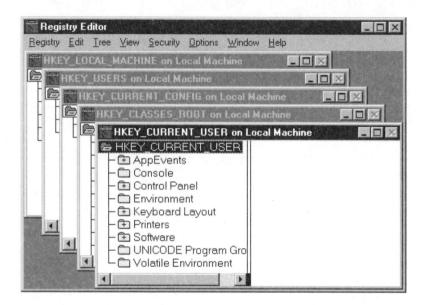

Administrators can also modify the Registry remotely, if permitted, by using REGEDT32.EXE from a workstation and choosing Registry ⇨ Select Computer. After entering the name of the server, two keys will open for the remote machine: HKEY_LOCAL_MACHINE and HKEY_USERS. However, it might appear as if remote administration limits the extent of what REGEDT32.EXE can do, but this is not true. These two keys encompass all other keys.

Table 11-1 explains briefly how to edit the Registry.

**Table 11-1. Registry Edit Commands and Data Types**

| Command | Description |
|---------|-------------|
| Add Key | Creates a new subkey under the key currently highlighted. |
| Add Value | Creates a new value entry for the key currently highlighted. |
| Delete | Deletes the highlighted item, whether a value or key. |
| Binary | Opens the highlighted value entry for editing. Regardless of the data type, it is converted to *Binary*. The inputted value is then converted back to its original data type and saved. |
| String | Opens the highlighted value entry for editing. Regardless of the data type, it is converted to *String*. The inputted value is then converted back to its original data type and saved. |
| DWORD | Opens the highlighted value entry for editing. Regardless of the data type, it is converted to *DWORD*. The inputted value is then converted back to its original data type and saved. |
| Multi String | Opens the highlighted value entry for editing. Regardless of the data type, it is converted to *Multi String*. The inputted value is then converted back to its original data type and saved. |

**Note** Windows NT comes with a utility called ROLLBACK.EXE, which is intended to facilitate installations of Windows NT Workstation. However, running this application removes all Registry settings and returns a Windows NT system back to the same settings that are on all Windows NT systems before any GUI options are configured. Because no warning is given, this utility should never be run on a production environment. ROLLBACK.EXE requires administrative privileges in order to run.

The Registry Editor has five windows, each representing a subtree of the Registry. Each subtree is displayed hierarchically in its respective window, similar to the way directories are displayed in Windows NT Explorer. Each subtree contains several individual keys that contain data items called *value entries*. These keys can also possess additional subkeys, with subkeys being analogous to subdirectories and values being analogous to files. Each root key name begins with *HKEY_* to indicate that the key is a unique identifier, called a *handle*, which can be used by a program to access resources.

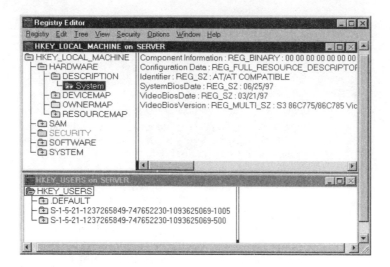

# HKEY_LOCAL_MACHINE

The HKEY_LOCAL_MACHINE (HKLM) subtree contains information about the local computer system. This information includes, but is not limited to, the type of hardware installed, application settings, and software settings. All users require this information when they log on the computer and access certain resources. HKLM contains five subtrees: HARDWARE, SAM, SECURITY, SOFTWARE, and SYSTEM. Only administrators can edit the SOFTWARE and SYSTEM keys.

### HARDWARE Subtree

The HARDWARE subtree contains information about the hardware that is detected upon system startup. Such information might include device settings, interrupts, and information about hardware components. All settings for this subtree are recomputed at system startup and discarded at system shutdown. The Hardware Recognizer accomplishes the method employed by Windows NT to determine some hardware information. NTDETECT.COM is the Hardware Recognizer on $x$86-based computers. Other hardware information comes from physical device settings and device drivers. Most values are presented in the REG_BINARY format, which is a binary representation of data, and should not be edited by administrators because of the difficulty in interpreting the values. The better method of viewing hardware information is using Windows NT Diagnostics and clicking the Devices button.

### SAM Subtree

The SAM subtree on a non-domain controller contains all account and security information for local users while a domain controllers SAM subtree contains all the account and security information for users in the current domain. This information is used by the *Security Account Manager (SAM)*. In addition, the User

Manager for Domains application obtains this information indirectly through system requests in order to display account information.

---

**Note**   In addition, 128-bit encryption can be implemented on the part of the SAM that stores the passwords. This feature comes with Service Pack 3 and is called SYSKEY.EXE. Run it and select the encryption radio button. Warning: After encryption is enabled, encryption cannot be disabled.

---

### SECURITY Subtree

The SECURITY subtree contains security information for the local machine on non-domain controllers and for the entire domain on domain controllers. Such information includes account policy, user rights, and group memberships. This data should not be edited here, rather it should be managed in User Manager for Domains.

The HKLM\SECURITY\SAM subtree points to the HKLM\SAM subtree, previously discussed, which contains account information. Both of these subtrees are grayed out because the access controls are set to disallow anyone from reading them, including administrators. Administrators who want to manage user accounts should use the User Manager for Domains application.

### SOFTWARE Subtree

The SOFTWARE subtree contains software configuration information pertaining to the local computer. Everyone needs this information for the computer on which they log so they can use *Object Linking and Embedding (OLE)* and file associations. The file associations defined here allow users to execute a data file and have it load the respective application with the data file opened.

The Classes subtree, located here, is mapped to HKEY_CLASSES_ROOT. The Microsoft subtree, also located here, contains important information about the system settings such as the version of Windows NT installed, the configuration settings, the security features, and other services. The Security subtree is where an application's configuration information is stored.

### SYSTEM Subtree

The SYSTEM subtree contains all data that is essential for starting the system. The ControlSet subkeys contain device and service parameters for the system. In addition, the ControlSet subkeys are backups for the CurrentControlSet. In case of a problem, the system can boot up in LastKnownGood configuration mode using an alternate ControlSet subkey.

The CurrentControlSet subkey is the control set currently active; however, it is only a pointer to one of the other ControlSet branches. Which branch depends on the current value of the Select subkey. The LastKnownGood control set is a clean control set that has actually worked in the past and is set by the LastKnownGood value in the Select subkey.

## HKEY_CURRENT_CONFIG

This subtree points to HKEY_LOCAL_MACHINE\SYSTEM\CurrentControlSet\Hardware Profiles\0001. CurrentControlSet actually points to the control set currently in use. This subtree contains the current configuration information about the hardware installed on the computer.

## HKEY_CLASSES_ROOT

This subtree points to HKEY_LOCAL_MACHINE\SOFTWARE\Classes that contains certain software settings, such as file-class association mappings and OLE. The sole purpose of this subtree is for Windows 3.1 registration database compatibility.

## HKEY_USERS

This subtree contains information (for both generic and user-specific settings) about active users. The generic information is represented by the DEFAULT key and contains information for settings that are common among multiple users. Other keys contain information for each user that logs on the computer.

## HKEY_CURRENT_USER

This subtree points to a branch of HKEY_USERS that contains information about the user who is currently logged on the system. This information includes the user's profile, groups, desktop settings, printers, application preferences, and network connections. When a user logs in, this subtree is used to propagate desktop and user settings across the system.

## HKEY_DYN_DATA

This sixth subtree will sometimes appear in the REGEDIT.EXE application. It points to the branch of HKEY_LOCAL_MACHINE that contains the dynamic status information for Plug and Play (PnP) devices. However, Windows NT 4.0 is not PnP-compliant without adding the PnPISA drivers. Therefore, the Dyn_Data subtree is not used in Windows NT.

# Registry and Security

There are two important security controls with regard to the Registry. The Registry keys should be secured through Registry permissions, and all files pertaining to the Registry data should be secured with NTFS permissions.

## Securing the Registry Files and Directories

By default, the HKEY_LOCAL_MACHINE Registry files are located in c:\winnt\ system-32\config. For that reason, this directory must be properly protected. In addition, the c:\winnt\repair directory, which stores a backed-up version of the Registry, must be secured in the same manner. The recommended permissions for securing these and other directories are shown in Table 11-2.

**Table 11-2. Recommended Permissions for Registry Directories**

| File and Directory | Users | Recommended Access |
| --- | --- | --- |
| \Winnt\System32\Config | Administrators | Full Control |
| | Everyone | List |
| | CREATOR OWNER | Full Control |
| | SYSTEM | Full Control |
| \Winnt\Profiles | Administrators | Full Control |
| \Winnt\Repair | Administrators | Full Control |

In addition, users should not be allowed to edit the Registry, whether remotely or locally. If Windows NT 4.0 is installed fresh, without being upgraded from Windows NT 3.x, users are prevented from remotely editing the Registry by default. However, when Windows NT 3.x is upgraded to 4.0, it does not always install a certain Registry key to prevent remote editing. This key can be inputted manually by adding the following key:

HKLM\System\CurrentControlSet\Control\SecurePipeServers\winreg

Users should not be allowed to log on locally at the console of the server. If they do, however, local editing of the Registry needs to be prohibited. It is very difficult to prevent users from accessing a file on a system locally because a specific task can be accomplished many ways. For example, if you restrict users from using REGEDT32.EXE, they will use REGEDIT.EXE. If that is prohibited, they will use a REGEDT32.EXE from the floppy disk. If the floppy disk is restricted, they will use a copy of REGEDT32.EXE stored on the network. The idea is that users should be denied at the source, within the Registry, because there are so many obstacles in the way of truly preventing their access.

## Securing the Registry Keys

Through REGEDT32.EXE, administrators can set permissions on trees and keys to protect them from unauthorized use. To change the security permissions on a key, display the Registry Key Permissions dialog box by choosing Security ➪ Permissions.

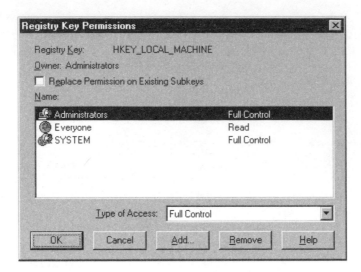

The top of the box displays the name of the Registry key being viewed. Below that, the owner of the key is displayed. Table 11-3 presents and describes the Registry Key Permissions dialog box.

**Table 11-3. Recommended Permissions for Registry Directories**

| Check Box | Description |
| --- | --- |
| Replace Permission on Existing Subkeys | Assigns changes made to the current key to all subkeys. |

| Section | Description |
| --- | --- |
| Name | Lists the group and user accounts that have permission to access the selected key. |

| Drop-Down List | Description |
| --- | --- |
| Type of Access | Allows one of three types of access to be given to the selected user: Full Control, Read, and Special |

| Button | Description |
| --- | --- |
| Add | Opens the Add Users and Group dialog box. This is where users and groups can be added to the Permissions list. |
| Remove | Removes the selected user or group from the Permissions list. |

As shown in the Type of Access drop-down list, there are three types of permissions: Full Control, Read, and Special. Table 11-4 describes each permission.

**Table 11-4. Registry Permissions: Standard and Special**

| Standard Permissions | Description |
| --- | --- |
| Full Control | Enables users to access, edit, and take ownership of a key |
| Read | Enables users to read the key contents but not to save any changes made to it |
| Special | Enables users to be granted one or more of ten specific rights |

| Special Permissions | Description |
| --- | --- |
| Query Value | Reads the settings of a value entry in a subkey |
| Set Value | Sets the value in a subkey |
| Create Subkey | Creates a new key or subkey within a selected key or subkey |
| Enumerate Subkeys | Identifies all subkeys within a key or subkey |
| Notify | Receives audit notifications generated by the subkey |
| Create Link | Creates symbolic links to the subkey(s) |
| Delete | Deletes selected keys or subkeys |
| Write DAC | Modifies the discretionary access control list (DAC) for the key |
| Write Owner | Takes ownership of the selected key or subkey |
| Read Control | Reads security information within selected subkey |

It is very critical to test all changes made to the Registry before implementing them in production. Depending on the applications that are installed, the Registry key access may be needed by applications and users. The following list provides some Registry permission recommendations to enhance security within the Registry. Only changes to default settings are listed. In addition, some Registry values may be changed to also further secure the system.

- **Registry Key:** HKCR (all subkeys)

  **Recommended Permissions:** Everyone: Special (Query Value, Enumerate Subkeys, Notify, and Read Control)

- **Registry Key:** HKLM\SOFTWARE

  **Recommended Permissions:** Everyone: Special (Query Value, Enumerate Subkeys, Notify, and Read Control)

  HKLM\SOFTWARE is an important registry hive to control, because it allows software to be installed. Changing the permissions restricts users from installing software, which may be a beneficial control for workstations.

- **Registry Key:** HKEY_LOCAL_MACHINE\SOFTWARE\MICROSOFT\RPC (and all subkeys)

  **Recommended Permissions:** Everyone: Special (Query Value, Enumerate Subkeys, Notify, and Read Control)

  Other Registry keys within HKEY_LOCAL_MACHINE\SOFTWARE\MICROSOFT carry similar permissions recommendations (see the table in Appendix A that provides baseline permissions settings for Registry keys). Certain Registry keys are vulnerable, by default, to the Everyone group, which means that anyone on the system can edit these keys and possibly place a Trojan Horse in one of them. This Trojan Horse can be anything from malicious code to a program that, when run as administrator equivalent, dumps the password hash.

- **Registry Key:** HKLM\SOFTWARE\MICROSOFT\WindowsNT\CurrentVersion\PerfLib

  **Recommended Permissions:** Remove Everyone: Read; Add Interactive: Read

  If Everyone had Read, remote users would be able to display performance data of the machine. Interactive read-only permits interactively logged on users to view performance data.

- **Registry Key:** HKLM\SOFTWARE\Microsoft\Windows\CurrentVersion\Run

  **Recommended Permissions:** Modify Everyone: Special (Query Value, Enumerate Subkeys, Notify, and Read Control)

  This Registry key allows programs to be run upon system startup, similar to the Start-Up Folder. With its default permission levels, any locally logged on user can change the value of a key to point to a Trojan Horse program.

  In addition, all programs listed in the Run key need to be secured by finding the actual executable file and making sure the Everyone group does not have the Change control on it. For example, usually when antivirus programs are installed, they commonly use an autoprotect virus scanner that is loaded at startup. The autoprotect scanner is opened because the Run key contains a link to it. The Run key might be secured, but the Everyone group might have Change permissions to the actual autoprotect executable. Therefore, anyone could simply delete the autoprotect file and rename a Trojan Horse to the autoprotect executable's original name. For greater security, all files listed in the Run key should have the Everyone: Read permission.

- **Registry Key:** HKLM\SOFTWARE\Microsoft\Windows\CurrentVersion\RunOnce

  **Recommended Permissions:** Modify Everyone: Special (Query Value, Enumerate Subkeys, Notify, and Read Control)

  This key is similar to the Run key, except that programs listed here are run after the machine starts up, and then it is removed from the list.

- **Registry Key:** HKLM\Software\Micorsoft\WindowsNT\CurrentVersion\Winlogon

  **Recommended Permissions:** Creator Owner: Full Control; Administrator: Full Control; System: Full Control; and Everyone: Read

  The Winlogon key contains information about starting Windows NT, like executables run during the logon process.

- **Registry Key:** HKLM\SYSTEM\CurrentControlSet\Control\LSA

  **Recommended Permissions:** Creator Owner: Full Control; Administrator: Full Control; System: Full Control; Everyone: Read

- **Registry Key:** HKLM\System\CurrentControlSet\Control\SecurePipeServers\WinReg

  **Recommended Permissions:** Administrators: Full Control

  The permissions set on this key define who is allowed to connect to the Registry remotely. No one except the administrators should be able to connect to the Registry remotely.

- **Registry Key:**
  HKLM\System\CurrentControlSet\Services\LanManServer\Shares\UPS

  **Recommended Permissions:** Modify Everyone: Special (Query Value, Enumerate Subkeys, Notify, and Read Control)

- **Registry Key:** HKEY_USERS\.default

  **Recommended Permissions:** Modify Everyone: Special (Query Value, Enumerate Subkeys, Notify, and Read Control)

## Registry Key Values

The following sections detail Registry key values that should be changed to secure the system.

### Disable Floppy Drive

Certain corporate environments might feel it is necessary to prevent users from accessing the floppy drive or other removable media. For example, a financial institution that stores sensitive information on employees' workstations that are physically accessible by co-workers and possibly the public would want to prevent the copying of data to a floppy disk.

Registry Key:   HKLM\SOFTWARE\Microsoft\WindowsNT\CurrentVersion\Winlogon

Value Name:   AllocateFloppies

Data Type:   String

Value:   1

### Disable CD-ROM

This Registry entry achieves the same goal as the floppy allocation, except for CD-ROMs. Administrators might want to disable access to the CD-ROM to prevent users from executing files from it, installing large applications, or, in the case of a CD-Recorder, to prevent users from burning data to the CD.

Registry Key:   HKLM\SOFTWARE\Microsoft\WindowsNT\CurrentVersion\Winlogon

Value Name:   AllocateCDROMS

Data Type:   String

Value:   1

## Automatic Logon

The AutoAdminLogon value allows a user (when used in conjunction with the DefaultUsername, DefaultDomain and DefaultPassword values in the same key) to by-pass the Authentication dialog box, which reduces the value of an authenticating operating system. Additionally, the password is stored unprotected in the Registry and is available for viewing. Users might alter the AutoAdminLogon setting if they thought the logon process was annoying, or if they did not want to enter a password each time. This option should never be used and by default, automatic logons are disabled. To make sure Automatic Logon is disabled, the value of this key should be set to 0.

Registry Key:   HKLM\SOFTWARE\Microsoft\WindowsNT\CurrentVersion\Winlogon

Value Name:   AutoAdminLogon

Data Type:   Binary

Value:   0

## Disable Caching of Logon Credential

Setting the value to 0 on a workstation disables it from caching the authentication credentials. This disablement means a user will not be able to authenticate unless she is connected to the network and the domain controllers are online.

Registry Key:   HKLM\Microsoft\Windows NT\CurrentVersion\Winlogon

Value Name:   CachedLogonsCount

Data Type:   Strings

Value:   0

## Do Not Display Last User to Log On

The fewer account names a hacker knows on a system, the fewer tools the hacker has to break into the system. One way to prevent user names from being known is to stop the display of the last user who logged on. Normally, when users attempt to log on, the Authentication dialog box displays the last user name. This display can be stopped if the key value is set to 1.

Registry Key:   HKLM\SOFTWARE\Microsoft\WindowsNT\CurrentVersion\Winlogon

Value Name:   DontDisplayLastUserName

Data Type:   String

Value:   1

## Legal Notice

Adjusting the value name enables you to create a logon banner. By default, there is no logon banner. To have a message displayed after a user executes the Secure Attention

Sequence (Ctrl+-Alt+Del) at logon, edit this string value. In addition, the LegalNoticeCaption should be modified to display a title bar for the legal notice.

Registry Key: HKLM\SOFTWARE\Microsoft\WindowsNT\CurrentVersion\Winlogon

Value Name: LegalNoticeText

Data Type: String

Value: 1

## Shut Down without Logging On

Windows NT allows administrators to set a value in the Registry that would permit anyone to shut down the computer without having to log on. This ability can only be accomplished at the Authentication dialog box. After users are authenticated, the Shut Down the System user right takes precedence. However, to prevent employees from shutting down a server, set the string value to 0.

Servers are usually not logged in because they can share files, run services, and authenticate users while still displaying the Authentication dialog box. If a critical server was not in a physically secure place and someone could inadvertently or deliberately shut it down, no users would be able to access any resources on it.

Registry Key: HKLM\SOFTWARE\Microsoft\WindowsNT\CurrentVersion\Winlogon

Value Name: ShutdownWithoutLogon

Data Type: String

Value: 0

## Shut Down on Full Audit Log

When this value is set to 1 and the system cannot for any reason log on an audit record, the system is brought down. If this flag is not set to 0, and the Audit Log is full, the system administrator receives an alert message warning that the Event Log is full.

Registry Key: SYSTEM\CurrentControlSet\Control\LSA

Value Name: CrashOnAuditFail

Data Type: DWORD

Value: 0

## Enable Auditing of Rights

By default, the auditing of all user rights is not enabled regardless of the settings in the audit policy. Therefore, if a user has the right to back up files, that user can access any file on the entire system; this would normally not be audited. To audit whether a user is using the backup files right, modify the binary value to 1. Note that this will cause the Audit Log to be filled quickly, because Bypass Traverse Checking will now be audited.

Registry Key:   HKLM\SYSTEM\CurrentControlSet\Control\LSA

Value Name:   FullPrivilegeAuditing

Data Type:    Binary

Value:        1

## LanManager Password Hash Support

Windows NT supports LanManager Challenge Response and Windows NT Challenge Response authentication. Windows NT, value 0, currently sends both types of authentication to a server. Because the LanManager uses a weaker form of encryption, a hacker may potentially be able to crack the password hash if they sniff it as it traverses the network. The LM hotfix enables this Registry value to be set. If this is set to 1, then the LM authentication will only be sent if it is requested (Windows 95 and NetWare clients). If this is set to 2, LM authentication will never be sent; in other words, Windows 95 and NetWare clients will never be able to authenticate.

Registry Key:   HKLM\System\CurrentControlSet\Control\LSA

Value Name:   LMCompatibilityLevel

Data Type:    DWORD

Value:        1

## Password Filtering

Employees usually do not adhere to password policies, and the original Windows NT installation does not allow the enforcement of complex password policies. For example, administrators should encourage their employees to have passwords consisting of letters, numbers, and symbols. With Service Pack 3, this can be imposed with an add-on enhancement called *PASSFILT.DLL*, which can be entered in the Notification Packages value, on the PDC's Registry.

The default setting of the Notification Packages value is FPNWCLNT. However, this file does not exist if you are not using File and Print Services for NetWare clients, and it allows a user to create a Trojan Horse called *FPNWCLNT.DLL* and possibly place it in the winnt\system32 directory. Regardless of whether PASSFILT.DLL is used, the FPNWCLNT entry should be deleted, unless the server is using the File and Print Services for NetWare clients.

Registry Key:   HKLM\SYSTEM\CurrentControlSet\Control\LSA

Value Name:   Notification Packages

Data Type:      Multi String

Value:          Passfilt

### Null Credentials Logon

Windows NT contains a type of logon known as the *Null Credentials* logon. Users may potentially be able to log on using NET USE \\servername\IPC$ "" /user:"". This logon cannot be controlled as if it was a user account nor can it be disabled. However, to force the Null Credentials logon to require authentication, edit the Registry key. The rights of this type of logon are derived from the rights assigned to the Everyone group.

The threat with the Null Credentials logon is a NULL session connection over the Named Pipes share (IPC$) that allows a potential intruder to obtain a listing of user account names, group memberships, password properties, user Security Identifiers, account policy details, and share names and permissions.

Registry Key:   HKLM\System\CurrentControlSet\Control\LSA

Value Name:     RestrictAnonymous

Data Type:      DWORD

Value:          1

### Schedule Service

The schedule service could potentially allow an unauthorized user to execute malicious code as an administrator. Scheduler works in such a way that it runs programs with the authority of the local system account. Setting SubmitControl to 0 restricts everyone except administrators from scheduling jobs.

Registry Key:   HKLM\SYSTEM\CurrentControlSet\Control\LSA

Value Name:     SubmitControl

Data Type:      DWORD

Value:          0

### Page File Clearing

The Windows NT page file stores a lot of information as a virtual memory space. Some of this information could have sensitive or valuable data contained within it, and the next user to log in might be able to read through the page file and find some of it. In a dual-boot system, a user may boot into the other operating system, which may not require authentication, and read the page file. When a user logs off, it is possible to have the page file cleared by setting the Registry value to 1.

Registry Key:   HKLM\SYSTEM\CurrentControlSet\Control\SessionManager
                \MemoryManagement

Value Name:   ClearPageFileAtShutdown

Data Type:   DWORD

Value:        1

### Disable Autorun

Normally a CD that has an AUTORUN.INF file will execute a program automatically when it is inserted in the CD-ROM drive. If an administrator puts a CD in their server and is not expecting a certain program to run, whether it be a resource-intensive application or a malicious executable, there could be undesirable results.

Registry Key:   HKLM\SYSTEM\CurrentControlSet\Services\CDROM

Value Name:   Autorun

Data Type:   DWORD

Value:        0

### Remote Access Auditing

A value of 0 enables Remote Access Services (RAS) auditing.

Registry Key:   HKLM\SYSTEM\CurrentControlSet\Services\RemoteAccess

Value Name:   Parameters

Data Type:   Binary

Value:        1

### Secure Event Log Viewing

Setting the value to 1 disables the guest account from viewing the System Event Log and the Application Event Log.

Registry Key:   HKLM\System\CurrentControlSet\Services\EventLog\*logname*

Value Name:   RestrictGuestAccess

Data Type:   DWORD

Value:        1

### System Policy Editor

The System Policy Editor provides the ability to configure and maintain the environment and actions of users, groups, and computers. Setting up policies is important to help standardize configurations as well as to protect the system from inadvertent mistakes and potential security holes. The System Policy Editor controls the same configurations as the Registry Editor. The System Policy Editor, however, is a GUI, user-friendly interface. Changes made in the System Policy Editor update the Registry.

To create a new policy or update the default policy, choose Start ⇨ Programs ⇨ Administrative Tools ⇨ System Policy Editor, which launches the System Policy Editor.

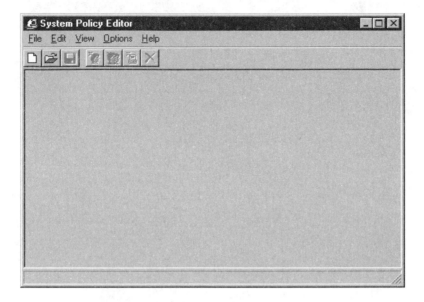

To create a new default policy or a policy for a particular user or computer, choose File ⇨ New Policy. The default Computer and User policies appear.

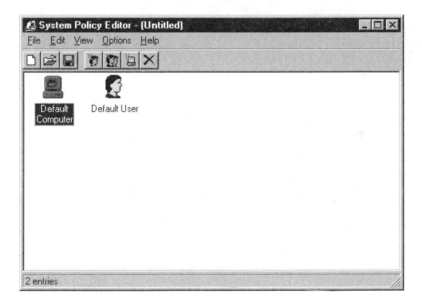

Double-click the Default Computer icon to make changes to the computer settings or double-click the Default User icon to make changes to the user settings. When finished making changes, choose File ➪ Save to save the settings. Save the settings with the filename NTCONFIG.POL in the NETLOGON share directory of the primary domain controller (usually located in *systemroot*\system32\repl\imports\scripts). This is the default policy that is used by all users and computers when they sign on the system.

If you want to create individual policies for certain users or computers, choose Edit ➪ Add User or Add Computer. A dialog box appears asking you to pick a user or computer. Choose a user and a new icon will appear for that user. Double-click the user icon to change the settings. To save these settings, choose File ➪ Save As. Save the policy under a new name and in the NETLOGON share directory of the primary domain controller.

When a user logs in, Windows NT defaults to the NTCONFIG.POL file. If you want it to use the individual policy, you need to include the following entry in the policy:

Local Computer ➪ Network ➪ System policies update ➪ Remote update

The first time you want to use the individual policies, you'll need to manually set the Remote Update parameter in the Registry, which will update the Registry setting. Then, each time a user logs on thereafter, the last Registry setting is used to look for the policy file.

To directly update the registry, choose File ➪ Open Registry. Any changes made to the settings will update the Registry directly.

The tricky part is enabling the features in the correct way. By default, all the options are grayed out, which means that the settings are taken from the Registry. To enable a setting, put a check in the box. To disable it, clear the box. Enabling and disabling the settings updates the Registry while the gray box leaves the setting in the Registry unchanged.

Users may belong to several different groups, each of which may have its own policy. To prioritize which group's policy takes precedence, choose Options ➪ Group Priority. Click a group in the Group Order dialog box, and then click Move Up or Move Down. The groups highest on the list have the highest priority.

### Recommendation

Many options can be customized according to aesthetic appeal and are not always vital security issues. However, some options can mitigate security risks that can arise. Because Fecha Manufacturing Corporation is a security-conscious corporation, it wants to limit any user potential to deliberately or inadvertently create security vulnerabilities. For this reason, they have gone through each System Policy Editor feature for Users and Computers (see Tables 11-5 and 11-6), and enabled (put a "checkmark" in) the ones that may create security implications.

### Table 11-5. System Policy Profile for Users

| Feature | Reason | Policy |
|---|---|---|
| Shell ⇨ Restrictions Remove Run Command from Start Menu | Fecha wants users to access only applications that have been installed on their desktop. Although, this does not completely prevent users from running unapproved software, it does deter them from using the Run command. | Select |
| Shell ⇨ Restrictions ⇨ No Entire Network in Network Neighborhood | Because users have no need to browse the Network Neighborhood, Fecha has disabled this capability. | Select |
| Shell ⇨ Restrictions ⇨ Don't Save Settings at Exit | This resets the system desktop back to its original setting in case users make changes. | Select |
| System ⇨ Restrictions ⇨ Disable Registry Editing Tools | Fecha does not allow employees to edit the Registry. Although this does not completely prevent users from opening the Registry for editing, it does add one level of deterrence. | Select |
| Windows NT Shell ⇨ Restrictions ⇨ Remove the Map Network Drive and Disconnect Network Drive Options | Other than the drives that are mapped when users logon, users should not have the ability to map other drives. | Select |

### Table 11-6. System Policy Profile for Computers

| Feature | Reason | Policy |
|---|---|---|
| Windows NT Remote Access ⇨ Max Number of Unsuccessful Authentication Retries | Fecha does not allow more than 5 authentication retries on its RAS Server before disconnecting a user. | Select, 5 |
| Windows NT Remote Access ⇨ Max Time Limit for Authentication | Fecha does not allow more than 60 seconds for RAS to continuously try and authenticate a user. | Select, 60 |
| Windows NT Remote Access ⇨ Auto Disconnect | Users are disconnected after 15 minutes of inactivity on Fecha's RAS Server. | Select, 15 |
| Windows NT System ⇨ Logon ⇨ Logon Banner | Designates caption and message text to be displayed after Secure Attention Sequence (Ctrl+Alt+Del) is executed at login. | Select, Input Legal Text |
| Windows NT System ⇨ Logon ⇨ Enable Shutdown from Authentication Dialog Box | Fecha denies users the ability to shut down a computer in which they are not logged. | Not Selected |

*(continued)*

**Table 11-6.** *(continued)*

| Feature | Reason | Policy |
|---|---|---|
| Windows NT System ⇨ Logon ⇨ Do Not Display Last Logged on User Name | The name of the last user who logged on will not be displayed. | Select |

## Workstation Lockout

Windows NT screen savers also allow for passwords to be implemented. This allowance will add another layer of security controls that will protect the servers and workstations from anyone just walking up to the keyboard and attempting to log in; in essence, creating a workstation lockout. Workstation lockout should be implemented on every server and workstation.

To implement Workstation Lockout, choose Start ⇨ Settings ⇨ Control Panel. Double-click on Display icon and then click the Screen Saver tab.

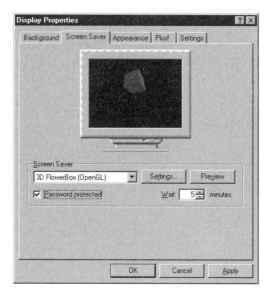

Click on the Screen Saver drop-down list and choose the screen saver. Then check the Password protected box. Enable the Wait box to be 15 minutes so that the Screen Saver is invoked after 15 minutes of inactivity.

# Chapter 12
# Ability to Recover from Operational Failure

Another security control that many corporations miss or do not spend enough resources on is the Ability to Recover from Operational Failure security control, which would meet their IT Availability objective. The ability to recover from operational failure means that if the system should go down or is disrupted for whatever reason, the business operations will not be able to continue. With many corporations, we are seeing highly critical systems that need to be available around the clock. Many of our clients are financial services firms and they require high availability. Every minute that their systems are down costs the business a lot of money. Therefore, controls should be in place to ensure that if the systems should go down or availability should be disrupted due to natural or other disasters, the business operations will continue.

Some of the security controls that can be implemented are systems-related such as disk mirroring, and creating and maintaining an Emergency Repair Disk (ERD). However, other controls are not system-related, such as having a disaster recovery plan or maintaining a recovery cold site. Often, resources are not spent on these items although they are critical. Some corporations do not realize the importance of a disaster recovery plan until a disaster strikes and it is too late. We describe disaster recovery plans and others operational recovery controls in the following section.

## Environmental Protection

To protect the integrity and availability of a corporation's data, the system and data facilities should be equipped to maintain proper environmental and safety controls. In addition, contingency plans should exist for the recovery of the systems in case of an emergency.

The security of the Computer Room should include protection against environmental factors. The likelihood of extreme weather or geological activity should dictate the strength of the building in order to withstand events such as hurricanes and earthquakes. The floors of a computer room should be surfaced with a material that does not generate static electricity, and should be elevated to protect equipment from pooled water. A room should be large enough to accommodate growth and space to move around while installing and maintaining equipment. Although it is generally advisable to have a window into the computer room from inside the building so unauthorized people or activity can be detected, there should never be an outside window to the room. This significantly increases the vulnerability to theft and to damage from natural events such as hurricanes and tornadoes.

Environmental controls, such as air conditioning and humidity control, are required in a room, which has the potential of reaching temperatures greater than 80 degrees Fahrenheit. Sensitive electronic components are prone to failure in these conditions, which is likely to happen when several large, heat-producing machines, such as computers, are put into an enclosed space without the proper environmental controls. Plans must also be made for the eventual failure of an air conditioner, either with a redundant unit or by increasing air circulation and monitoring conditions closely. Systems equipment should be shut down automatically if the environmental conditions deteriorate beyond a certain point.

Fire is a very real danger in the operation of a computer room. Equipment is prone to "shorting" or burning up a circuit board that has failed. This is often caused by faulty components or by power surges. The following is a list of some steps you can take to prevent fire in a computer room:

- Ensure an adequate supply of grounded electricity.
- Prohibit smoking.
- Remove all flammable material.
- Inspect equipment upon failure.

Heat and smoke detectors should also be installed to alert staff of a fire or short so that it can be quickly extinguished. Fire extinguishers should be located in strategic areas in the computer room. If a fire has started and cannot be smothered or put out with a hand-held extinguisher, it is important that a fire-suppression system be in place. Such a system should be charged with material that will not damage equipment when it is discharged, such as Halon. Other materials suitable for computer rooms include special mixtures primarily consisting of $CO_2$. Water is not considered a good extinguishing agent for computer rooms because of the danger of electrocution and because of the damage it can cause to surrounding equipment. However, water systems are in widespread use.

## Backing Up the Registry

Backing up the Registry can be used as a control, in that if the system crashes, a system administrator can use the backup of the Registry to return to the latest settings rather than reinstalling Windows NT. A number of methods exist for backing up the Registry, and each has its pros and cons. We discuss the following three methods and the differences between them: Emergency Repair Disk (ERD), Tape Backup, and REGBACK.EXE.

It is very difficult to get a complete and timely backup of the Registry because it is constantly changing. Sometimes parts of the Registry are changing or in use by the system and will not be backed up. The first two methods suffer from this problem, but REGBACK.EXE does a good job of including most of the Registry.

The most basic way of backing up the Registry is to create an ERD that contains the system boot data. (For details about how to create an ERD, see the "Emergency Repair Disk" section, later in this chapter.) This operation backs up a copy of the Registry to a floppy disk, which should be stored separately from the server, and can be used to update the contents of the %systemroot%\repair directory. However, in our experience, we have seen that most corporations' Registry is too big to fit on a floppy disk. Therefore, the NT Backup utility would probably be better.

Administrators can also use the Windows NT Backup utility that is also described later in this chapter, under the "Backup" section. From within the Backup utility, select the Backup Local Registry option in the Backup Information dialog box. For the Windows NT Backup program, the tape drive must be installed on the primary domain controller (PDC) in order to back up the Registry. Third-party, tape backup programs can be used instead of Windows NT Backup, in which case the drive does not need to be on the PDC.

The third method, and most effective way to back up the Registry, is to use a tool that comes with the Windows NT Resource Kit, called REGBACK.EXE. This utility has one major advantage over the other methods; it can back up parts of the Registry even if they are opened by the system. To restore parts of the Registry, another utility called REGREST.EXE must be used, which also comes with the Resource Kit.

# Viruses

A virus is a destructive program that can cause varying amounts of damage, from corrupting files to shutting down entire systems. Viruses could attack executable files and macros within word processing programs. Viruses execute when the macro or the executable program is run.

A virus does its destructive work by attaching itself to a program and modifying it so that the virus code gains control when the legal procedure of the program is invoked by a legitimate user. Viruses can be introduced into the system from floppy disks or by programs from the Internet. Due to the increased use of the Internet, the threat of viruses from the Internet has grown stronger.

Several forms of protection against viruses include disabling the floppy drive, implementing strong policies against users downloading information from the Internet, and bringing diskettes into the computer system. Users should be fully educated on the harmful effects of viruses and the how they are introduced into the system. Other things that should be considered are:

- Set file permissions to Read and Execute only for all program directories available on the Windows NT server and workstation, thus preventing them from being changed or replaced by viruses.

- Install new applications on a test computer not attached to the network and check them with a virus checker before migrating them into production.

Virus detection programs should be installed on your system to prevent viruses from causing destructive events. Virus detection programs check for viruses on the disk and in memory. Virus detection programs can be updated to check for new viruses as they are invented. It is recommended to have resident scanning turned on, which is constantly scanning for viruses.

Although Windows NT does not come with a built-in virus checker, there are many third-party vendors that provide virus checkers that are compatible with Windows NT.

# Fault Tolerance

Fault tolerance is a recovery from operational failure control because it provides the ability to withstand hardware failures and software errors. The reliability of a system is as strong as its weakest component. One of the most vulnerable parts of a system is the integrity of its magnetic media. Hard disks and other related media store information by magnetizing and demagnetizing specific areas on a rapidly spinning surface. In a heavily accessed piece of equipment such as a file server, this continuous movement and change in state exposes the media to wear and a higher potential for failure.

Windows NT provides fault tolerance by allowing the redundancy of data by simultaneously writing files to multiple disks, and by replicating the contents of file directories to other servers on the network. By writing files to redundant disks and directories, the risk of losing data due to failed media is reduced considerably. This is because the average life span for a hard disk is measured in the thousands of hours, thereby making the probability of multiple disks failing, at the same time, from wear extremely small. Fault tolerance should not be viewed as a replacement for a comprehensive backup plan, but as a control mechanism to minimize system downtime and to prevent data loss or corruption.

Microsoft Windows NT supports fault tolerance in the following ways:

- Disk Mirroring
- Data Striping with Parity
- Replication (Discussed in Chapter 10, "Managing Server Security")
- Integrated Uninterruptable Power Supply (UPS)

## Disk Mirroring

*Disk mirroring* enables Windows NT to read files from, and write files to, two disks simultaneously. Entire disks (or sets of disks) can be mirrored or just partitions on each disk. If one drive fails, the second continues to function as normal. These drives can either share a common disk controller card, or an additional controller card can be installed to run the second disk (referred to as *disk duplexing*). Though not required by Windows NT to perform mirroring, it is recommended that an additional disk controller be installed. Because data can be read from, or be written to, either drive, access times are improved using disk duplexing. Installing a second controller enables even better performance than having just one controller, and provides another layer of redundancy in case of component failure. The downside to disk mirroring is that you need to double your disk space to provide this level of fault tolerance. This expansion can get expensive if used for large data sets.

To set up disk mirroring, you should have first installed at least two disks with free partitions. One partition will be your data partition; the other will be the mirrored partition. The mirrored partition will have to be equal to or larger than the data partition in order to hold a copy of all the data.

**To configure a mirrored set,**

    1. Choose Start, select Administrator Tools, and then select Disk Administrator.

       The Disk Administrator utility launches.

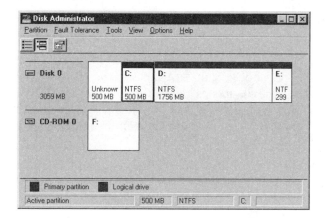

    2. Highlight the partition that is to be mirrored.

    3. Press the Ctrl key while clicking on the duplicate partition.

    4. Choose Fault Tolerance and then Establish Mirror.

A single drive letter will be automatically assigned to both partitions. If one of the disks or controllers fails, you will need to break the mirror set before removing it. To do this, choose Fault Tolerance and select Break Mirror Set. When the disk is replaced and another mirror is established, data from the original drive would then automatically populate the new drive.

Any changes you make will not be saved until you choose Partition ⇨ Commit Changes Now.

## Data Striping

Another technology supported by Windows NT is *RAID*, or *Redundant Array of Inexpensive Disks*. RAID technology enables a system to segment data and store pieces of it on several different drives, a process known as *data striping*. *Data striping* allocates data evenly among the drives, improving reliability and access times. If one drive fails, the data from that drive is automatically reconstructed from the parity information stored on the other disks. Data striping requires more disks be used than in disk mirroring, but it is more efficient due to the fact that only a small level of data duplication needs to occur to provide full recoverability of the information.

**Note** RAID technology supports the use of "hot-swappable" drives. This hardware configuration allows for the removal of an individual drive by simply opening a panel and sliding the hard drive out of its bay. Because removal of the drives is so quick and requires no tools, there exists an increased risk of losing data from theft.

Windows NT provides disk striping and disk striping with parity. The disk striping without parity method is not considered a fault-tolerant mechanism. Because there is no parity stripe, there is no way to recover the data. When a stripe is lost, its data is gone; therefore, setting up disk striping without parity is not recommended.

To set up disk striping with parity, you need to have installed at least three disks of approximately the same size. Choose Start ⇨ Administrator Tools ⇨ Disk Administrator. The Disk Administrator utility launches. Select three or more areas of free space by selecting the first area of space on the first disk, and then by pressing Ctrl and clicking on the areas in each of the other hard disks. Choose Fault Tolerance ⇨ Create Striped Set with Parity.

Any changes you make will not be saved until you choose Partition ⇨ Commit Changes Now.

## Uninterruptable Power Supply (UPS)

Systems failure due to electrical power outage can often be prevented by installing an *Uninterruptable Power Supply (UPS)* on all mission-critical components. A UPS is a device consisting of a stand-alone power source (a battery or a generator) and circuitry that will automatically and instantaneously switch from building power to backup power in the case of an outage.

Windows NT Server can be configured to work with many brands of UPS units to ensure a proper shutdown of the server when the power source is almost drained, preventing potential data corruption or component damage from sudden loss of power.

UPS units feature a wide range of capacities and features. A UPS can be as simple as a battery, which will provide enough time after a power outage to enable the administrator to shut down the servers properly. A more robust UPS can consist of a series of diesel generators with sophisticated power conditioning and monitoring capabilities. When evaluating the needed capacity and features for a UPS, issues such as the regularity of power failures, the availability of "clean" power (free of voltage spikes or dips), and the required time that standby power must be available.

To configure the UPS system, choose Start ⇨ Settings ⇨ Control Panel, and then double-click the UPS applet. The UPS dialog box appears on screen.

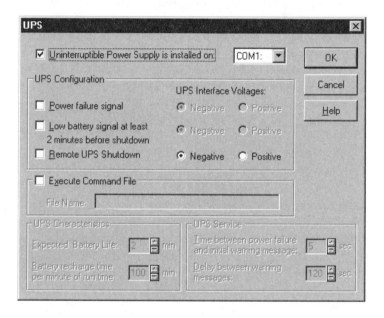

The UPS service uses the Alerter, Messenger, and Event Log services. Using UPS with these other services ensures that events related to the UPS service, such as a power failure or a UPS connection failure, are recorded in Event Viewer's System Log; it also ensures that designated users are notified of these events over the network. The Computer ⇨ Properties ⇨ Alert option in Server Manager should be used to designate which users and computers should receive UPS alerts and warning messages.

## Data Backup and Recovery

The development, execution, and testing of data backup procedures are one of the most important precautions a corporation can take to protect the integrity of its data. Backups will enable an administrator to quickly and completely recover the most recent data possible, regardless of the severity of the initial failure. Data backups must be viewed as a core business security control rather than an activity that an individual is supposed to perform.

## Backups

Many different strategies can be employed for backing up and archiving data. Variables include type of media (tape, hard disk, optical media, and floppy disk), backup application (NT Backup utility and third-party application), type of backup (full, incremental, and differential), rotation and archive schedule (real time, daily, weekly, and monthly) and storage location (onsite vs. offsite). An appropriate strategy for a corporation is one that is cost effective, that will allow the restoration of data files in a timely manner, and that will maintain data integrity. In addition, a corporate backup strategy should be reviewed and updated periodically (especially when there is a change in technology) and controls should be in place to ensure it is executed. A corporation can spend a great deal of money and effort developing a sophisticated backup strategy, but if it is not followed consistently, it is essentially useless. A backup strategy should include testing of the backed-up data at least twice per year.

## Backup Media

Any type of data storage media can be used for backing up and archiving data. If backup needs are limited to a group of key files, a floppy disk or higher-capacity removable drive may be sufficient. For most business operations, large volumes of files and operating system data are required to quickly recover from a destructive event. For this purpose, tapes currently provide the best ratio of cost, capacity, and speed. Tapes are also the only media that the Windows NT Backup utility supports.

Because backup media usually contains full copies of all a corporation's data, secure storage of backup media is critical to protect it from theft or destruction. Fireproof safes are a relatively inexpensive way to protect onsite data, though access to the safe must be strictly controlled. Locks or key combinations to the backup onsite storage should be controlled in the same manner as the computer room access key. Access should be limited and reviewed on a regular basis. It is also very important to have an additional copy of the backup tapes stored offsite. Third-party services are available, which will pick up backup media on a regular schedule and store it in a facility that is designed to protect it against natural events. Although the services can be expensive, they ensure the availability of backup tapes. When selecting a third-party service, make sure that the service is bonded, and that it has a secure method for authenticating individuals to whom media is given.

## Backup Types

When preparing a backup plan, the type of backup to be performed must be determined. The types of backup schemes include normal, incremental, and differential. A normal backup scheme is where the complete set is backed up every session, writing over any previous data on the backup media. Although this is the simplest method for backing up data, it is slow and causes excessive wear on media and equipment due to the fact that you are backing up all data instead of just the data that has been changed.

An incremental backup scheme calls for first completing a normal backup, then backing up only those files that have been changed. This method completes backups more quickly than if you were to backup the whole set; however, the series of incremental backups must be loaded in order to restore the most current data. This method also increases the complexity, as well as the chance of failure due to lost or corrupted media.

A differential backup stores data changed since the last normal backup, resulting in longer backup times than incremental backups, but a less complex recovery because only the latest normal backup and the latest differential backup are needed to restore the data.

Choosing a backup type depends on the size of the corporation, the amount of data that needs to be backed up, and the media type used. An incremental backup strategy for most corporations is the most cost effective. Corporations need to complete a full backup of their systems either on a weekly or monthly basis and whenever the systems change. One copy is kept offsite and two copies should be kept onsite, one inside the computer room and one outside the computer room. Daily incremental backups should be executed and taken offsite immediately. The previous week's incremental backup tape should be brought onsite and stored in the fireproof safe or cabinet. This way the previous week's data is onsite and the current data is offsite.

## Rotation Schedules

It is important that tapes be rotated to provide the greatest number of potentially successful backup copies and to limit the wear on a particular tape. There is no "correct" tape rotation strategy. Rotation schedule strategy should ensure that there are at least two week's worth of backup tapes to recover from, that no individual tape is cycled too many times, and that a tape is removed from the cycle and archived at least on a monthly basis. Tapes can be labeled by the day of the week or by sequential numbering, but should clearly indicate that the tape that has been added to the cycle is different from the archive tape it replaced in order to aid later retrieval.

A good recommended strategy is to keep one week's worth of data in a fireproof safe or cabinet onsite, a week's worth of data offsite, and a week's worth of data archived.

## Configuring a Backup Set

The Windows NT Backup utility allows you to back up and restore volumes, directories, and files onto tape in the form of a backup set. The backup set can consist of multiple volumes on a single tape, or of a single volume comprised of several tapes. To configure a backup set, you must first install a tape drive on the server, as well as the driver software to interface with the system.

To begin using the Windows NT Backup utility, choose Start ⇨ Administrative Tools ⇨ Backup. The Backup window appears.

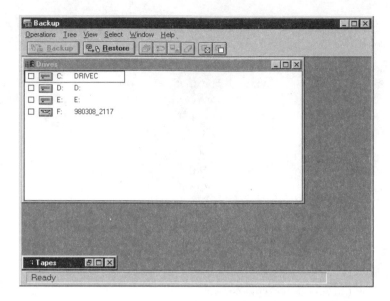

To prepare a new tape for backing up data, choose Operations ➪ Format Tape. If the tape has been used previously but you want to write over the data that is on it, select Erase Tape. Make sure it is a tape that you no longer need data from, as once you erase the tape, the data is irretrievable.

In the Drives window, select the drives that contain data you want to backup by clicking the check box next to the drive letter. If you want to back up only specific directories or files on the drive, double-click the drive and navigate to the directories or files desired. Click the check boxes next to the directories and files to select them for backup.

When you click the Backup button, the Backup Information dialog box appears.

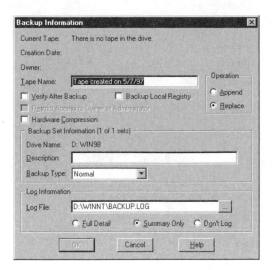

Table 12-1 presents and describes the options in the Backup Information dialog box.

**Table 12-1.  Backup Information Options**

| Option | Meaning |
| --- | --- |
| Verify After Backup | Initiates a process validating the integrity of the backup after completion |
| Restrict Access to Owner or Administrator | Limits access to the files on tape |
| Hardware Compression | Compresses data while it is being backed up, assuming the tape drive you are using supports this feature |
| Backup Local Registry | Adds a copy of the Registry to the backup set |

## Recommendations

Though it will increase the length of time for a backup to finish, Verify After Backup is very important to ensure the accuracy of a backup and should be selected. Restrict Access to Owner or Administrator is also very important for security reasons, as backup tapes contain valuable information and are vulnerable. Backup tapes can be stolen and then restored on another system to gain the information. Backup tape data should be secured especially if you check Backup Local Registry. Backup Local Registry is available only if the local drive is selected. Windows NT Backup cannot be used to back up registries on remote computers.

You can create a log file in the Backup Information dialog box by specifying a path and a filename. Choices for log file capturing include the following:

| Logging Option | Meaning |
| --- | --- |
| Full Detail | Logs all backup activities, including tape function, files and directories backed up, and processing errors |
| Summary Detail Only | Logs activities related to the successful or unsuccessful processing of the backup set |
| Don't Log | Logs no information |

Though the log file can grow quickly, it is recommended that Full Detail be selected to provide as much audit data as possible. At a minimum, Summary Detail should be kept. In addition to logging backup information in the Windows NT Backup utility, manual logs should be considered for recording summary information about the session. Keeping a manual log enables you to choose the right tape in the rotation schedule for recovery in cases where the backup log file is corrupted and inaccessible.

There are several security issues surrounding the use of the Windows NT Backup utility. Configuring the Windows NT Backup utility to back up and restore data requires that you either have Administrator or Backup Operator rights, or that you have ownership or write access to the data. The backup set can also be configured to limit the ability to restore the data to the Backup Operator by selecting the Restrict Access to Owner or Administrator setting. However, anyone with read access can back up data (though they cannot restore it without write access).

Another security issue involves the role of the Backup Operators group. Because this group can back up and restore data that it does not own, any member of this group has full access to data in the backup set. Members of this group should be acknowledged as having administrator privileges and be held to the same high standards of integrity and professional competence.

As mentioned earlier, great care must be taken to protect backup media. Possession of the backup tape means likely access to the data it contains, thanks to the many tools available to extract backup data. Damaged media can also lead to corrupted backups, which can go undetected if not verified during each session.

## Recovery

To restore a file, set, or tape, first make sure the tape that has been backed up most recently is loaded. Then choose Window ⇨ Tape to open the Tape window. Select the tape or backup set you want to restore, and then choose Operations ⇨ Catalog. The Catalog Status dialog box appears. Check the files that need to be recovered. To begin restoring, choose Operations ⇨ Restore.

In the Restore Information screen, verify by the Tape Name, Backup Set, and Creation Date that this is the tape from which you want to restore. Next, in the Restore to Drive field, select the drive to which you want to restore. If you want to restore to a directory path other than the path from which the data was backed up, enter the desired path in the Alternate Path field. To verify the integrity of the restored data, select the Verify After

Restore option. To restore the Registry on the drive from which the data was backed up, select Restore Local Registry. To restore the original file permissions for the items being restored, instead of having the files inherit the permissions for the new directory, select Restore File Permissions. When using this option, files should only be restored into the domain from which they were created; otherwise, the new domain will not recognize the file permissions.

As with the backups, Log Information can be captured by designating a log filename and path. Again, Full Detail, Summary Detail, or Don't Log can be selected to capture all, some, or none of the restore information.

## Recovery Recommendations

It is recommended that regular restore tests of the backups should be conducted on a test machine. This testing will ensure the availability of the backups in the event they are actually needed.

Restoring files is very similar to backing them up. The important security feature to be aware of is the Restore File Permissions option in the Operations ⇨ Restore ⇨ Restore Information dialog box. When restoring, make sure this is checked to restore the permission information along with the file. If you do not select Restore File Permissions check box, the restored files inherit the permissions of the directory into which they are restored.

## Last Known Good Configuration

The *Last Known Good Configuration* feature allows the user to restore the system to the last working system configuration. When used, it discards any changes to the configuration since the last working system configuration. The feature can be selected upon booting the system when the user is prompted to respond if he wants Windows NT Server to boot with the Current Startup Configuration feature or the Last Known Good Configuration feature. To invoke the Last Known Good Configuration feature, while Windows NT is booting, press the spacebar when prompted.

## Emergency Repair Disk (ERD)

The *Emergency Repair Disk (ERD)* allows the user to restore the system to a previous setup state. The ERD can be used if system files are corrupt and the user is unable to recover the previous startup configuration (Last Known Good Configuration).

During installation, you will be prompted whether you want to create an ERD. Insert a diskette and click Yes to create a disk. To create the ERD after you install Windows NT, choose Start ⇨ Run and type **RDISK** in the Open field. Click OK. The Repair Disk Utility box appears.

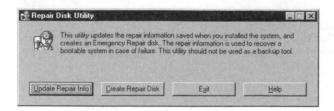

Click Create Repair Disk to create a new ERD. The Repair Disk utility will format the disk before saving the configuration files; all data currently on the disk will be lost. If you choose Update Repair Info, the files in the \Repair directory will be replaced with new updated information. When the Repair Disk utility finishes saving this information, you will be prompted to create a new ERD.

The Repair Disk program does not update the default, SAM, and security files if it is run from Windows NT Explorer. To update these files, choose Start ⇨ Run and type **rdisk /s** in the Open field and click OK. The /s switch forces the Repair Disk program to update all the files.

## ERD Recommendations

An ERD should be created at installation time. Every time significant configuration changes are made to the system, Update Repair should be used within the Rdisk utility to update the files on the system, especially if the Disk Administrator utility is used to configure volume sets, stripe sets, mirror sets, or stripe sets with parity. In addition, an ERD should be made right before a software upgrade or addition.

Once a month, a new ERD should be created and kept in a safe place. A copy of the ERD should also be made and kept in a separate safe place. The ERD should only be used with the computer by which it was created. It should not be used to restore another machine and it should not be used as a replacement for backups.

## Disaster Recovery and Business Continuity Planning

It is critical that corporations develop contingency plans for catastrophic events that can disrupt or destroy their ability to conduct business. A comprehensive risk analysis should be done and strategies should be developed to ensure the recoverability of systems and business processes. Two types of contingency plans that are critical to all corporations are Disaster Recovery Planning (DRP) and Business Continuity Planning (BCP).

### Disaster Recovery Planning (DRP)

The goal of a *Disaster Recovery Plan (DRP)* is to recover the necessary systems and data to support the core processes necessary to run the business. Depending on the needs of the business, the plan can be as basic as reloading backup tapes on a PC, or as complex as maintaining full redundancy for all systems and networks.

If the systems in place are highly complex or if timeliness of systems and data recovery is an issue, extensive documentation, planning and testing by experienced professionals is required to ensure that recovery can be achieved. As is the case with other security issues, a DRP should balance the estimated risk of a particular event taking place with the relative value of the asset being protected.

The first step in a DRP is a *risk analysis*. Only the systems that are critical to the business need to be up and running during a disaster. The Risk Analysis matrix completed in the Chapter 3, "Effective Management Security," can be used as a building block. This matrix maps all the corporation's critical systems and applications, the possible threats to those systems and applications, and the impact of the threat to the corporation. For Disaster Recovery Planning, an extra column can be added to the matrix. This column will contain an assessment of how long the corporation can operate without the systems or applications. If it is determined that the corporation cannot operate without the system, an assessment of the daily financial impact to the corporation must be analyzed.

For example, an order entry system is a critical application of Chris's Catalogs (a mail-order company). If a disaster should destroy the computer room that houses the systems, the order entry system will be unusable. Although the order entry system is a critical application, the corporation can operate for a certain amount of time without it by taking orders manually. However, a financial services firm cannot operate without its systems. In addition to the financial services firm not being able to conduct business, it will also lose money every day its systems are not working.

These risk analyses and assessments are very important in determining the corporation's disaster recovery strategy. There are several major strategies a corporation can use and each one has a cost associated with it. The least expensive strategy is backing up all the corporate data and restoring when necessary. When a disaster strikes, a corporation will have to call vendors to get a new site and new hardware. They then need to restore all the data onto the systems. This strategy is the least costly but takes the most time. Another strategy consists of obtaining a cold site. A cold site is another site with all the hardware needed, ready, and available to run a corporation's systems. The site can be contracted from a third-party vendor or it can be another corporate site. When a disaster strikes, backups are restored onto the new system. This strategy is more expensive, but takes less time to restore operations. The most expensive strategy is a hot site. A hot site is another site with an exact duplicate of your systems including hardware, software, and data. The duplicate system can be updated in real time or can be updated on a periodic basis, such as every two days.

Chris's Catalogs may choose the cold site strategy, as this strategy is more cost effective for them. Because they can operate manually for three days without a system, Chris's Catalogs can wait for the backups to be restored without having a major financial impact on the business. However, after three days, the cost of operating manually becomes too high. Therefore, having a cold site is justified because it ensures that they do not go more than three days without a system. The financial services firm loses money every day it cannot operate without its systems. Therefore, it is able to justify investing in the hot site strategy.

Disaster Recovery Plans should contain detailed step-by-step procedures of how to load and operate the new systems, including job responsibilities. In addition, a DRP should contain all necessary phone numbers and contacts, and it should be distributed to all employees. All employees who play a role in the DRP should keep a copy of the plan at work and at home. They also should be trained in the plan. In addition, a walk-through of the plan should be done periodically.

The keys to a successful DRP are maintenance and testing. The plan must be continually updated to reflect any substantive changes in staff, equipment, software, or policies. With technology's rapid evolution, this is a frequent occurrence in most IT environments. Testing enables participants to become comfortable with the process so that performance under emergency conditions is less prone to mistakes. It also becomes a method for ensuring the plans accurately, reflect the existing environment.

## Business Continuity Planning (BCP)

Where Disaster Recovery is primarily concerned with the restoration of critical business systems in the case of an emergency, the objective of a *Business Continuity Plan (BCP)* is for a corporation to continue the business processes needed for a company to function in a disaster. A BCP would include or reference the DRP and build upon it.

For example, if an earthquake were to destroy the data center of Chris's Catalogs customer support center, a successful DRP could have systems operational in the prescribed timeframe. However, what if this earthquake also destroys the buildings in which the employees work or the roads that the employees use to get to work? Functioning systems are useless unless employees are able to use and support them. A BCP would analyze and document critical processes and the steps needed to recover those processes so that the business can continue operating at the minimum level necessary. Many corporations in the World Trade Center did not have a BCP. Not only did they not know how to react to the disaster of a bomb going off and disrupting business operations, but they did not know how or where to continue their business operations afterwards. Many of the corporations in the World Trade Center subsequently went out of business.

As with the DRP, a risk assessment of the business processes needs to be completed. Only the core critical processes that a business needs to operate without having a major financial impact are needed during a disaster. This assessment of needs may result in half the functions in a corporation being restored. This assessment is also a good way of eliminating any non value-added functions. The procedures, either manual or with systems, needed to re-create these processes must be fully documented within the BCP.

The BCP should be a fully comprehensive plan that includes roles and responsibilities, critical numbers to call, press release information, detailed second site information, and detailed steps and procedures to re-create the business processes.

As is the case with the DRP, testing and employee awareness is a key component of a successful BCP. Processes for running a corporation can change rapidly, and new activities may go without contingency procedures until being discovered by the testing process. Because it is impossible to predict every conceivable emergency scenario that would affect the functioning of a business, simulations should be conducted at all levels of the corporation to test group and individual responses to various emergency scenarios. This type of activity makes people more comfortable with ambiguity and enables them to come up with creative solutions in times of crisis. In addition, all employees should keep a copy of the BCP at work and at home. They should sign off that they have received BCP training and have gone through a simulation.

# Chapter 13
# Auditing Windows NT Security Features and Controls

In Chapters 1 through 12, we discuss security objectives and controls. We also explain the various security controls within Windows NT and how to implement them. Most of our clients have implemented Windows NT in multiple configurations, and have concerns about Windows NT controls meeting their IT control objectives. For example, Enright Bank recently asked us to assist them in evaluating the strength of their Windows NT controls because they were not sure they implemented the Windows NT features which would accomplish their control objectives. One of Enright Bank's IT control objectives is: "The systems that support our client accounts will be secured from unauthorized access." PricewaterhouseCoopers (PwC) can perform this service for Enright Bank, but believes it is far more valuable for Enright Bank's IT department to understand this review process and perform it for themselves. PwC will analyze the results of the review, and assist in developing corrective action recommendations. Therefore, we explain the vehicle used to perform these reviews, more commonly known as a systems audit.

A *systems audit* is an independent examination designed to determine whether adequate controls exist to ensure that the following corporate IT objectives have been met: Effectiveness, Efficiency, Compliance, Reliability of Information, Confidentiality, Integrity, and Availability. A systems security audit is designed to determine whether the information system has adequate security controls to ensure that the following IT security objectives have been met: Confidentiality, Integrity, and Availability. Systems audits are based on audit objectives, which are the goals an auditor wants to achieve through the audit. Methods and guides have been developed to help perform the systems audit. PwC has developed systems audit guides for many operating systems including Windows NT. In this chapter, we help you conduct a systems security audit on Windows NT by presenting the systems audit process and PwC's Windows NT Security Audit Program ("PwC-NTSAP").

# The Systems Security Audit Process

The *systems security audit process* should be used as the framework for performing the PricewaterhouseCoopers' Windows NT Security Audit Program. The steps in the systems audit process are as follows:

1. Gain an understanding.
2. Define the scope.
3. Review the controls.
4. Report the findings.

Gaining an understanding involves gathering and reviewing background information about the IT organization, IT operations, network, applications, and Windows NT environment. Defining the scope involves reviewing the risk assessment conducted in Chapter 3, "Effective Security Management," and deciding on which systems should be audited. These systems should be the same as those deemed critical by the organization. Reviewing the controls involves inquiring and examining for appropriateness which Windows NT security control features have been implemented. Reporting findings involves drafting an audit report, which conveys the audit findings to management. The report should focus on corrective actions, which are steps that need to be taken to implement the deficient controls.

# PricewaterhouseCoopers' Windows NT Security Audit Program (PwC-NTSAP)

PwC-NTSAP is designed to assist you in performing the systems audit process, focusing on IT security controls and Windows NT configurable security features. PwC-NTSAP accomplishes this process by identifying Windows NT security control features. PwC-NTSAP makes this identification by posing questions, presenting audit procedures that assist in answering the questions, and explaining how to examine the features.

**Note** The features should be analyzed using the descriptions and guidance provided on configuring each security feature in Chapters 2 through 12, and the Baseline Security Configuration Matrix in Appendix A.

The PwC-NTSAP is primarily aimed at a Windows NT server installed as a PDC, but selectively applies to the following six different types of servers:

1. Domain Controller
2. File and Print Member Server
3. Application Server: Web Server
4. Application Server: Database Server
5. Remote Access Server
6. Workstation

All these servers come with network components fully enabled. When performing PwC-NTSAP, be aware that most Windows NT environments contain other components that include other servers using other operating systems, and network components such as hubs, routers, and firewalls. In addition, a Windows NT server may have applications resident, such as Microsoft Exchange or Microsoft SQL Server. The addition of applications adds another layer of risk that needs to be analyzed in conjunction with the Windows NT servers. Application change management, development, and implementation as well as the applications' use of Windows NT server security needs to be reviewed and audited to ensure that risks have been identified. PwC-NTSAP is not designed to identify these risks.

## Background of the IT Environment

Before assessing the control environment, you need to understand the environment you plan to audit. The minimum amount of data required to understand the environment is subjective. However, we believe the following provide a reasonable basis to gain this understanding.

The objective of this audit is to understand the systems environment. The following sections detail the procedures involved in performing this audit.

### Contacts in the IT Function and User Departments

If the audit is being performed in a sizeable IT department or by someone other than the system administrator, a list of primary IT contacts and their titles should be created. This point is very basic, but auditors can attest to how important it is to know who is responsible for what function. A handy way to gather contact information is to create a document that specifies each contact's name, job title, telephone number, fax number, and e-mail address.

### Organizational Structure of the IT Function or User Departments

Understanding the organizational structure of the IT function or user departments will help the auditor understand whether IT duties are properly segregated, whether the company places importance on IT, and if the IT function is decentralized or highly leverages the user community. The auditor can answer the following questions to gain a better understanding of this.

- What is the organizational structure of the IT department?

  Obtain an organization chart for the IT department. Focus on the number of people in the department, their segregation of duties, and where your primary contacts reside in the organization.

- What is the organizational structure of the corporation?

  Obtain an organization chart for the corporation. Focus on the IT reporting structure to the company. This is an indicator of the level of importance the company places on IT.

- Do any other departments have significant IT responsibilities for critical systems?

  Focus on the segregation of duties and potential points of security control failure due to decentralization of duties outside the span of IT control. For example, does the financial department download files to Excel spreadsheets that are manipulated and used to present financial data? At our clients' offices we have seen that most IT managers give a *no* answer to this question because they do not regard systems out of their control as being critical. However, it is common to find remote offices with a low user count and a strong user with administrator privileges who does not report to the IT department.

### Operation of the IT Function

The operation of the IT function provides an understanding on whether the IT objectives that have been documented are aligned to the corporate business objectives, and whether the IT organization is capable of meeting these objectives. The following questions should provide this understanding:

- Are the IT roles and responsibilities defined clearly?
- Are the IT roles and responsibilities appropriate to the size of the organization?
- Is the number of IT personnel appropriate to support the size of the organization?
- Has the IT personnel significantly turned over during the year?
- Are the IT staff's skills appropriate to the complexity of the IT environment and industry?
- Are there documented IT objectives consistent with the corporate business objectives?
- Have the IT objectives been communicated and agreed to by senior management?
- Do the users have a positive regard for the quality of service provided?

### Overall System Structure

After reviewing the structure of the IT department and its relation to the corporation, gather an understanding of the overall system and network environment. A logical network diagram should suffice. Through this diagram, you should also gain a preliminary understanding of where the domain controller, backup domain controllers, file and print servers, application and database servers, RAS servers, Web servers, workstations, and any external connections reside. You should also note the instances and direction of trust relationships. The following points of focus should be covered for the overall system structure:

- Is there a network diagram?

- What Windows NT domain model is deployed?
- Where are the PDCs and BDCs located?
- Where are the other critical servers located?
- What are the trust relationships?
- Is there a connection to the Internet?

## Computer Environment

After gaining an understanding of the system environment, focus on the detailed components of the system environment (such as hardware and application software), which is more commonly known as the *computer environment*. To fully analyze the system environment, consider the following questions:

- What are the specifications of the critical computers?
  - Examine the Windows NT version and service pack installed by choosing Start ⇨ Programs ⇨ Administrative Tools ⇨ Windows NT Diagnostics ⇨ Version.
  - Examine which domain or workgroup the computer is a member of by choosing Start ⇨ Settings ⇨ Control Panel ⇨ Network ⇨ Identification.
  - Examine whether the computer is a primary or backup domain controller or a workstation or a member server by choosing Start ⇨ Programs ⇨ Administrative Tools ⇨ Server Manager.
  - Examine the file system by choosing Start ⇨ Programs ⇨ Administrative Tools ⇨ Disk Manager.
  - Compile a list of your group's machines (specifying manufacturer and model # for each machine), their primary functions, the versions of Windows NT and Service Pack running on the machines, the domains or workgroups to which each machine is assigned, whether the machines are running PDC/BDC or Workstation, and whether the machines are using NTFS or FAT.
- Do hardware service maintenance agreements exist for all major hardware components documented?
- Does the number of Windows NT users equal the amount of licenses purchased?
- What are the drives and their mappings? Examine the Drives dialog box by choosing Start ⇨ Programs ⇨ Administrative Tools ⇨ Windows NT Diagnostics ⇨ Drives.
- How much memory resides on each computer? Examine the Memory tab by choosing Start ⇨ Programs ⇨ Administrative Tools ⇨ Windows NT Diagnostics ⇨ Memory.

## Key Applications

Understanding the IT environment should include a review of the significant applications. This review identifies the computers where critical applications reside. Also, you should identify what versions of these applications are running on the machines and then ask the questions that follow. (Note that these questions do not pertain to only Windows NT, but contribute to the understanding of the overall IT environment.)

- Do any of the applications utilize the Windows NT Remote Procedure Call facility?
- Do any of the applications utilize NT account security?

# Effective Security Management

The Effective Security Management control is often overlooked because most of the controls that are not features are "touchy feely" or intangible. Therefore, implementing and auditing these controls can be difficult. Effective Security Management involves corporate security awareness, senior management support on security issues, and a corporate security policy.

The objective of this audit is to determine whether security is being managed effectively. The following sections detail the procedures for this audit.

## Corporate Security Policy

To ascertain the state of the current corporate security policy and to better direct the future of such a policy, answer the following questions:

- Is there a documented corporate security policy?
- Does the corporate security policy include the following sections: Mission Statement, Objectives and Scope, Definition of the Assets, Asset Owners, Security Roles and Responsibilities, Risk Assessment of the Assets, and Security Procedures Regarding the Assets?
- Is there an awareness of and a commitment to the corporate security policies?
- Did senior management review, support, and communicate their support of the corporate security policies?
- Are users trained in security policies and procedures?

## Legal Notice

Has a legal notice been implemented? To examine the legal notice, choose Start ⇨ Programs ⇨ Windows NT Explorer and execute Systemroot\system32\Regedt32.exe. Select HKLM\Software\Microsoft\WindowsNT\CurrentVersion\WinLogon LegalNotice Caption: REG_SZ LegalNoticeText: REG_SZ.

## Effective Security Monitoring

Monitoring controls are often overlooked, but can really aid management in determining whether systems have been secured. Monitoring controls include violation and exception reporting, which help management determine whether their systems are being compromised.

The objective of this audit is to determine whether security is being monitored effectively. The following sections detail the procedures for this audit.

### Performance Monitor

Determine how effectively you are using the Performance Monitor by considering the following questions.

- Is the Performance Monitor utility used to gather, analyze, and graphically display vital information? Examine Performance Monitor by choosing Start ⇨ Program ⇨ Administrative Tools ⇨ Performance Monitor. Then answer the following questions.

- Is Chart View used? Examine Chart View by choosing View ⇨ Chart.
  - What objects are tracked?
  - Why are these objects being tracked?
  - On what frequency are the charts viewed?

- Is Alert View used? Examine Alert View by choosing View ⇨ Alert.
  - What objects are tracked?
  - Why are these objects being tracked?
  - What are the threshold values?
  - To whom are the alerts sent?

- Is Log View used? Examine Log View by choosing View ⇨ Log.
  - What objects are tracked?
  - Why are these objects being tracked?
  - On what frequency are the logs viewed?
  - Are critical logs updated manually or periodically? If they are updated periodically, what is the interval set for updates?

- Is Report View used? To access Report View, choose View ⇨ Report.
  - What objects are tracked?
  - Why are these objects being tracked?
  - On what frequency are the reports viewed?
  - Are critical reports updated manually or periodically? If they are updated periodically, what is the interval set for updates?

### Network Monitor

To better direct your use of the Network Monitor utility, consider the following questions:

- Is the Network Monitor utility being used to watch network traffic? If so, on what frequency is the Network Monitor utility used to monitor this traffic to and from the server? Examine Network Monitor by choosing Start ⇨ Administrative Tools ⇨ Network Monitor.

- What network addresses, protocols, and protocol properties are monitored?

- What triggers have been set for what conditions? Examine Triggers by choosing Capture ⇨ Triggers.

- Are reviews conducted for identifying unauthorized copies of Network Monitor? Examine who else on the network has installed and is using Network Monitor by choosing Tools ⇨ Identify Network Monitor.

- Are any third-party network monitoring tools used?

### Auditing User Accounts

When preparing to perform an audit of User Accounts, consider the following questions:

- Has User Account auditing been enabled? Examine User Account auditing by choosing Start ⇨ Administrative Tools ⇨ User Manager for Domains ⇨ Policies ⇨ Audit. Focus on whether the User and Group Management option is selected for success and/or failures. If this option is not selected, User Account auditing is not possible.

- Which permissions are audited?

### File and Directory Auditing

When preparing to perform a File and Directory audit, consider the following questions:

- Has File and Directory auditing been enabled? Examine File and Directory auditing by choosing Start ⇨ Administrative Tools ⇨ User Manager for Domains ⇨ Policies ⇨ Audit. Focus on whether the Audit These Events option is selected. If this option is not selected, File and Directory auditing is not possible. Also focus on whether the File and Object Access option is highlighted.

- On which Windows NT implementations do critical directories and files reside?

- What auditing settings have been selected on these critical directories? Examine the audit settings selected by choosing Start ⇨ Programs ⇨ Windows NT Explorer, highlighting a directory and right-clicking the object to open its drop-down menu, and then choosing Properties. The Properties dialog box appears. Click on the Security tab and then click the Auditing button. A Directory Auditing dialog box appears. Focus on the appropriateness of the selected auditing settings.

## Registry Auditing

When preparing to perform an audit of the Registry, consider the following questions:

- Has Registry auditing been enabled? Examine whether Registry auditing is possible by choosing Start ⇨ Administrative Tools ⇨ User Manager for Domains ⇨ Policies ⇨ Audit. Focus on whether the Audit These Events option is selected. If this option is not selected, Registry auditing is not possible. Also focus on whether the File and Object Access option is highlighted. Examine the auditing selected on the Registry by choosing Start ⇨ Programs ⇨ Windows NT Explorer ⇨ Regedt32.exe. Select the subkey or value in question and choose Security ⇨ Auditing, and then answer the following questions.
- Which Registry keys and subkeys are audited?
- Which permissions are audited?

## Printer Auditing

When preparing to perform an audit of your printers, consider the following questions:

- Which printers are critical?
- Is Printer auditing selected on critical printers? Examine whether Printer auditing is possible by choosing Start ⇨ Administrative Tools ⇨ User Manager for Domains ⇨ Policies ⇨ Audit. Focus on whether the Audit These Events option is selected. If this option is not selected, Printer auditing is not possible. Also, focus on whether the File and Object Access option is highlighted. Examine Printer auditing by choosing Start ⇨ Settings ⇨ Printers. Double-click on the printer you want to audit. Choose Printer ⇨ Properties. Click the Security tab and then click the Auditing button. The Printer Auditing dialog box appears. Ask which permissions are audited.

## Remote Access Server (RAS) Auditing

When preparing to perform an audit of a Remote Access Server, consider the following questions:

- Which computers offer remote access services?
- Examine whether RAS auditing is possible by choosing Start ⇨ Administrative Tools ⇨ User Manager for Domains ⇨ Policies ⇨ Audit. Focus on whether the Audit These Events option is selected. If this option is not selected, RAS auditing is not possible. Examine if auditing is enabled on computers offering remote access services by choosing Start ⇨ Programs ⇨ Windows NT Explorer, executing Systemroot\system32\Regedt32.exe, and then selecting the HKLM\SYSTEM\CurrentControlSet\Services\RemoteAccess\Parameters\EnableAudit key. Focus on whether the DWORD value is 1.

### Event Viewer

When attempting to utilize the Event Viewer in creating security logs, consider the following questions:

- Is the Event Viewer used to log and monitor User Account, File and Directory, Registry, Printer, and RAS audit events? Examine the Security Log by choosing Start ⇨ Programs ⇨ Administrative Tools ⇨ Event Viewer ⇨ Log ⇨ Security. Focus on the nature of the events. To categorically view events, choose View ⇨ Filter events.
- What is the policy for archiving the Event Logs? Examine the log settings by choosing Log ⇨ Log Settings. Click on Change Settings.
- Which log settings are selected?
- Is the Crash On Audit Fail feature implemented? Examine whether the feature is implemented by choosing Start ⇨ Programs ⇨ Windows NT Explorer, and then executing Systemroot\system32\Regedt32.exe. Select HKLM\SYSTEM\CurrentControlSet\Control\Lsa, and then focus on whether the flag in the CrashOnAuditFail Registry key exists.

### Securing Audit Logs

To ensure that your audit logs are secure, address this question—are the Audit Logs properly secured? Examine the permissions on the Security Logs by choosing Start ⇨ Programs ⇨ Windows NT Explorer, and then selecting the systemroot\System32\CONFIG directory. Select each of the APPEVENT.EVT, SECEVENT.EVT, and SYSEVENT.EVT files, choose File ⇨ Properties ⇨ Security, and then choose Permissions.

## Securing Physical Access to All Critical Systems

Physical access to all critical systems should be restricted. Implementing these controls ensures that unauthorized users cannot physically access your systems, which is the easiest way to access data.

The objective of this audit is to determine whether physical access to all critical systems is restricted. The following sections detail the procedures involved in performing this audit.

### Computer Room and Communications Room Security

To assess the security of your computer room and your communications room, consider the following questions.

- Does a lock restrict access to the computer room?
- Are keys or locks to the computer room controlled by the Security Administrator?
- For high traffic rooms, do visitors record their access to the computer room in a log?

- Is access to the computer room limited to the operations staff?
- Is the access list to the computer room reviewed on a regular basis?
- Is the computer room monitored by cameras or a security guard?
- Are backup tapes and other sensitive electronic media stored in a locked fire-proof cabinet within the computer room?
- Are backup tapes and other sensitive electronic media stored offsite?
- Does the computer room contain a window viewable from the inside of the building?
- Does the computer room contain a window viewable from the outside of the building?

## Workstation Security

You should also ensure that the individual workstations within your system are secure. To assess the security of these workstations, consider the following questions:

- Do cables or alarms secure workstations?
- Are removable media drives, such as floppy, removable hard drives, writable CD-ROM, and portable streaming tape units, present on any workstations?
- Have floppy drives been disabled? To examine whether floppy drives have been disabled, choose Start ➪ Programs ➪ Windows NT Explorer and execute Systemroot\system32\Regedt32.exe. Then select HKLM\Software\Microsoft\WindowsNT\CurrentVersion\Winlogon\AllocateFloppies key. Focus on whether the String value is 0.
- Have compact disk drives been disabled? To examine whether compact disk drives have been disabled, choose Start ➪ Programs ➪ Windows NT Explorer and execute Systemroot\system32\Regedt32.exe. Then select HKLM\Software\Microsoft\WindowsNT\CurrentVersion\Winlogon\AllocateCDRoms key. Focus on whether the String value is 0.
- Do workstations contain modems connected to telephone lines?
- If workstations contain modems connected to telephone lines, is remote dial-in restricted? To examine the port configuration, choose Start ➪ Settings ➪ Control Panel ➪ Network ➪ Services ➪ Remote Access Service ➪ Properties. Highlight the device you want to examine and click the Configure button.
- If workstations contain modems connected to telephone lines, is the Callback option enabled? To examine whether Callback is enabled, choose Start ➪ Programs ➪ Administrative Tools ➪ Remote Access Admin. Users ➪ Permissions. Focus on whether Callback is selected for each of the users who appear in the Grant Dial-in Permission to User field.
- Are any of the telephone lines restricted to "dial-out only" by the telephone company?

### Network Access Points

Assess the security of your network access points by considering the following questions:

- Are network access points restricted to active computers?
- Are unused network access points physically secured via locking devices or disconnected?

## Securing All External and Internal Network Connections

Most systems today are made up of many networked computers, which may physically reside in one room or across the world. Each connection to this network of computers creates a potential point of vulnerability. In addition, the transport of data across the network creates a potential vulnerability for the data. The controls assessed in this section focus on the network points of connection as well as data traversing the network.

The objective of this audit is to determine whether external and internal network connections are secure. The following sections detail the procedures involved in performing this audit.

### Domain Administration

To perform the domain administration portion of this audit, consider the following questions:

- What Windows NT domain model is deployed? To examine the domains in the network, choose Start ⇨ Programs ⇨ Administrative Tools ⇨ User Manager for Domains ⇨ User menu ⇨ Select Domain. Compare the visible domains with those presented in the network diagram.
- Where are the PDC(s) and BDC(s) located? To examine the PDC(s) and BDC(s), choose Start ⇨ Programs ⇨ Administrative Tools ⇨ Server Manager.
- What are the trust relationships? For each PDC examined, examine the trust relationships (trusted domains and trusting domains) between the domain being examined and other domains on the network by choosing Start ⇨ Programs ⇨ Administrative Tools ⇨ User Manager for Domains ⇨ Policies ⇨ Trust Relationships. Compare whether the relationships match those in the logical network diagram. You may find it helpful to create your own logical network diagram of the domains, using one- and two-way arrows to indicate trust relationships between the domains in the network.

### Protocols

You should audit the security of the general protocols within your system. What protocols are deployed on the network and why were they selected? To examine the deployed protocols, choose Start ⇨ Settings ⇨ Control Panel ⇨ Network ⇨ Protocols tab.

To examine the security of your system's use of the TCP/IP protocol, consider the following questions:

- Are simple TCP/IP services installed? To examine simple TCP/IP services, choose Start ➪ Settings ➪ Control Panel ➪ Network ➪ Services tab ➪ Simple TCP/IP Services.

- What are the TCP/IP settings? To examine the TCP/IP settings, choose Start ➪ Settings ➪ Control Panel ➪ Network ➪ Protocols tab ➪ TCP/IP Protocol ➪ Properties. Examine the IP address schema specified. Click the TCP/IP Advanced button and examine the Gateways, whether Enable PPTP Filtering and Enable Security have been selected. Click the Configure button. For each adapter, focus on whether packet filtering has been enabled by viewing the allowable TCP ports, UDP ports, and IP protocols.

## Denial of Service Security Attacks

Have solutions been applied to some of the potential denial of service attacks? To examine whether solutions have been applied by examining the level of Service Pack applied, choose Start ➪ Programs ➪ Administrative Tools ➪ Windows NT Diagnostics ➪ Version tab. To examine whether hot fixes have been applied, go to Microsoft's web site and download HOTFIX.EXE. Run HOTFIX.EXE on the local computer and examine the list of hot fixes installed.

## External Networking

To examine the external networking of your system, address the following questions:

- Is there a connection to the Internet?
- Is RAS being used?
- Is any remote control software being used?

## Windows NT Remote Access Services

To examine the Remote Access Services of your system, address the following questions:

- Are remote access users monitored?
- How is remote access authorization granted?
- Are the RAS Servers domain members? To examine the Windows NT RAS configuration, choose Start ➪ Programs ➪ Administrative Tools ➪ Remote Access Admin.
- What remote access permissions are users granted? To examine these permissions, choose Start ➪ Programs ➪ Administrative Tools ➪ Remote Access Admin ➪Users ➪ Permissions. Focus on whether the users who appear in the Grant Dial-in Permission to User field should have remote access capability. In addition, for each user (if feasible), focus on whether the Callback option is selected, and how Callback is configured.
- Are any of the telephone lines restricted to "dial-out only" by the telephone company?

- What is the configuration for each RAS port? To examine the port configuration, choose Start ⇨ Settings ⇨ Control Panel ⇨ Network ⇨ Services tab ⇨ Remote Access Service ⇨ Properties. Highlight the device you want to examine and click the Configure button. Focus on the dial-out and dial-in protocols used. Click the Network button. Focus on the level of encryption settings.

## Securing the System

Auditing whether the system is secure encompasses evaluating all the controls available to ensure your system and data are not accessible by unauthorized users. Because Windows NT's control capabilities are numerous, evaluating these controls can be a massive undertaking. To aid you in this task, we focus on four areas:

- User Security Management
- Resource Security Management
- Server Security Management
- System Security Management

These areas focus on overall user policies and rights, the use of groups, the file systems, services, and specifics on the Registry. The objective of this audit is to determine whether Users, Resources, the Server, and the System are secure. The following sections detail the procedures involved in performing this audit.

### User Security Management—Group Accounts

To examine the group accounts within your system, address the following questions:

- How are users and groups managed? Focus on whether users are assigned to global groups as a method of managing common permissions, rights and privileges, and whether users are ever assigned directly to local groups.
- What are the rights assigned to the built-in local groups? To examine the built-in local groups, choose Start ⇨ Programs ⇨ Administrative Tools ⇨ User Manager for Domains ⇨ Policies ⇨ User Rights. Examine the rights assigned to the built-in local groups by scrolling through the various user rights. Don't forget to select Show Advanced Rights so all user rights can be viewed. Focus on the differences between our recommended group rights and those assigned to these groups. Table 13-1 and Table 13-2 can be used as a basis for documenting these rights and capabilities. Do not attempt to fill out the table from scratch; just document the changes.

**Table 13-1.  Domain Controllers Rights and Capabilities**

| | Accout Oper- ators | Admin- istra- tors | Backup Oper- ators | Guests | Print Oper- ators | Rep- lica- tors | Server Oper- ators | Users |
|---|---|---|---|---|---|---|---|---|
| ***Standard Rights*** | | | | | | | | |
| Log On Locally | X | X | X | X | X | X | X | X |
| Access This Computer from Network | | X | | | | | | |
| Take Ownership of Files or Other Objects | | X | | | | | | |
| Manage Auditing and Security Log | | X | | | | | | |
| Change the System Time | | X | | | | | X | |
| Shut Down the System | X | X | X | | X | X | X | |
| Force Shutdown from a Remote System | | X | | | | | X | |
| Back Up Files and Directories | | X | X | | | | X | |
| Restore Files and Directories | | X | X | | | | X | |
| ***Advanced Rights*** | | | | | | | | |
| Act As Part of the Operating System | | | | | | | | |
| Bypass Traverse Checking | | | | | | | | |
| Create a Pagefile | | X | | | | | | |
| Create a Token Object | | | | | | | | |
| Create Permanent Shared Objects | | | | | | | | |
| Debug Programs | | X | | | | | | |
| Generate Security Audits | | | | | | | | |
| Increase Quotas | | X | | | | | | |
| Increase Schedul- ing Priority | | X | | | | | | |

*(continued)*

**Table 13-1.** *(continued)*

| | Accout Oper- ators | Admin- istra- tors | Backup Oper- ators | Guests | Print Oper- ators | Rep- lica- tors | Server Oper- ators | Users |
|---|---|---|---|---|---|---|---|---|
| Load and Unload Device Drivers | | X | | | | | | |
| Lock Pages in Memory | | | | | | | | |
| Log On As a Batch Job | | | | | | | | |
| Log On As a Service | | | | | | | | |
| Modify Firm- ware Environ- ment Variables | | X | | | | | | |
| Profile Single Process | | X | | | | | | |
| Profile System Performance | | X | | | | | | |
| Replace a Process Level Token | | | | | | | | |
| ***Built-in Capabilities*** | | | | | | | | |
| Create and Manage User Accounts | X | X | | | | | | |
| Create and Manage Local Groups | X | X | | | | | | |
| Create and Manage Global Groups | X | X | | | | | | |
| Assign User Rights | | X | | | | | | |
| Lock the Work- station/Server | | X | | | | | | X |
| Override the Lock of the Work- station/Server | | X | | | | | | X |
| Format Work- station/Server's Hard Disk | | X | | | | | | X |

*(continued)*

**Table 13-1.**   *(continued)*

| | Accout Oper- ators | Admin- istra- tors | Backup Oper- ators | Guests | Print Oper- ators | Rep- lica- tors | Server Oper- ators | Users |
|---|---|---|---|---|---|---|---|---|
| Create Common Groups | X | | | | | | | X |
| Keep Local Profile | X | X | X | | | X | X | X |
| Share and Stop Sharing Directories | | X | | | | | | X |
| Share and Stop Sharing Printers | | X | | | | X | | X |

## Table 13-2. Non-Domain Controllers Rights and Capabilities

| | Admin- istra- tors | Backup Oper- ators | Guests | Rep- licators | Power Users | Users |
|---|---|---|---|---|---|---|
| ***Standard Rights*** | | | | | | |
| Log On Locally | X | X | X | X | X | X |
| Access This Computer from Network | X | | | | X | |
| Take Ownership of Files or Other Objects | X | | | | | |
| Manage Auditing and Security Log | X | | | | X | |
| Change the System Time | X | | X | | X | |
| Shut Down the System | X | X | | X | X | X |
| Force Shutdown from a Remote System | X | | | | X | |
| Back Up Files and Directories | X | X | | | | |
| Restore Files and Directories | X | X | | | | |

*(continued)*

**Table 13-2** *(continued)*

| | Admin-istra-tors | Backup Oper-ators | Guests | Rep-licators | Power Users | Users |
|---|---|---|---|---|---|---|
| **Advanced Rights** | | | | | | |
| Act As Part of the Operating System | | | | | | |
| Bypass Traverse Checking | | | | | | |
| Create a Pagefile | | X | | | | |
| Create a Token Object | | | | | | |
| Create Permanent Shared Objects | | | | | | |
| Debug Programs | | X | | | | |
| Generate Security Audits | | | | | | |
| Increase Quotas | | X | | | | |
| Increase Scheduling Priority | | X | | | | |
| Load and Unload Device Drivers | | X | | | | |
| Lock Pages in Memory | | | | | | |
| Log On As a Batch Job | | | | | | |
| Log On As a Service | | | | | | |
| Modify Firmware Environment Variables | | X | | | | |
| Profile Single Process | | X | | | | |
| Profile System Performance | | X | | | | |
| Replace a Process Level Token | | | | | | |
| **Built-in Capabilities** | | | | | | |
| Create and Manage User Accounts | | X | | | | X |

**Table 13-2**   *(continued)*

| | Admin-istra-tors | Backup Oper-ators | Guests | Rep-licators | Power Users | Users |
|---|---|---|---|---|---|---|
| Create and Manage Local Groups | | X | | | | X |
| Create and Manage Global Groups | | | | | | |
| Lock the Work-station/Server | | X | | | | X |
| Override the Lock of the Work-station/Server | | X | | | | |
| Format Work-station/Server's Hard Disk | | X | | | | |
| Create Common Groups | | X | | | | X |
| Keep Local Profile | | X | X | | X | X |
| Share and Stop Sharing Directories | | X | | | | X |
| Share and Stop Sharing Printers | | X | | | | X |

- Are the groups' members administratively and functionally appropriate?
- What are the rights assigned to the additional local groups? To examine the additional local groups' rights, choose Start ➪ Programs ➪ Administrative Tools ➪ User Manager for Domains ➪ Policies ➪ User Rights. Examine the rights assigned to the local group by scrolling through the various user rights. Don't forget to select Show Advanced Rights so all user rights can be viewed. Focus on assessing whether the global groups or possibly users are administratively and functionally appropriate for the groups they are assigned.
- What are the rights assigned to the built-in and additional significant global groups? To examine the global groups, choose Start ➪ Programs ➪ Administrative Tools ➪ User Manager for Domains ➪ Policies ➪ User Rights. Examine the local group(s) of which the global group is a member by scrolling through the various user rights. Don't forget to select Show Advanced Rights so all user rights can be viewed. Focus on assessing whether the

users are administratively and functionally appropriate members of the group. Focus only on critical global groups.

## User Security Management—User Accounts

To examine the user accounts within your system, address the following questions:

- What are the properties of the two built-in user accounts? To examine the accounts, choose Start ⇨ Programs ⇨ Administrative Tools ⇨ User Manager for Domains. Determine whether the Administrator or Guest accounts exist in the User Account list. Either double-click on the desired account or highlight it and select User ⇨ Properties. If either account is enabled, examine whether the following check boxes are selected:

  - User Cannot Change Password
  - Password Never Expires
  - Account Disabled

- Has the Administrator account been renamed? If the Administrator account has been renamed, execute the preceding procedure for the renamed account.

- Is a password set for each of the built-in accounts? To examine whether these accounts have passwords, try to log on the accounts from the Windows NT Login dialog box.

- What are the properties for all other significant accounts? To examine the properties, choose Start ⇨ Programs ⇨ Administrative Tools ⇨ User Manager for Domains ⇨ User ⇨ Properties.

- To which groups do the significant user accounts belong? To examine the groups to which the user belongs, click the Groups button. Focus on whether the user is an administratively and functionally appropriate member of the groups of which it is a member.

- What is the User Environment Profile configuration for the significant accounts? To examine the profiles, click the Profile button. Focus on whether logon scripts and profiles have been implemented. Also focus on whether a home directory has been established. Inquire on the specific contents of the logon script.

- What are the valid logon hours for all significant accounts? To examine the logon hours click the Hours button. Focus on whether all users have all hours allowed, and whether hours are commensurate with a user's functional and administrative need.

- Which workstations can the significant accounts log on? To examine which workstations the account is able to log on, click the Logon To button. Focus on comparing the applicability of the feature to the environment, and the users who are restricted.

- Which accounts have expiration dates? Focus on any temporary accounts. For those identified accounts, examine whether the account has an expiration date by clicking the Account button.

- Which accounts have dialin capability? To examine whether an account has dialin capability, click the Dialin button. Focus on comparing whether the access granted is commensurate with a user's functional and administrative need.

### User Security Management—Account Policies

To examine the account policies within your system, answer this question: What is the account policy? Examine the account policy for all accounts by choosing Start ⇨ Programs ⇨ Administrative Tools ⇨ User Manager for Domains ⇨ Policies Account. Focus on each of the following account policy settings:

- Maximum Password Age (days)
- Minimum Password Age (days)
- Minimum Password Length (characters)
- Password Uniqueness (passwords)
- Account Lockout
- Account Lockout (bad attempts)
- Account Lockout (reset count in minutes))
- Lockout Duration (minutes)
- Forcibly disconnect remote users from server when logon hours expire
- Users log on to change password

## Auditing User Rights

To audit the user rights within your system, address the following questions:

- Which accounts have been granted which user rights? For each right, examine the user rights policy by choosing Start ⇨ Programs ⇨ Administrative Tools ⇨ User Manager for Domains ⇨ Policies ⇨ User Rights. Focus on the functional and administrative appropriateness of the users or groups who were granted the right.

- Which accounts have been granted which advanced user rights? For each right, examine the advanced user rights policy by choosing Start ⇨ Programs ⇨ Administrative Tools ⇨ User Manager for Domains ⇨ Policies ⇨ select Show Advanced User Rights and scroll down through the list of various rights. For each right, focus on the functional and administrative appropriateness of the users or groups who were granted the right.

### Resource Security Management—File Systems

To examine the security of file systems within your network, address this question: Which file system is deployed? To examine the deployed file system, choose Start ⇨ Programs ⇨ Administrative Tools ⇨ Disk Administrator. If NTFS is not the deployed file system, inquire on the reasoning for selecting FAT.

### Resource Security Management/File and Directory Permissions

To audit the file and directory permissions within your network, address the following questions:

- Which directories, subdirectories, and files are critical?
- What are the permissions on the critical files? To examine the permissions, choose Start ⇨ Programs ⇨ Windows NT Explorer. Select the file and choose File ⇨ Properties ⇨ Security. Choose Focus on whether the owner, and user, and group access is functionally and administratively appropriate.
- What are the permissions on the critical directories? To examine the permissions, choose Start ⇨ Programs ⇨ Windows NT Explorer. Select the directory and then choose File ⇨ Properties ⇨ Security. Choose Permissions. Focus on whether the owner, and user and group access is functionally and administratively appropriate.
- What are the permissions on the critical systems directories? To examine these permissions, choose Start ⇨ Programs ⇨ Windows NT Explorer. Select the directory or file, choose File ⇨ Properties ⇨ Security, and then choose Permissions. Document any differences between the default permissions and the actual permissions.

### Resource Security Management—Shared File and Directory Permissions

To audit the security of the shared file and directory permissions within your network, address this question: What shares and permissions have been placed on the previously identified directories? To examine each significant directory shares, choose Start ⇨ Programs ⇨ Administrative Tools ⇨ Server Manager ⇨ Computer menu ⇨ Shared Directories. For each share, click Properties. Focus on whether user and group access is functionally and administratively appropriate.

### Resource Security Management—Managing Printers

To manage the printers within your network, address the following questions:

- What printers are critical?
- What permissions have been set on the critical printers? To examine each printer, choose Start ⇨ Settings ⇨ Printers. Select the critical printer and choose File ⇨ Properties ⇨ Security tab. Choose Permissions. Focus on whether user and group access is functionally and administratively appropriate.

## Server Security Management

What computers reside on the domain? To examine the list of computers on the domain, choose Start ⇨ Programs ⇨ Administrative Tools ⇨ Server Manager. Then choose Domain Members Only. With the administrator, review the list of computers that are members of the domain for appropriateness. One should note that Windows 95 and 98 boxes as well as Windows For Workgroup and DOS clients would not appear using this method.

### Server Security Management—Computer Properties

Is the Properties dialog box (Computer ⇨ Properties) used as a method of monitoring and controlling connections to the server and domain?

### Server Security Management—Users

Is the User Sessions dialog box (Computer ⇨ Properties ⇨ Users button) used as a method of monitoring and controlling the users connected to the server and domain?

### Server Security Management—Shares

Is the Shared Resources dialog box (Computer ⇨ Properties ⇨ Shares button) used as a method of monitoring and controlling shares on the server and other computers in the domain?

### Server Security Management—In Use

Is the Open Resources dialog box (Computer ⇨ Properties ⇨ In Use button) used as a method of monitoring and controlling network usage of shares?

### Server Security Management—Replication

Is replication used to maintain identical directory trees and files on multiple servers and workstations? Focus on the nature of the directories and files being replicated.

Is there a replication user account with appropriate rights? To examine the account, choose Start ⇨ Programs ⇨ User Manager for Domains. To focus on whether the account exists and is a member of the Replicator local group, choose User ⇨ Properties and click the Groups button.

Does the Replicator local group have appropriate rights? To examine the rights of the Replicator group, choose Start ⇨ Programs ⇨ Administrative Tools ⇨ User Manager for Domains ⇨ Policies ⇨ User Rights. Examine each right and focus on the rights that have been granted to the Replicator group.

Is the Replicator service running? To examine whether the Replicator service is running, choose Start ⇨ Programs ⇨ Administrative Tools ⇨ Server Manager ⇨ Computer ⇨ Services, and double-click on the Directory Replicator service. Focus on whether the service is started automatically, and whether the account specified is the one designated for replication.

Are the files and computers designated for import and export replication appropriate? To examine the configuration of the Replication dialog box, choose Start ⇨ Programs ⇨ Administrative Tools ⇨ Server Manager ⇨ Computer ⇨ Properties, and then click the Replication button.

Do locks exist on the subdirectories in the replicated directory? To examine the Manage Exported Directories dialog box, click the Manage button for Export Directories. Also, focus on whether the Wait Until Stabilized and Entire Subtree check boxes are selected.

### Server Security Management—Alerts

Who is receiving administrator alerts? To examine the list of users receiving alerts, choose Start ⇨ Programs ⇨ Administrative Tools ⇨ Server Manager ⇨ Computer ⇨ Properties and then click the Alerts button. Focus on the appropriateness of the users selected to receive alerts.

### Server Security Management—Services

Which services are running on critical computers? To examine the services, choose Start ⇨ Programs ⇨ Administrative Tools ⇨ Server Manager, highlight the critical computer, and choose Services from the Computer menu.

### System Security Management—Registry

To examine the security of the Registry, address the following questions:

- Has REGEDT32.EXE been removed from workstations? To examine a sample of workstations, choose Start ⇨ Programs ⇨ Windows NT Explorer ⇨ systemroot\system32\.

- Are Registry file and directory permissions appropriate for groups with access? To examine the Registry directory permissions, choose Start ð Programs ð Windows NT Explorer and select the directory. Choose File ð Properties ð Security, and then choose Permissions. Focus on any changes from the following table.

| File and Directory Permissions | Recommendations | |
| --- | --- | --- |
| \winnt\system32\config | Administrators | Full Control |
| | Everyone | List |
| | CREATOR OWNER | Full Control |
| | SYSTEM | Full Control |
| \winnt\repair | Administrators | Full Control |

- Does the Prevent Remote Editing key exist? To examine whether the key exists, choose Start ⇨ Programs ⇨ Windows NT Explorer and execute Systemroot\system32\Regedt32.exe. Select HKLM\SYSTEM\CurrentControlSet\Control\SecurePipeServers\winreg.

- What permissions have been set for the Registry keys? To examine the permissions, choose Start ➪ Programs ➪ Windows NT Explorer, execute Systemroot\system32\Regedt32.exe, and then choose Security ➪ Permissions. Focus on comparing the permissions with those in the following table.

| Registry HKEY | Permissions |
| --- | --- |
| HKCR (all subkeys) | Modify Everyone: Special (Query Value, Enumerate Subkeys, Notify, Read Control) |
| HKLM\SOFTWARE | Modify Everyone: Special (Query Value, Enumerate Subkeys, Notify, Read Control) |
| HKEY_LOCAL_MACHINE\SOFTWARE\MICROSOFT<br>\RPC (and all subkeys)<br>\WindowsNT\CurrentVersion\<br>\WindowsNT\CurrentVersion\AeDebug<br>\WindowsNT\CurrentVersion\Compatibility<br>\WindowsNT\CurrentVersion\Drivers<br>\WindowsNT\CurrentVersion\Embedding<br>\WindowsNT\CurrentVersion\Fonts<br>\WindowsNT\CurrentVersion\FontSubstitutes<br>\WindowsNT\CurrentVersion\FontDrivers<br>\WindowsNT\CurrentVersion\FontMapper<br>\WindowsNT\CurrentVersion\FontCache<br>\WindowsNT\CurrentVersion\GRE_Initialize<br>\WindowsNT\CurrentVersion\MCI<br>\WindowsNT\CurrentVersion\MCI Extensions<br>\WindowsNT\CurrentVersion\Port (all subkeys)<br>\WindowsNT\CurrentVersion\Type1Installer<br>\WindowsNT\CurrentVersion\ProfileList<br>\WindowsNT\CurrentVersion\Windows3.1MigrationStatus(all subkeys)<br>\WindowsNT\CurrentVersion\WOW (all subkeys) | Modify Everyone: Special (Query Value, Enumerate Subkeys, Notify, Read Control) |
| HKLM\SOFTWARE\MICROSOFT\WindowsNT\CurrentVersion\PerfLib | Remove Everyone: Read, Add Interactive: Read |
| HKLM\SOFTWARE\MICROSOFT\WindowsNT\CurrentVersion\PerfLib | Remove Everyone: Read, Add Interactive: Read |
| HKLM\SOFTWARE\Microsoft\Windows\CurrentVersion\Run | Modify Everyone: Special (Query Value, Enumerate Subkeys, Notify, Read Control) |
| HKLM\SOFTWARE\Microsoft\Windows\CurrentVersion\RunOnce | Modify Everyone: Special (Query Value, Enumerate Subkeys, Notify, Read Control) |
| HKLM\Software\Microsoft\WindowsNT\CurrentVersion\Winlogon | Creator Owner: Full Control, Administrator: Full Control, System: Full Control, Everyone: Read |

*(continued)*

*(continued)*

| Registry HKEY | Permissions |
|---|---|
| HKLM\SYSTEM\CurrentControlSet\Control\LSA | Creator Owner: Full Control, Administrator: Full Control, System: Full Control, Everyone: Read |
| HKLM\System\CurrentControlSet\Control\SecurePipeServers\WinReg | Administrators: Full Control |
| HKLM\System\CurrentControlSet\Services \LanManServer\Shares \UPS | Modify Everyone: Special (Query Value, Enumerate Subkeys, Notify, Read Control) |
| HKEY_USERS\.default | Modify Everyone: Special (Query Value, Enumerate Subkeys, Notify, Read Control) |

- What are the Registry key values? To examine the values, choose Start ⇨ Programs ⇨ Windows NT Explorer, execute Systemroot\system32\Regedt32.exe, and then choose Security ⇨ Permissions. Focus on comparing the values with those in the following table.

| Description | Registry Key | Value Name | Data Type |
|---|---|---|---|
| Disable CD-ROM | HKLM\SOFTWARE\Microsoft\ WindowsNT\CurrentVersion\ Winlogon | AllocateCDROMs | String |
| Disable Floppy Drive | HKLM\SOFTWARE\Microsoft\ WindowsNT\CurrentVersion\ Winlogon | AllocateFloppies | String |
| Automatic Logon | HKLM\SOFTWARE\Microsoft\ WindowsNT\CurrentVersion\ Winlogon | AutoAdminLogon | Binary |
| Disable of Caching of Logon Credential | HKLM\Microsoft\Windows NT\ CurrentVersion\Winlogon | CachedLogonsCount | Strings |
| Do Not Display Last User to Log In | HKLM\SOFTWARE\Microsoft \WindowsNT\CurrentVersion\ Winlogon | DontDisplayLastUserName | String |
| Legal Notice | HKLM\SOFTWARE\Microsoft\ WindowsNT\CurrentVersion\ Winlogon | LegalNoticeText | String |
| Shut Down without Logging On | HKLM\SOFTWARE\Microsoft\ WindowsNT\CurrentVersion\ Winlogon | ShutdownWithoutLogon | String |
| Shutdown on Full Audit Log | SYSTEM\CurrentControlSet\ Control\Lsa | CrashOnAuditFail | DWORD |

*(continued)*

*(continued)*

| Description | Registry Key | Value Name | Data Type |
|---|---|---|---|
| Enable Auditing Of Rights | HKLM\SYSTEM\CurrentControlSet\Control\LSA | FullPrivilegeAuditing | Binary |
| LanManager Password Hash Support | HKLM\System\CurrentControlSet\Control\LSA | LMCompatibilityLevel | DWORD |
| Password Filtering | HKLM\SYSTEM\CurrentControlSet\Control\LSA | Notification Packages | Multi String |
| Null Credentials Logon | HKLM\System\CurrentControlSet\Control\LSA | RestrictAnonymous | DWORD |
| Schedule Service | HKLM\SYSTEM\CurrentControlSet\Control\LSA | SubmitControl | DWORD |
| Page File Clearing | HKLM\SYSTEM\CurrentControlSet\Control\ SessionManager\MemoryManagement | ClearPageFileAtShutdown | DWORD |
| Disable Autorun | HKLM\SYSTEM\CurrentControlSet\Services\CDROM | Autorun | DWORD |
| Auditing | HKLM\SYSTEM\CurrentControlSet\Services\RemoteAccess | Parameters | Binary |
| Secure Event Log Viewing | HKLM\System\CurrentControlSet\Services\EventLog\ *logname* | RestrictGuestAccess | DWORD |

## System Security Management—System Policy Editor

What system policies have been established? To examine the policies, choose Start ⇨ Programs ⇨ Administrative Tools ⇨ System Policy Editor ⇨ File ⇨ Open Policy. Focus on any .POL and .ADM files. Open each .POL or .ADM file and document the groups and policies. Focus on the policies for the following network and computer features:

- Network Features

  Shell ⇨ Restrictions ⇨ Remove Run command from Start menu

  Shell ⇨ Restrictions ⇨ No Entire Network in Network Neighborhood

  Shell ⇨ Restrictions ⇨ Don't save settings at exit

  System ⇨ Restrictions ⇨ Disable Registry editing tools

  Windows NT Shell ⇨ Restrictions ⇨ Remove the "Map Network Drive" and "Disconnect Network Drive" options

- Computer Features

  Windows NT Remote Access ⇨ Max number of unsuccessful authentication retries

  Windows NT Remote Access ⇨ Max time limit for authentication

  Windows NT Remote Access ⇨ Auto disconnect

Windows NT System ⇨ Logon ⇨ Logon banner

Windows NT System ⇨ Logon ⇨ Enable shutdown from Authentication dialog box

Windows NT System ⇨ Logon ⇨ Do not display last logged on user name

### System Security Management—Workstation Lockout

Is the Workstation Lockout feature utilized? To examine the feature for critical computers and sample noncritical computers, choose Start ⇨ Settings ⇨ Control Panel ⇨ Display ⇨ Screen Saver. Focus on whether the password protection feature has been selected and if the value for the number of minutes before the lockout invokes is reasonable.

## Ability to Recover from Operational Failure

The ability to recover from operational failure is often neglected. However, the ramifications of not being able to recover from a failure may be devastating to the business. Therefore, we focus on examining the security controls relating to recoverability.

The objective of this audit is to determine the level of ability to recover from operational failure. The following sections detail the procedures involved in performing this audit.

### Environmental Protection

To perform the Environmental Protection section of the Ability to Recover from Operational Failure audit, address the following questions:

- Are the building and computer room structurally sound enough to resist any probable weather or geological activity?
- Is the computer room floor static resistant?
- Is the computer room floor elevated?
- Is the computer room large enough to accommodate growth?
- Is the computer room large enough to move within while installing and maintaining equipment?
- Is the computer room humidity and temperature controlled, and are these systems redundant?
- Are systems designed to shut down in the event humidity or temperature exceeds a predetermined critical point?
- Is power to the computer room clean (free from significant spikes or surges), and supplied through wiring that is fire- and smoke-retardant?
- Is the computer room equipped with smoke and fire detectors?
- Is the computer room equipped with fire extinguishers that are nondamaging to equipment?
- Is the computer room equipped with a fire suppression system that is nondamaging to equipment?

### Fending off Viruses

To perform the Fending off Viruses section of the Ability to Recover from Operational Failure audit, address the following questions:

- Are precautions taken to minimize the potential introduction of viruses? Focus on the following points.

  - Are floppy and CD-ROM drives disabled? To examine whether floppy drives have been disabled, choose Start ⇨ Programs ⇨ Windows NT Explorer and execute Systemroot\system32\Regedt32.exe. Select HKLM\Software\Microsoft\WindowsNT\CurrentVersion\Winlogon\AllocateFloppies key. Focus on whether the String value is 0. Select HKLM\Software\Microsoft\WindowsNT\CurrentVersion\Winlogon\AllocateCDRoms key. Focus on whether the String value is 0.

  - Do strong company policies exist to discourage users from downloading information from the Internet?

  - Are file permissions set to Read Only and Execute Only for all program directories available on the Windows NT server and workstation? To examine the permissions, choose Start ⇨ Programs ⇨ Windows NT Explorer. Select the file and choose File ⇨ Properties ⇨ Security. Then choose Permissions.

  - Are new applications installed on a test computer not attached to the network?

- Are virus detection programs installed to prevent viruses from causing destructive events?

### Fault Tolerance

To perform the Fault Tolerance section of the Ability to Recover from Operational Failure audit that deals with disk mirroring and data striping, address the following question: Is and on what level of redundancy are the storage drives? To examine the drives, choose Start ⇨ Programs ⇨ Administrative Tools ⇨ Disk Administrator. Focus on the number and type of drives, and configurations, including whether they are stripe or mirror sets. If a stripe set is used, focus on whether the stripe set is configured with parity.

### Fault Tolerance—UPS

To perform the Fault Tolerance section of the Ability to Recover from Operational Failure audit that deals with the uninterruptable power supply, address the following questions:

- Is an uninterruptable power supply used to ensure "clean" reliable power? If the Windows NT UPS feature is used, examine it by choosing Start ⇨ Settings ⇨ Control Panel. Then double-click the UPS icon. Focus on comparing the values selected to those in the following table.

| UPS Feature | Policy |
|---|---|
| Power Failure Signal | Select |
| Low Battery Signal (at least 2 minutes before shutdown) | Select |
| Remote UPS Shutdown | Select |
| Execute Command File | Select |
| Time between Power Failure and Initial Warning Message | 5 Seconds |
| Delay between Warning Messages | 300 seconds |

- Which users receive the UPS Alerts? To examine which users receive Alerts, choose Start ⇨ Programs ⇨ Administrative Tools ⇨ Server Manager ⇨ Computer ⇨ Properties ⇨ Alert.

### Data Backup

To perform the Data Backup section of the Ability to Recover from Operational Failure audit, address the following questions:

- What is the company's backup and archiving strategy? Focus on the type of media (tape, hard disk, optical media, and floppy disk), backup application (NT Backup Utility, third-party application), type of backup (full, incremental, and differential), rotation and archive schedule (real time, daily, weekly, and monthly), and storage location (onsite versus offsite).

- Is the Backup Operators group membership appropriate? To examine the membership, choose Start ⇨ Programs ⇨ Administrative Tools ⇨ User Manager for Domains. Double-click on the Backup Operators group. Examine the group's members. Are the rights assigned to the Backup Operators group appropriate? To examine the rights, choose Start ⇨ Programs ⇨ Administrative Tools ⇨ User Manager for Domains ⇨ Policies ⇨ User Rights. Examine each right and focus on which rights are granted to the Backup Operators group.

- Is the Registry backed up through Emergency Repair Disk, tape backup (either Windows NT Backup selecting the Backup Local Registry check box or Third-Party Tape Backup system), or REGBACK.EXE? If the Registry is backed up with the Windows NT Backup utility, inquire how registries on other computers are backed up.

- Is a backup log maintained? Examine the log file. The path for the log file is displayed in the Backup Information dialog box, which can be launched by choosing Start ⇨ Programs ⇨ Administrative Tools ⇨ Backup ⇨ Operations ⇨ Backup. Focus on whether a log is maintained, and whether log in Full Detail is selected.

### Data Recovery

To perform the Data Recovery section of the Ability to Recover from Operational Failure audit, address the following question: What is the frequency of backup testing? To examine any backups recovered to a test computer, load the backup tape and choose

Start ⇨ Administrator Tools ⇨ Disk Administrator ⇨ Window ⇨ Tape. Select the tape or backup set that you want to restore, and then choose Operations ⇨ Catalog. Select the first file, hold down the Ctrl key, and select the other files. Choose Select ⇨ Check and then choose Operations ⇨ Restore.

## Business Continuity Planning

To perform the Business Continuity Planning section of the Ability to Recover from Operational Failure audit, address the following question: What are the company's contingency plans? Focus on the appropriateness of the Disaster Recovery and Business Continuity plans based on the risk analysis.

## Last Known Good Configuration

To perform the Last Known Good Configuration section of the Ability to Recover from Operational Failure audit, address the following question: Has the company ever invoked Last Good Known Configuration? Focus on whether the staff knows the conditions for when the Last Known Good Configuration should be used.

## Emergency Repair Disk (ERD)

To perform the ERD section of the Ability to Recover from Operational Failure audit, address the following question: Is there an ERD and what is the practice for creating and updating the ERD? Inquire on when the last ERD was updated. Inquire on whether the ERD is updated using the /s option in order to force the Repair Disk program to update all the files.

# Appendix A
# Baseline Security Configurations

PricewaterhouseCoopers recognizes the hectic and fast-paced life of the information technologist. We understand that sometimes it is hard to sift through all the material in a book. Therefore, we have combined some important Windows NT security control features in the various Windows NT implementations and our recommended settings into the following matrix to be used as a baseline security configuration and as a quick reference. Systems administrators should use this appendix as a guide when building their Windows NT security environment.

| Feature | Domain Controller | File and Print Server | Database Server | Web Server | RAS Server | Workstation |
|---|---|---|---|---|---|---|
| **Built-in Accounts** | | | | | | |
| Administrator | This account should be renamed to an obscure value to disguise its function. | This account should be renamed to an obscure value to disguise its function. | This account should be renamed to an obscure value to disguise its function. | This account should be renamed to an obscure value to disguise its function. | This account should be renamed to an obscure value to disguise its function. | This account should be renamed to an obscure value to disguise its function. |
| | Set strong password and change regularly. | Set strong password and change regularly. | Set strong password and change regularly | Set strong password and change regularly. | Set strong password and change regularly. | Set strong password and change regularly. |
| | Disable from network access with Passprop.exe (see Password Enhancements below). | Disable from network access with Passprop. | Disable from network access with Passprop. | Disable from network access with Passprop. | Disable from network access with Passprop. | Disable from network access with Passprop. |

*(continued)*

*(continued)*

| Feature | Domain Controller | File and Print Server | Database Server | Web Server | RAS Server | Workstation |
|---|---|---|---|---|---|---|
| Guest | Disable and set a random, complex password on disabled account. | Disable and set a random, complex password on disabled account. | Disable and set a random, complex password on disabled account. | Disable and set a random, complex password on disabled account. | Disable and set a random, complex password on disabled account. | Disable and set a random, complex password on disabled account. |
| **User Properties** | | | | | | |
| User Must Change Password at Next Logon | Enable for newly created accounts. | N/A since all accounts exist on DC | N/A since all accounts exist on DC | N/A since all accounts exist on DC | Enable for newly created accounts | N/A since all accounts exist on DC |
| Password Never Expires | Disable, except for accounts that log on as a service. | N/A since all accounts exist on DC | N/A since all accounts exist on DC | N/A since all accounts exist on DC | Disable, except for accounts that log on as a service | N/A since all accounts exist on DC |
| Account Disabled | Select when an employee is on vacation, suspended, terminated, or access is denied. | N/A since all accounts exist on DC | N/A since all accounts exist on DC | N/A since all accounts exist on DC | Select when an employee is on vacation, suspended, terminated, or access is denied. | N/A since all accounts exist on DC |
| Logon Hours | Set a valid login-hours range based on users' requirements and Corporate Security Policy. | N/A since all accounts exist on DC | N/A since all accounts exist on DC | N/A since all accounts exist on DC | Set a valid login-hours range based on users' requirements and Corporate Security Policy. | N/A since all accounts exist on DC |
| Logon to | Depending on the environment, administrators may have accounts that have specific station needs. | N/A since all accounts exist on DC | N/A since all accounts exist on DC | N/A since all accounts exist on DC | Administrators may want to allow users to log on to only certain database servers or file servers. | N/A since all accounts exist on DC |

*(continued)*

*(continued)*

| Feature | Controller | Domain Print Server | File and Server | Database Web server | RAS Server | Workstation |
|---|---|---|---|---|---|---|
| Account | Use when required to have an account expire. | N/A since all accounts exist on DC | N/A since all accounts exist on DC | N/A since all accounts exist on DC | Use when required to have an account expire | N/A since all accounts exist on DC |
| Dial-in | RAS is not installed. | N/A since all accounts exist on DC | N/A since all accounts exist on DC | N/A since all accounts exist on DC | Only users that must have access via remote access should be given this permission. | N/A since all accounts exist on DC |

### *User Account Policy*

| Feature | Controller | Domain Print Server | File and Server | Database Web server | RAS Server | Workstation |
|---|---|---|---|---|---|---|
| Account Type | Domain Accounts | Local Accounts | Local Accounts | Local Accounts | Local Accounts | Local Accounts |
| Maximum Password Age (days) | 30–60 | 30–60 | 30–60 | 30–60 | 30–60 | 30–60 |
| Minimum Password Age (days) | 7 | 7 | 7 | 7 | 7 | 7 |
| Minimum Password Length (characters) | 8 | 8 | 8 | 8 | 8 | 8 |
| Password Uniqueness (passwords) | 6–12 | 6–12 | 6–12 | 6–12 | 6–12 | 6–12 |
| Account Lockout | Yes | Yes | Yes | Yes | Yes | Yes |
| Account Lockout (bad attempts) | 3 | 3 | 3 | 3 | 3 | 3 |
| Account Lockout (reset count in minutes) | 1440 | 1440 | 1440 | 1440 | 1440 | 1440 |

*(continued)*

*(continued)*

| Feature | Controller | Domain Print Server | File and Server | Database Web Server | RAS Server | Workstation |
|---|---|---|---|---|---|---|
| Lockout Duration (minutes) | Forever | Forever | Forever | Forever | Forever | Forever |
| Forcibly Disconnect Remote Users from Server When Logon Hours Expire. Select N/A Since All Accounts Exist on DC. | Select. | N/A since all accounts exist on DC | N/A since all accounts exist on DC | N/A since all accounts exist on DC | Select. | N/A since all accounts exist on DC |
| Users Must Log on in Order to Change Password | Do not select. | Do not select. | Do not select. | Do not select. | Do not select. | Do not select. |

***Password Enhancement***

| Feature | Controller | Domain Print Server | File and Server | Database Web Server | RAS Server | Workstation |
|---|---|---|---|---|---|---|
| Passprop.exe | Install and use to lock Administrator account over the network. | Install and use to lock Administrator account over the network. | Install and use to lock Administrator account over the network. | Install and use to lock Administrator account over the network. | Install and use to lock Administrator account over the network. | Install and use to lock Administrator account over the network. |
| Passfilt.dll | Install and use to enforce strong user passwords. | Not needed since all accounts exist on DC. | Not needed since all accounts exist on DC. | Not needed since all accounts exist on DC. | Install and use to enforce strong user passwords. | Not needed since all accounts exist on DC. |
| Syskey | Install and implement 128-bit encryption. | Install and implement 128-bit encryption. | Install and implement 128-bit encryption. | Install and implement 128-bit encryption. | Install and implement 128-bit encryption. | Install and implement 128-bit encryption. |

***User Rights Policy***

| Feature | Controller | Domain Print Server | File and Server | Database Web Server | RAS Server | Workstation |
|---|---|---|---|---|---|---|
| Access This Computer from Network | Domain Users Server Operators | Domain Users | Domain Users | Domain Users | Domain Users | None |

*(continued)*

*(continued)*

| Feature | Domain Controller | File and Print Server | Database Server | Web Server | RAS Server | Workstation |
|---|---|---|---|---|---|---|
| Account Operators | | | | | | |
| Print Operators | | | | | | |
| Backup Operators | | | | | | |
| Add Workstations and Member Servers to Domain | Domain Admins | None | None | None | None | None |
| Back Up Files and Directories | Backup Operators | Backup Operators | Backup Operators | Backup Operators | Backup Operators | Backup Operators |
| Change the System Time | Administrators<br>Server Operators | Administrators | Administrators | Administrators | Administrators | Administrators<br>Power Users |
| Force Shut Down from a Remote System | None | None | None | None | None | None |
| Log on Locally | Administrators<br>Server Operators<br>Backup Operators | Administrators | Administrators tors | Administrators tors | Administrators tors | Administrators<br>Users |
| Manage Auditing and Security Log | Administrators<br>Auditors (must be created) | Administrators<br>Auditors (must be created) | Administrators<br>Auditors (must be created) | Administrators<br>Auditors (must be created) | Administrators<br>Auditors (must be created) | Administrators |

*(continued)*

*(continued)*

| Feature | Domain Controller | File and Print Server | Database Server | Web Server | RAS Server | Workstation |
|---|---|---|---|---|---|---|
| Restore Files and Directories | Backup Operators | Backup Operators | Backup Operators | Backup Operators | Backup Operators | Backup Operators |
| Shut Down the System | Administrators | Server Operators | Administrators | Administrators | Administrators | Administrators<br><br>Users |
| Take Ownership of Files or Other Objects | Administrators | Administrators | Administrators | Administrators | Administrators | Administrators |

**User Advanced Rights Policy**

| Feature | Domain Controller | File and Print Server | Database Server | Web Server | RAS Server | Workstation |
|---|---|---|---|---|---|---|
| Act as Part of the Operating System | None | None | None | None | None | None |
| Bypass Traverse Checking | Administrators<br><br>Server Operators<br><br>Backup Operators | Administrators | Everyone | Everyone | Everyone | Everyone |
| Create a Pagefile | Administrators | Administrators | Administrators | Administrators | Administrators | Administrators |
| Create a Token Object | None | None | None | None | None | None |
| Create Permanent Shared Objects | None | None | None | None | None | None |
| Debug Programs | Administrators | Administrators | Administrators | Administrators | Administrators | Administrators |

*(continued)*

*(continued)*

| Feature | Domain Controller | File and Print Server | Database Server | Web server | RAS Server | Workstation |
|---|---|---|---|---|---|---|
| Generate Security Audits | None | None | None | None | None | None |
| Increase Quotas | Administrators | Administrators | Administrators | Administrators | Administrators | Administrators |
| Increase Scheduling priority | Administrators | Administrators | Administrators | Administrators | Administrators | Administrators |
| Load and Unload Device Drivers | Administrators | Administrators | Administrators | Administrators | Administrators | Administrators |
| Lock Pages in Memory | None | None | None | None | None | None |
| Log on as a Batch Job | None | None | None | None | None | None |
| Log on as a Service | None | None | None | None | None | None |
| Modify Firmware Environment Variables | Administrators | Administrators | Administrators | Administrators | Administrators | Administrators |
| Profile Single Process | Administrators | Administrators | Administrators | Administrators | Administrators | Administrators |
| Profile System Performance | Administrators | Administrators | Administrators | Administrators | Administrators | Administrators |
| Replace a Process Level Token | None | None | None | None | None | None |

### Replicator Account Properties

| Feature | Domain Controller | File and Print Server | Database Server | Web server | RAS Server | Workstation |
|---|---|---|---|---|---|---|
| Password Never Expires | Select | N/A since all accounts exist on DC | N/A since all accounts exist on DC | N/A since all accounts exist on DC | N/A | N/A since all accounts exist on DC |

*(continued)*

*(continued)*

| Feature | Domain Controller | File and Print Server | Database Server | Web Server | RAS Server | Workstation |
|---|---|---|---|---|---|---|
| User Must Change Password At Next Logons | Do not select. | N/A since all accounts exist on DC | N/A since all accounts exist on DC | N/A since all accounts exist on DC | N/A | N/A since all accounts exist on DC |
| User Cannot Change Password | Select. | N/A since all accounts exist on DC | N/A since all accounts exist on DC | N/A since all accounts exist on DC | N/A | N/A since all accounts exist on DC |
| Account Disabled | Do not select. | N/A since all accounts exist on DC | N/A since all accounts exist on DC | N/A since all accounts exist on DC | N/A | N/A since all accounts exist on DC |
| Groups | Replicator | N/A since all accounts exist on DC | N/A since all accounts exist on DC | N/A since all accounts exist on DC | N/A | N/A since all accounts exist on DC |
| Profile | Do not define a user profile. | N/A since all accounts exist on DC | N/A since all accounts exist on DC | N/A since all accounts exist on DC | N/A | N/A since all accounts exist on DC |
| Hours | Enable 24 hours a day, 7 days a week. | N/A since all accounts exist on DC | N/A since all accounts exist on DC Automatic | N/A since all accounts exist on DC | N/A | N/A since all accounts exist on DC |
| User Rights for Replicator Group | Permit Log-on as a Service.<br><br>Deny Logon Locally.<br><br>Deny Access to this Computer from the Network. | N/A since all accounts exist on DC | | N/A since all accounts exist on DC | N/A | N/A since all accounts exist on DC |

### Directory Replicator Service Features

| Feature | Domain Controller | File and Print Server | Database Server | Web Server | RAS Server | Workstation |
|---|---|---|---|---|---|---|
| Startup Type | Automatic | Automatic | Automatic | Automatic | N/A | N/A |
| Log On As | Select the This Account radio button. | Select the This Account radio button. | Select the This Account radio button. | Select the This Account radio button. | N/A | N/A |

*(continued)*

*(continued)*

| Feature | Domain Controller | File and Print Server | Database Server | Web server | RAS Server | Workstation |
|---|---|---|---|---|---|---|
| This Account | Input the user account and password created for Directory Replicator. | Input the user account and password created for Directory Replicator. | Input the user account and password created for Directory Replicator. | Input the user account and password created for Directory Replicator. | N/A | N/A |

### Audit Policy

| Feature | Domain Controller | File and Print Server | Database Server | Web server | RAS Server | Workstation |
|---|---|---|---|---|---|---|
| Logon and Logoff | Select Failure. | Select Failure. | Do not select. | Select Failure. | Do not select. | Do not select. |
| File and Object Access | Select Failure. | Select Failure. | Do not select. | Select Failure. | Do not select. | Do not select. |
| Use of User Rights | Select Success. Select Failure. | Select Success. Select Failure. | Do not select. Do not select. | Do not select. Do not select. | Do not select. Do not select. | Do not select. Do not select. |
| User and Group Management | Select Success Select Failure. | Select Success. Select Failure. | Do not select. Do not select. | Do not select. Do not select. | Do not select. Do not select. | Do not select. Do not select. |
| Security Policy Changes | Select Failure. | Select Failure. | Select Failure. | Select Success. Select Failure. | Do not select. | Do not select. |
| Restart, Shutdown, and System | Select Success. Select Failure. | Select Success. Select Failure. | Select Success. Select Failure. | Select Success. Select Failure. | Select Success. Select Failure. | Do not select. Do not select. |
| Process Tracking | Do not select. | Do not select. | Do not select. | Do not select. | Do not select. | Do not select. |

### Registry Auditing (an Advanced Option, Not a Baseline) Implemented on HKLM\Software, HKLM\System, and HKCR

| Feature | Domain Controller | File and Print Server | Database Server | Web server | RAS Server | Workstation |
|---|---|---|---|---|---|---|
| Query Value | Do not select. | Do not select. | Do not select. | Do not select. | Do not select. | Do not select. |
| Set Value | Select Success. Select Failure. | Select Success. Select Failure. | Select Success. Select Failure. | Select Success. Select Failure. | Select Success. Select Failure. | Select Success. Select Failure. |

*(continued)*

*(continued)*

| Feature | Domain Controller | File and Print Server | Database Server | Web Server | RAS Server | Workstation |
|---|---|---|---|---|---|---|
| Create Subkey | Select Success. | Select Success. | Select Success. | Select Success. | Select Success. | Select Success. |
| | Select Failure. | Select Failure. | Select Failure. | Select Failure. | Select Failure | Select Failure. |
| Enumerate Subkeys | Do not select. | Do not select. | Do not select. | Do not select. | Do not select. | Do not select. |
| Notify | Do not select. | Do not select. | Do not select. | Do not select. | Do not select. | Do not select. |
| Create Link | Select Success. | Select Success. | Select Success. | Select Success. | Select Success. | Select Success. |
| | Select Failure. | Select Failure. | Select Failure. | Select Failure. | Select Failure. | Select Failure. |
| Delete | Select Success. | Select Success. | Select Success | Select Success. | Select Success. | Select Success. |
| | Select Failure. | Select Failure. | Select Failure. | Select Failure. | Select Failure. | Select Failure. |
| Write DAC | Select Success. | Select Success. | Select Success. | Select Success. | Select Success. | Select Success. |
| | Select Failure. | Select Failure. | Select Failure. | Select Failure. | Select Failure. | Select Failure. |
| Read Control | Do not select. | Do not select. | Do not select. | Do not select. | Do not select. | Do not select. |

### Event Viewer Log File Overwrite Policy

| | Domain Controller | File and Print Server | Database Server | Web Server | RAS Server | Workstation |
|---|---|---|---|---|---|---|
| Security Log | Overwrite events older that 14 days. | Overwrite events older that 14 days. | Overwrite events older that 14 days. | Overwrite events older that 14 days. | Overwrite events older that 14 days. | Overwrite events as necessary. |
| System Log | Overwrite events older that 14 days. | Overwrite events older that 14 days. | Overwrite events older that 14 days. | Overwrite events older that 14 days. | Overwrite events older that 14 days. | Overwrite events as necessary. |
| Application Log | Overwrite events as necessary. | Overwrite events as necessary. | Overwrite events as necessary. | Overwrite events as necessary. | Overwrite events as necessary. | Overwrite events as necessary. |

### Event Viewer Log File Size

| | Domain Controller | File and Print Server | Database Server | Web Server | RAS Server | Workstation |
|---|---|---|---|---|---|---|
| Security Log | 5–10 MB (large enough to contain 2 weeks of data) | 2–4 MB (large enough to contain 2 weeks of data) | 2–4 MB (large enough to contain 2 weeks of data) | 2–4 MB (large enough to contain 2 weeks of data) | 5–10 MB (large enough to contain 2 weeks of data) | 1024 KB |

*(continued)*

*(continued)*

| Feature | Domain Controller | File and Print Server | Database Server | Web server | RAS Server | Workstation |
|---|---|---|---|---|---|---|
| System Log | 1–2 MB | 1–2 MB | 1–2 MB | 1–2 MB | 1–2 MB | 1024 KB |
| Application Log | 1–2 MB | 1–2 MB | 1–2 MB | 1–2 MB | 1–2 MB | 1024 KB |

**Windows NT Services**

| Feature | Domain Controller | File and Print Server | Database Server | Web server | RAS Server | Workstation |
|---|---|---|---|---|---|---|
| Alerter | Running if sending alerts | Running if sending alerts | Running if sending alerts | Running if sending alerts | Stopped | Running only on machines that should receive the alerts |
| Computer Browser | No change | No change | No change | No change | No change | No change |
| Directory Replicator | Running if replicating directories. Use Replicator account. | Running if replicating directories. Use Replicator account. | Running if replicating directories. Use Replicator account. | Running if replicating directories. Use Replicator account. | Stopped | Stopped |
| Event Log | No change | No change | No change | No change | No change | No change |
| FTP Publishing Service | Do not use. | Do not use. | Do not use. | Do not use. | Do not use. | Do not use. |
| Messenger | Running if Alerter service is running | Running if Alerter service is running | Running if Alerter service is running | Running if Alerter service is running | Stopped | Running if Alerter service is running |
| Net Logon | Running | Running | Running | Running | Running | Running |
| Net Logon | No change | No change | No change | No change | No change | No change |
| Network DDE | No change | No change | No change | No change | No change | No change |
| DDE DSDM | No change | No change | No change | No change | No change | No change |
| NT LM Security Support Provider | Running | Running | Running | Running | Running | Running |

*(continued)*

*(continued)*

| Feature | Domain Controller | File and Print Server | Database Server | Web Server | RAS Server | Workstation |
|---|---|---|---|---|---|---|
| Remote Procedure Call (RPC) Locator | No change | No change | No change | No change | No change | No change |
| Remote Procedure Call (RPC) Service | No change | No change | No change | No change | No change | No change |
| Schedule | Running if using scheduler. Use Scheduler account. | Running if using scheduler. Use Scheduler account. | Running if using scheduler. Use Scheduler account. | Running if using scheduler. Use Scheduler account. | Running if using scheduler. Use Scheduler account. | Stopped |
| Server | No change | No change | Stopped, if not required for database use | Stopped | Stopped | No change |
| Spooler | No change | No change | No change | No change | No change | No change |
| UPS | No change | No change | No change | No change | No change | No change |
| Workstation | No change | No change | No change | No change | No change | No change |
| **Alerts** | | | | | | |
| Errors Access Permissions | Select | N/A | Select | Select | Select | N/A |
| Errors Granted Access | Select | N/A | Select | Select | Select | N/A |
| Errors Logon | Select | N/A | Select | N/A | Select | N/A |
| Logon Total | Select | N/A | Select | N/A | Select | N/A |
| **RAS configuration** | | | | | | |
| Port Usage | N/A | N/A | N/A | Dial out and receive calls | N/A | N/A |

*(continued)*

*(continued)*

| Feature | Domain Controller | File and Print Server | Database Server | Web Server | RAS Server | Workstation |
|---|---|---|---|---|---|---|
| Administrator Access | N/A | N/A | N/A | N/A | Denied | N/A |
| Guest or Anonymous Access | N/A | N/A | N/A | N/A | Denied | N/A |
| Call Back | N/A | N/A | N/A | N/A | Set by caller | N/A |
| Network Access | N/A | N/A | N/A | N/A | Entire network | N/A |
| Network Protocols | N/A | N/A | N/A | N/A | TCP/IP | N/A |
| TCP/IP | N/A | N/A | N/A | N/A | Assign IP addresses | N/A |
| Encryption | N/A | N/A | N/A | N/A | Requires Microsoft encrypted authentication | N/A |

**Auditing**

| Auditing | N/A | N/A | N/A | N/A | Enabled | N/A |
|---|---|---|---|---|---|---|

The following table provides baseline permissions to be implemented on critical directories and files.

| File and Directory Permissions | Recommendations |
|---|---|
| \ (Root on an NTFS volume) | Administrators: Full Control<br>Server Operators: Change<br>Everyone: Read<br>CREATOR OWNER: Full Control<br>SYSTEM: Full Control |
| \WINNT\ | Administrators: Full Control<br>Server Operators: Change<br>Everyone: Read<br>CREATOR OWNER: Full Control<br>SYSTEM: Full Control |
| \WINNT\SYSTEM32 | Administrators: Full Control<br>Server Operators: Change<br>Everyone: Read |

*(continued)*

*(continued)*

| File and Directory Permissions | Recommendations |
| --- | --- |
| \WINNT\SYSTEM32\CONFIG | CREATOR OWNER: Full Control<br>SYSTEM: Full Control<br>Administrators: Full Control<br>Everyone: List |
| \WINNT\SYSTEM32\DRIVERS | CREATOR OWNER: Full Control<br>SYSTEM: Full Control<br>Administrators: Full Control<br>Server Operators: Full Control<br>Everyone: Read |
| \WINNT\SYSTEM32\SPOOL | CREATOR OWNER: Full Control<br>SYSTEM: Full Control<br>Administrators: Full Control<br>Server Operators: Full Control<br>Print Operators: Full Control<br>Everyone: Read |
| \WINNT\SYSTEM32\REPL | CREATOR OWNER: Full Control<br>SYSTEM: Full Control<br>Administrators: Full Control<br>Server Operators: Full Control<br>Everyone: Read |
| \WINNT\SYSTEM32\REPL\IMPORT | CREATOR OWNER: Full Control<br>SYSTEM: Full Control<br>Administrators: Full Control<br>Server Operators: Change<br>Everyone: Read |
| \WINNT\SYSTEM32\REPL\EXPORT | CREATOR OWNER: Full Control<br>Replicator: Change<br>NETWORK: No Access<br>SYSTEM: Full Control<br>Administrators: Full Control<br>Server Operators: Change |
| \WINNT\REPAIR | CREATOR OWNER: Full Control<br>Replicator: Read<br>SYSTEM: Full Control<br>Administrators: Full Control |

The following section provides baseline permissions to be implemented on critical Registry Keys and Hives.

| Registry Key Permissions | Recommendations |
| --- | --- |
| HKLM\System\CurrentControlSet\Control\SecurePipeServers\winreg | Add this key to prevent remote Registry editing.<br><br>Administrators: Full Control |
| HKLM\SOFTWARE\Microsoft\Windows\CurrentVersion\Run<br><br>And all files listed in the Run key should have the Everyone: Read permission. | Everyone: Special (Query Value, Enumerate Subkeys, Notify, and Read Control) |
| **_RunOnce_**<br>HKLM\SOFTWARE\Microsoft\Windows\CurrentVersion\RunOnce | Everyone: Special (Query Value, Enumerate Subkeys, Notify, and Read Control) |
| **_Shut Down without Logging On_**<br>HKLM\SOFTWARE\Microsoft\WindowsNT\CurrentVersion\Winlogon\ShutdownWithoutLogon | 0 |
| **_Disable Floppy Drive_**<br>HKLM\SOFTWARE\Microsoft\WindowsNT\CurrentVersion\Winlogon\AllocateFloppies | 1 |
| **_Disable CD-ROM_**<br>HKLM\SOFTWARE\Microsoft\WindowsNT\CurrentVersion\Winlogon\AllocateCDROMS | 1 |
| **_Automatic Logon_**<br>HKLM\SOFTWARE\Microsoft\WindowsNT\CurrentVersion\Winlogon\AutoAdminLogon | 0 |
| **_Do Not Display Last User to Log In_**<br>HKLM\SOFTWARE\Microsoft\WindowsNT\CurrentVersion\Winlogon\DontDisplayLastUserName | 1 |
| **_Enable Auditing of Rights_**<br>HKLM\SYSTEM\CurrentControlSet\Control\LSA\ FullPrivilegeAuditing | 1 |
| **_Password Filtering_**<br>HKLM\SYSTEM\CurrentControlSet\Control\LSA\ | Delete FPNWCLNT PASSFILT. |
| **_Schedule Service_**<br>HKLM\SYSTEM\CurrentControlSet\Control\LSA\SubmitControl | 0 |

*(continued)*

*(continued)*

| Registry Key Permissions | Recommendations |
|---|---|
| ***Disable Autorun***<br>HKLM\SYSTEM\CurrentControlSet\Services\<br>CDROM\Autorun | 0 |
| ***Remote Access Auditing***<br>HKLM\SYSTEM\CurrentControlSet\Services\<br>RemoteAccess\Parameters | 1 |

### Other Registry Keys

| | |
|---|---|
| HKEY_LOCAL_MACHINE\SOFTWARE\MICROSOFT<br>\RPC (and all subkeys)<br>\WindowsNT\CurrentVersion\ <br>\WindowsNT\CurrentVersion\AeDebug<br>\WindowsNT\CurrentVersion\Compatibility<br>\WindowsNT\CurrentVersion\Drivers<br>\WindowsNT\CurrentVersion\Embedding<br>\WindowsNT\CurrentVersion\Fonts<br>\WindowsNT\CurrentVersion\FontSubstitutes<br>\WindowsNT\CurrentVersion\GRE_Initialize<br>\WindowsNT\CurrentVersion\MCI<br>\WindowsNT\CurrentVersion\MCIExtensions<br>\WindowsNT\CurrentVersion\Port (and all subkeys)<br>\WindowsNT\CurrentVersion\ProfileList<br>\WindowsNT\CurrentVersion\ <br>Windows3.1MigrationStatus<br>\WindowsNT\CurrentVersion\WOW (and all subkeys)<br>\WindowsNT\CurrentVersion\Winlogon | Everyone should be granted Query Value, Enumerate Subkeys, Notify, and Read Control access. |
| HKEY_CLASSES_ROOT (and all subkeys) | Everyone should be granted Query Value, Enumerate Subkeys, Notify, and Read Control access. |
| HKEY_LOCAL_MACHINE\\SYSTEM<br>\CurrentControlSet\Control\SessionManager<br>\Environment | |

| Miscellaneous Registry Settings | Recommendations |
|---|---|
| **Legal Notice**<br>HKLM\Software\Microsoft\WindowsNT\<br>CurrentVersion\Winlogon\LegalNoticeCaption,<br>and HKLM\Software\Microsoft\WindowsNT\<br>CurrentVersion\Winlogon\LegalNoticeText | "Legal Notice" or "Warning" or other acceptable heading, and approved message |

# Appendix B
# Service Pack 3 Features and Enhancements

This appendix lists the features and enhancements provided with Service Pack 3 that either improve security features within Windows NT or fix any security problems that may have existed. This appendix is not meant to be a comprehensive discussion on the features, but only a security summary.

## CryptoAPI 2.0

The CryptoAPI, version 2.0, enables developers to use cryptographic and certificate functions inside applications. Version 2 includes cryptographic as well as certificate-based functionality that can be integrated into applications. It supports current standards such as X.509 v.3. certificate formats, DES and RSA algorithms, and extended key lengths for popular cipher functions such as RC2 and RC4.

## Server Message Block Signing

The update of the *Server Message Block (SMB)* authentication protocol, also known as *Common Internet File System (CIFS)* file sharing protocol, has two major security improvements:

- Mutual authentication, preventing the so-called "man-in-the-middle" attack
- Message authentication, preventing active message attacks in which messages are modified between the client and the server

The SMB-signing mechanism places a digital signature into each SMB for verification by both the client and server.

## Password Filtering

A password filter (PASSFILT.DLL) included in Service Pack 3 enables administrators to increase password strength. The password policy, when implemented appropriately, is as follows:

- Passwords must be at least six characters long.
- Passwords cannot contain the user name or any part of the user's full name.
- Passwords must contain characters from at least three of the following four classes: English uppercase, English lowercase, digits (0–9), and non-alphanumeric characters.

To enable the filter, the password filtering mechanism must be installed on both the primary and backup domain controller, and a Registry key must be added to each of the machines.

## Restricting Anonymous Access

When Service Pack 3 is installed, the ability for anonymous users to list domain user names and enumerate hidden- and public-share names through the NULL credential logon, can be restricted. To enable the restriction, a change must be made in the Registry.

In addition, anonymous access over the network to the Registry can be restricted. Remote access to the Registry is restricted to administrators. Finally, the Everyone group has been replaced with Authenticated Users, containing only those users who successfully authenticate to a domain controller within the domain or from a trusted domain.

## Unencrypted Passwords No Longer Sent by Default

Service Pack 3 provides the ability to prevent user authentication on SMB-enabled Windows NT servers with unencrypted passwords. By default, connections to SMB servers running Windows NT with unencrypted passwords are refused.

## Strong Encryption of Password Information

Service Pack 3 provides the option to further enhance the security of the Security Account Manager (SAM) by encrypting the information stored in the SAM database. The purpose of this feature is to prevent members of the Administrators group from reading encrypted passwords in the Registry on both the primary and backup domain controllers. Each machine can have its own unique key. To enable this option, Administrators must create a 128-bit cryptographic system key using the SYSKEY.EXE utility. This key will be used to encrypt the encrypted password; in addition, it is required to boot the system. The system key can be protected in three ways:

- Use of a machine-generated random key as System Key that is stored on the local system using a difficult obfuscation method.
- Use of a machine-generated random key stored on a diskette. This diskette is required to start the system.
- Use of a chosen password to obtain the system key. Every time the system is booted, the administrator must enter the password to start the system.

The first two methods are the most secure and offer the strongest protection, because the key is not stored on the system.

## 128-bit Support for Networking Components

The North American version of Service Pack 3 automatically enables the following networking components to use 128-bit encryption for securing network connections:

- **Remote Access Server.** RAS connections between NT workstation and server will use a 128-bit key to encrypt data.
- **Secure Socket Layer.** Internet and Intranet connections using the SSL protocol will be able to use 128-bit encryption for ensuring confidentiality, integrity, and, optionally, authentication.
- **Secure Remote Procedure Call.** Any application requesting secure RPC will automatically use 128-bit encryption.
- **Remote Access Service PPP CHAP MD5 Authenticator Support.** Service Pack 3 provides the option for limited PPP MD5-CHAP authenticator support for the Remote Access Server. This option could be useful in small user environments to provide secure PPP non-RAS-based dial-in access. A separate MD5 account database is stored in the Remote Access Server's Registry. Integration into the domain user database is planned in a later release. Creating a new Registry key for the MD5-CHAP authenticator enables this option.

# Appendix C
# Option Pack

This appendix lists the Option Pack features. It is not meant to be a comprehensive discussion on the features and their implementation, but only a brief summary of any potential security implications that administrators need to be aware of if they choose to implement the feature.

## Internet Information Server (IIS) 4.0

Provides core, as well as expanded, Internet services. Internet Information Server (IIS), version 4.0, includes the following fundamental services: World Wide Web, FTP, and Gopher. Many of the following components of Option Pack are designed to support and enhance the core Internet services, which are provided by IIS. Besides providing Internet service, IIS also enables the remote administration of IIS and Windows NT through a web browser.

Installation of IIS should only be performed after careful planning and preparation. Furthermore, IIS should only be installed on a dedicated machine and rarely, if ever, installed on a company's PDC.

## Microsoft Transaction Server (MTS) 2.0

Microsoft Transaction Server (MTS), version 2.0, is designed for the development and management of Internet workflow applications. Applications supported by MTS may use a variety of languages, including scripts, CGI, Java, and Active X controls. MTS is designed specifically to handle applications delivered using an Internet-type model. As with all Internet-based applications, steps should be taken to secure the integrity of the server and to prevent inappropriate access from Internet users.

## Index Server 2.0

The Index Server, version 2.0, catalogues the contents of an entire web site to enable the quick and effective searching of the web site by end-users. Because the Index Server does not change the actual content of the web site, its security implications are minimized.

## Certificate Server 1.0

The Certificate Server, version 1.0, handles the administration of digital certificates for a company's Intranet or Internet. Certification Server supports SSL and PCT for the encryption of data between a web server and a browser. Furthermore, digital certificates can be used to establish identity when a user authenticates to a web server. If remote administration of the IIS server or Windows NT server through a web browser is planned, it is imperative that the Certificate Server be used to verify identity and to encrypt the communication.

## Data Access Components 1.5

Data Access Components, version 1.5, are components that can be used by MTS and IIS to provide integrated connectivity to a database from a web browser or Internet application. Care should be taken to ensure that database controls and authentication are not bypassed by the Data Access Components.

## Site Server Express 2.0

Site Server Express, version 2.0, can be utilized to provide efficient management capabilities for a web site. Site Server allows you to access a map, a web site, troubleshoot, post content, and collect and analyze web server logs from various sites. Site Server should be restricted in use to only those who need to manage and administer the company's web sites.

## Message Queue (MSMQ) 1.0

Message Queue (MSMQ), version 1.0, allows various Microsoft applications to communicate with one another. Specifically, it allows various Internet-based applications to communicate with Windows-based applications or services, and vice-versa. This area is currently being developed by Microsoft technology, and as such, the security implications are not yet clearly defined. However, any communication channel, beyond that defined by the standard Internet protocol, can pose a serious risk to overall system security.

## Internet Connection Services 1.0

Internet Connection Services, version 1.0, allows remote connections to a corporate network, either through dial-in, Internet access, or a VPN-type solution. The Internet Connection Service authenticates users using the RADIUS standard, allows administrators to specify the level of network access and types of services allowed for a particular connection, and can track information relating to each connection (such as services used, connection time, site visited, and so on). As these services are a form of remote network access, they should be treated with the same security considerations.

## Microsoft Management Console (MMC)

The Management Console (MMC) is a newly developing platform for the development and management of a user console (that is, desktop services and operations specific to each user). Many of the current Option Pack components, including IIS and MTS, use MMC to manage their operation. Microsoft plans to integrate all BackOffice products, as well as Windows NT Server itself, into the MMC model.

# Appendix D
# Windows NT Commands

The following table lists most of the Windows NT commands that may have security implications. Security implications indicate that the use of these commands may provide hackers a means of thwarting system security. We have described potential security implications but this does not mean that the command is a security risk and needs to be removed. Administrators should use this table to review the commands and their potential security implications as a guideline. This table is not meant to be a comprehensive discussion on the commands and their implementation, but only a brief summary to be used as a guideline.

| Command | Description |
|---------|-------------|
| ARP | Displays and modifies the IP-to-physical address translation tables used by the address resolution protocol (ARP). This command is available only if the TCP/IP protocol has been installed. ARP tables are extremely sensitive resources and should only be viewed and modified by authorized employees. |
| AT | Schedules commands and programs to run on a computer at a specified time and date. The Schedule service must be running to use the AT command. |
| | The capability of scheduling commands is a relatively powerful privilege. It should only be given to necessary users, and auditing of scheduled jobs should be turned on. |
| CACLS | Displays or modifies a file's access control list (ACL). |
| | Modification of ACLs is another privilege that is extremely sensitive. Permissions on files should be set to prevent unauthorized users from modifying them. |
| CMD.EXE | Starts a new instance of the Windows NT command interpreter, CMD.EXE. A command interpreter is a program that displays the command prompt at which you type commands. |
| | Users may be able to access the command prompt and execute command utilities. |
| CONVERT | Converts FAT volumes to NTFS. If the CONVERT command cannot lock the drive, it will offer to convert it the next time the computer reboots. |

*(continued)*

*(continued)*

| Command | Description |
|---------|-------------|
|  | Anytime you convert a drive there may be security implications. Data can be corrupted, deleted, destroyed, or modified. Care should be taken when using CONVERT. |
| DATE | Displays the date or allows you to change the date from your terminal or from a batch program. |
|  | Changing the system date is a sensitive privilege. By changing the date, modification times on files and system times on log records become useless. Systems administrators should only make date changes. |
| DEBUG | Allows you to test and debug MS-DOS executable files. |
|  | This command is extremely useful for developers, but unauthorized users can use it to test for weaknesses in programs. The DEBUG command should not be available to a production machine. And administrators should manage the use of the command. |
| FINGER | Displays information about a user on a specified system running the Finger service. Output varies based on the remote system. This command is available only if the TCP/IP protocol has been installed. |
|  | Unauthorized users could use this command to find information about users on a system. The command should be limited to authorized employees. |
| FORMAT | Formats the disk in the specified drive to accept Windows NT files. You must be a member of the Administrators group to format a hard drive. |
|  | Because a user has to have Administrator rights to run this command, security is not a major issue. Firms should remember, however, that formatting disks erases all data so use of the command might be limited to certain administrators. |
| FTP | Transfers files to and from a computer running an FTP server service. The FTP command can be used interactively. This command is available only if the TCP/IP protocol has been installed. |
|  | Transferring files between machines can be a sensitive event, especially if anonymous connections are allowed. In general, unless necessary, the service should be disabled. |
| IPCONFIG | Displays all current TCP/IP network configuration values. This diagnostic command is of particular use on systems running DHCP, allowing users to determine which TCP/IP configuration values have been configured by DHCP. |
|  | IPCONFIG provides TCP/IP information that can readily be used by intruders to piece together details about systems and networks. Only authorized individuals should run this command. |
| IPXROUTE | Displays and modifies information about the routing tables used by the IPX protocol. The command has different options for IPX routing and for source routing. Separate all options with spaces. |

*(continued)*

*(continued)*

| Command | Description |
|---|---|
| | Normal users should not perform an update of routing rules. By modifying these rules, malicious traffic may be allowed access to the system. Administrators should be the only users who can update routing settings. |
| NBTSTAT | Displays protocol statistics and current TCP/IP connections using NBT (NetBIOS over TCP/IP). This diagnostic command is available only if the TCP/IP protocol has been installed. |
| | NBTSTAT provides TCP/IP information that can readily be used by intruders to piece together details about systems and networks. Only authorized individuals should run this command. |
| NET ACCOUNTS | Updates the User Account Database and modifies password and logon requirements for all accounts. The Net Logon service must be running on the computer for which you want to change account parameters. |
| | Account policies are extremely sensitive resources and should only be modified by appropriate personnel in your corporation. |
| NET COMPUTER | Adds or deletes computers from a domain database. This command is available only on computers running Windows NT Server. |
| | Modifying the domain structure is an extremely sensitive action and should only be performed by appropriate personnel in your corporation. |
| NET CONFIG | Displays the configurable services that are running, or displays and changes settings for a service. |
| | Service configurations are sensitive settings that should only be modified by appropriate personnel in your corporation. |
| NET CONTINUE | Reactivates suspended services. |
| | Reactivating suspended services might be a sensitive event, depending on the service. Only appropriate personnel in your corporation should control this command. |
| NET FILE | Displays the names of all open shared files on a server and the number of file locks, if any, on each file. This command also closes individual shared files and removes file locks. |
| | Shares and file locks are sensitive resources that should only be managed by appropriate personnel in your corporation. |
| NET GROUP | Adds, displays, or modifies global groups on Windows NT Server domains. This command is available for use only on Windows NT Server domains. |
| | Groups are extremely sensitive resources that should only be modified by appropriate personnel in your corporation. |
| NET LOCALGROUP | Adds, displays, or modifies local groups. |
| | Groups are extremely sensitive resources that should only be modified by appropriate personnel in your corporation. |

*(continued)*

*(continued)*

| Command | Description |
| --- | --- |
| NET NAME | Adds or deletes a messaging name (sometimes called an alias), or displays the list of names for which the computer will accept messages. The Messenger service must be running to use net name.<br><br>Only appropriate personnel in your corporation should modify aliases for computers. |
| NET PAUSE | Pauses running services.<br><br>Services are extremely sensitive resources and should only be modified by appropriate personnel in your corporation. |
| NET SEND | Sends messages to other users, computers, or messaging names on the network. The Messenger service must be running to receive messages.<br><br>Although this command is a powerful messaging tool, Net Send can be used to inundate a machine with messages or send unauthorized messages. Use of this command should be limited to necessary employees. |
| NET SESSION | Lists or disconnects the sessions between a local computer and the clients connected to it.<br><br>Only Administrators should perform managing computer sessions. |
| NET SHARE | Creates, deletes, or displays shared resources.<br><br>The ability to share resources is very powerful and should only be reserved for authorized employees. |
| NET START | Starts a service, or displays a list of started services. Service names of two or more words, such as Net Logon or Computer Browser, must be enclosed in quotation marks.<br><br>Services are extremely sensitive resources and only Administrators should manage them. |
| NET STATISTICS | Displays the Statistics Log for the local workstation or server service.<br><br>The command should be limited to authorized employees. |
| NET STOP | Stops a Windows NT network service.<br><br>Services are extremely sensitive resources and could be used as a Denial of Service attack. Only Administrators should manage them. |
| NET TIME | Synchronizes the computer's clock with that of another computer or domain. Used without the /set option, displays the time for another computer or domain.<br><br>Changing the system time is a sensitive privilege. By changing the time, modification times on files and system times on log records become useless. Only system administrators should perform time changes. |
| NET USE | Connects a computer to or disconnects a computer from a shared resource, or displays information about computer connections. The command also controls persistent net connections.<br><br>The ability to share resources is very powerful and should only be reserved for authorized employees. |

*(continued)*

*(continued)*

| Command | Description |
| --- | --- |
| NET USER | Adds or modifies user accounts or displays user-account information. |
| | Account policies are extremely sensitive resources and should only be modified by administrators. |
| NET VIEW | Displays a list of domains, a list of computers, or the resources being shared by the specified computer. |
| | The command should be limited to authorized employees. |
| NETSTAT | Displays protocol statistics and current TCP/IP network connections. This command is available only if the TCP/IP protocol has been installed. |
| | Netstat provides TCP/IP information that can readily be used by intruders to piece together details about systems and networks. Only authorized individuals should run this command. |
| NSLOOKUP | This diagnostic tool displays information from Domain Name System (DNS) name servers. NSLOOKUP is available only if the TCP/IP protocol has been installed. |
| | DNS provides information about systems that can readily be used by intruders to piece together details of systems and networks. Only authorized individuals should run this command. |
| PING | Verifies connections to a remote computer(s). This command is available only if the TCP/IP protocol has been installed. |
| | PING can be used to launch systematic attacks against machines. The use of this command should be limited to authorized individuals. |
| PORTUAS | Merges a LAN Manager 2.x User Account Database into an existing Windows NT User Account Database. |
| | Only administrators should perform operations on user accounts. Merging the databases is a sensitive action and should be seriously considered before being executed. |
| RCP | Copies files between a Window NT computer and a system running RSHD, the remote shell daemon. This connectivity command can also be used for third-party transfer to copy files between two computers running RSHD when the command is issued from a Windows NT computer. The RSHD daemon is available on UNIX computers, but not on Windows NT, so the Windows NT computer can only participate as the system from which the commands are issued. The remote computer must also provide the RCP utility in addition by running RSHD. |
| | Remote commands are security-sensitive because the programs they use often do not require authentication. These commands, unless necessary, should be disabled. |
| REXEC | Runs commands on remote computers running the REXEC service. REXEC authenticates the user name on the remote computer before executing the specified command. This command is available only if the TCP/IP protocol has been installed. |

*(continued)*

(continued)

| Command | Description |
|---|---|
| | Remote commands are security-sensitive because the programs they use often do not require authentication. These commands, unless necessary, should be disabled. |
| ROUTE | Manipulates network routing tables. This command is available only if the TCP/IP protocol has been installed. |
| | Routing tables are extremely sensitive resources. By manipulating them, a user could allow malicious traffic to access the system. Only authorized individuals should use this command. |
| RSH | Runs commands on remote computers running the RSH service. This command is available only if the TCP/IP protocol has been installed. |
| | Remote commands are security-sensitive because the programs they use often do not require authentication. These commands, unless necessary, should be disabled. |
| TIME | Displays the system time or sets your computer's internal clock. |
| | Similar to Date: Changing the system time is a sensitive privilege. By changing the time, modification times on files and system times on log records become useless. Only systems administrators should perform time changes. |
| TFTP | Transfers files to and from a remote computer running the TFTP service. This command is available only if the TCP/IP protocol has been installed. |
| | Depending on the implementation, TFTP might be a security-sensitive application. In many cases, no authentication is required so intruders have an open door to systems. Unless necessary, the command should be disabled. |
| TRACERT | Determines the route taken to a destination by sending Internet Control Message Protocol (ICMP) echo packets with varying Time-to-Live (TTL) values to the destination. Each router along the path is required to decrement the TTL on a packet by at least 1 before forwarding it, so the TTL is effectively a hop count. When the TTL on a packet reaches 0, the router is supposed to send back an ICMP Time Exceeded message to the source system. TRACERT, a diagnostic utility, determines the route by sending the first echo packet with a TTL of 1 and incrementing the TTL by 1 on each subsequent transmission until the target responds or the maximum TTL is reached. The route is determined by examining the ICMP Time Exceeded messages sent back by intermediate routers. Note that some routers silently drop packets with expired TTLs and will be invisible to TRACERT. |
| | TRACERT gives extremely detailed information about network topology, which intruders can use to launch appropriate attacks. Only authorized individuals should use this command. |

# Appendix E
# Resource Kit Security Programs

The following table lists most of the Windows NT Resource Kit utilities that may have security considerations. Security considerations indicate that the use of these commands may facilitate and deter system security in the Windows NT environment. This table is not meant to be a comprehensive discussion on the utilities and their implementation, but only a brief summary to be used as a guideline.

| Tool | Description |
| --- | --- |
| Add Users to a Group (USERTOGRP.EXE) | Adds users to a local or global group using a user-specified text file. If the group does not exist, the utility will create it. If adding to a local group, the command will search trusted domains to find it. If adding to a global group, trusted domains will not be searched. |
| AddUsers (ADDUSERS.EXE) | Creates, writes, and deletes user accounts using a comma-delimited input file. |
| Applications as a Service Utility (SVRANY.EXE) | Allows any application to run as a service under a specified user account. It allows an application to continue running when one user has logged off and another has logged on, and it allows server applications to service requests even when nobody is logged on the server. |
| AuditPol (AUDITPOL.EXE) | Allows a user to modify audit policies for the local machine or remote machine. The user must have administrator privileges on the specified machine. |
| | Auditing is a critical portion of security controls on a system, and changing the way files, directories, and so on are audited can render the log file useless if the changes are not well-configured. |
| AutoExNT Service (AUTOEXNT.EXE) | Allows the batch file AUTOEXNT.BAT to run at boot time without logging on the machine. |

*(continued)*

*(continued)*

| Tool | Description |
|---|---|
| | The batch file includes an interactive option, which allows the users to see the processes started. |
| Command Prompt Here (CMDHERE.EXE) | When an object in Explorer is right-clicked, this allows the creation of a command prompt with that object's path. |
| Command Scheduler (WINAT.EXE) | Schedules commands and programs to run on a computer at a specified time and date. This is an updated version of the AT command. The Schedule service must be running to use this utility. |
| Command Line Service Controller (NETSVC.EXE) | This utility is used on a server only. It is used to remotely start, stop, and query services. |
| Crystal Reports Event Log Viewer (CRW.EXE) | This utility is used on a server only. Allows viewing, saving, and publishing of Windows NT Event Logs. These reports are created in an easy-to-read format and can be saved for future reference. |
| Disk Mapper (DISKMAP.EXE) | Produces a report on the configuration of the hard disk specified. It includes information about the Registry disk characteristics, and it displays data about all the partitions and logical drives defined on the disk. |
| DiskProbe (DISKPROBE.EXE) | Allows edit of hard disks on a sector-by-sector basis. Only local administrators may use the command to modify the physical hard drive. |
| | Although only administrators can use this command, physically modifying hard disks is a sensitive operation and should be performed only after all the consequences have been determined and all recovery options have been evaluated to ensure the integrity of the data on the hard disk. |
| Domain Monitor (DOMMON.EXE) | Displays the domain controller name and the list of trusted domains. Also monitors the status of servers on the domain, secure channels to the domain controller, and secure channels to trusted domain controllers. |
| Dump Event Log (DUMPEL.EXE) | Dumps the Event Log contents for a system into a tab-separated text file. When running this command there is the issue of |

*(continued)*

*(continued)*

| Tool | Description |
|---|---|
| | who has permissions to the file that is created. The utility can be used, but precautions must be taken to assign appropriate permissions to the output file. |
| Enumerating Remote Access Users (RASUSERS.EXE) | This utility is used on servers only. Lists all users who have permission to dial into the network via an RAS server. |
| | An unauthorized user might use this list of users to conduct a test of dial-in controls. Part of the security of RAS lies in the secrecy of which users can access RAS. This utility should be restricted to administrative users. |
| Event Logging Utility (LOGEVENT.EXE) | Allows a user to send entries to the Event Log on a local or remote computer using the command prompt or a batch file. |
| | Writing entries to the Event Log is privileged action. If too many records are added, the log could get overloaded and begin to overwrite legitimate records. Use of this utility should be restricted to administrative users. |
| File Copy with Security (SCOPY.EXE) | Copies files with security attributes intact. The Backup Files and Folders user right is required. This is a powerful tool for keeping security permissions intact while copying or backing up files. |
| Find Group (FINDGRP.EXE) | Lists all direct and indirect group memberships for a specified user in a domain. Administrative access is *not* required. |
| FT Registry Information Editor (FTEDIT.EXE) | Allows a user to create, edit, and delete fault tolerance settings for disk drives and partitions on local and remote computers. To edit or delete settings, the user must have permissions to write to the SYSTEM hive of the Registry. These fault tolerance settings are critical for ensuring disk drive integrity and availability. |
| GetMAC (GETMAC.EXE) | Obtains MAC (Ethernet) layer address and binding order for the system or across a network. This is helpful for figuring out what protocols are in use and what MAC address might need to be entered as a target field in a network sniffer. |

*(continued)*

*(continued)*

| Tool | Description |
| --- | --- |
| Global Groups (GLOBAL.EXE) | Displays members of global groups on remote servers or domains. |
| Graphical IPConfig Utility (WNTIPCFG.EXE) | Allows management of IP address and IP information for systems running the TCP/IP protocol. |
| Group Copy (GRPCPY.EXE) | This utility is used on servers only. Enables a user to copy the usernames in an existing group to another group that exists in the same or another domain or on a Windows NT member server. Users must at least have Account Operator privileges to use this utility. |
| KiXtart 95 (KIX32.EXE) | A logon script processor and enhanced batch language for NT. Scripts can be written to display information, set environment variables, start programs, connect to network drives, read or edit the Registry, and change the current drive and directory. |
| KiXtart Group Utility (KIXGRP.EXE) | Used with KIX32.EXE, it allows logon scripts to process parameters conditionally based on users' group memberships. The utility reads the Registry to determine all group memberships. |
| LeakyApp (LEAKYAPP.EXE) | A testing tool that appropriates memory to see how applications or the system run(s) in low-memory situations. The utility allocates all available memory to itself until it is stopped or reset. |
| Local Groups (LOCAL.EXE) | Displays members of local groups on remote servers or domains. |
| Lock Floppy Drives (FLOPLOCK.EXE) | Controls access to floppy drives on a system. On Windows NT Workstation, only administrators and power users can access the floppy drive if the service is started. On a Windows NT Server, only administrators can access the floppy drive if the service is started. |
| Logon and FAT File System Setting (REGKEY.EXE) | Can set several Registry settings, without manually editing the Registry, using a GUI. The settings that can be set, include: displaying the Shutdown button in the Logon dialog box, displaying the last user who logged on in the Logon dialog box, parsing AUTOEXEC.BAT for SET and PATH commands, setting the number of user profiles to cache, setting the default |

*(continued)*

*(continued)*

| Tool | Description |
| --- | --- |
| | background wallpaper, and allowing long filenames in FAT. |
| Near-Future Command Scheduler (SOON.EXE) | Schedules commands to run in the near future on either the local system or remote machines. The utility generates and executes the appropriate AT command. |
| Net Domains (NETDOM.EXE) | Allows administrators to manage domains from the command prompt. Available actions are: joining computers to domains, managing computer accounts for members, managing computer accounts for BDCs, establishing trust relationships, and managing resource domain computer accounts. |
| Net Watch (NETWATCH.EXE) | Displays which users are connected to shared folders, and allows a user to disconnect users and unshare folders. This utility can monitor multiple machines at the same time. To use the Net Watch utility, the Server service must be started and the user must be a member of the Administrators group. |
| NLMonitor (NLMON.EXE) | Used to list and test trust relationships. NLMonitor uses the Browser service to enumerate the lists so if the service is not functioning properly, incorrect results will be displayed. |
| NLTEST (NLTEST.EXE) | Performs administrative tasks including: forcing a user-account database into sync, getting a list of primary domain controllers (PDCs), forcing a shutdown, and querying and checking on the status of trust. |
| Windows NT Rights (NTRIGHTS.EXE) | Grants or revokes any Windows NT rights to or from users or groups. |
| Password Properties (PASSPROP.EXE) | Used to set two domain policy flags: whether passwords have to be complex and whether the Administrator account can be locked out. To satisfy password complexity, a user must choose a password of mixed case or one that contains numbers or symbols. If the Administrator account is locked out, then it can only be used to log on interactively to domain controllers. |
| Path Manager (PATHMAN.EXE) | Allows modification of the user path and the system path. Any user can modify his or her portion of the path (user path), |

*(continued)*

*(continued)*

| Tool | Description |
| --- | --- |
| | but a user needs administrator privileges to modify the system path. |
| PerfLog: Performance Data Log Service | Logs data from performance counters to either a tab- or comma-separated variable file. |
| Performance Monitor MIB Builder Tool (PERF2MIB.EXE) | Enables developers to create new ASN.1 syntax MIBs (Management Information Bases) for their applications, services, or devices that use Performance Monitor counters. Administrators can then track performance of these components by using any system-management program that supports SNMP. |
| Performance Data Logging Service and Configuration Tool (MONITOR.EXE) | Installs and controls the Data Logging service, which performs the same function as Performance Monitor Alert and Logging Facility. |
| Permission Copy (PERMCOPY.EXE) | Copies share-level permissions (ACLs) from one share to another. If copying from an administrative share to a target share, the target share's ACLs will not change. Note that copying permissions to an administrative share located on an x86 machine will cause SERVICES.EXE to crash. |
| Process and Thread Status (PSTAT.EXE) | Lists all running processes and threads, and displays their status. |
| Process Viewer (PVIEWER.EXE) | Displays information about a running process and allows you to stop (kill) processes. |
| Processes/Usernames List (PULIST.EXE) | Tracks processes running on local or remote computers. This utility can list the names and IDs of all processes running on one or more remote systems. When run on the local system, it will list the user associated with the process. |
| Remote Access Server List (RASLIST.EXE) | This utility is run on servers only. Displays RAS service announcements from the network. |
| Remote Command Service (RCMD.EXE) | This utility is run on servers only. It allows the execution of commands on a remote server. |
| REG (REG.EXE) | Allows a user to add, change, delete, list, and perform other operations on Registry entries. This utility can be run from the command prompt or a batch file. |

*(continued)*

*(continued)*

| Tool | Description |
| --- | --- |
| Registry Backup (REGBACK.EXE) | Allows backup of the Registry without using a tape drive. It also can back up more parts of the Registry than typical backup software products. |
| Regina REXX Scripting Language (REXX.EXE) | A full scripting language with Registry access, Event Log functions, and OLE automation support. |
| Registry Change by Script (REGINI.EXE) | Allows a user to add keys to the Registry using a batch file. |
| Registry Restoration (REGREST.EXE) | Restores Registry files from backup copies. The user must have the Backup Files and Folders user right to run this utility. |
| Remote Access Manager (\APPS\RASMGR\) | Allows management of RAS separately for each user. Actions include: display RAS server and port status, disconnect RAS sessions from any port, and enable or disable RAS privileges for any user. |
| Remote Console (RCLIENT.EXE) | Used to run a remote command-line session on another system. A CMD.EXE process is started on every client, and Remote Console takes full control of this process. It does not redirect input and output.

This utility, which is similar to Telnet, could pose a security risk. Running commands on a remote machine without proper authentication is a common problem with these types of utilities. |
| Remote Command Line (REMOTE.EXE) | Allows the execution of command-line programs on remote machines. This remote utility does no security authorization. Any machine with a remote client can connect to any machine with a remote server. |
| Remote Kill (RKILLSRV.EXE) | Allows a user to enumerate and kill processes on a remote machine. Killing a process remotely requires a user to be a member of the Administrator group. |
| Remote Shutdown (SHUTDOWN.EXE) | Allows a user to remotely shut down or reboot a computer running Windows NT. |
| Remote Shutdown GUI (SHUTGUI.EXE) | Same as SHUTDOWN.EXE but execution without parameters will present a GUI interface to the user. |
| Remote Share (RMTSHARE.EXE) | Allows authorized users to set up or delete shares remotely. |

*(continued)*

*(continued)*

| Tool | Description |
|---|---|
| Reset System File Permissions (FIXACLS.EXE) | Resets NTFS file and folder permissions to their default values. A user needs to be a member of the Administrator group, and needs the Backup Files and Folders user right to run this utility. |
| Security Power Toy (RSHXMENU) | Adds a Security menu to items right-clicked in Explorer. |
| Service List (SCLIST.EXE) | Shows currently running services, stopped services, or all services on a local or remote computer. |
| SECADD (SECADD.EXE) | Removes the Everyone group from the access control list (ACL) on a specified Registry key, or adds read permissions for a specified user. |
| Security Context Editor (SECEDIT.EXE) | Allows a user to modify security privileges of the logged-on users and running processes. It can also be used to list the security contexts that are in use. |
| Service Installation Wizard (SRVINSTW.EXE) | Method of installing and deleting services and device drivers. The user must have Administrator privileges to run this utility. |
| Share Directories User Interface (SHAREUI.EXE) | Configures properties of network shares for any local or remote computer. The user must have privileges to view and configure shares on a remote computer. A user must be a member of the Administrator group to run the utility. With ShareUI, administrators can configure directory sharing for remote computers from a single window, which is normally done on a per-share basis using the Server Manager. |
| Show ACLs (SHOWACLS.EXE) | Displays permissions on files and directories. This is another mechanism for displaying file and directory permissions through Explorer. |
| Show Disk (SHOWDISK.EXE) | Reads and displays the Registry subkey HKEY_LOCAL_MACHINE\SYSTEM\DISK. It displays information about each of the primary partitions and logical drives defined on the computer. It also identifies which of the primary partitions and logical drives are members of volume sets, stripe sets, mirror sets, and stripe sets with parity. |
| Show Groups (SHOWGRPS.EXE) | Displays the groups to which a user belongs. |

*(continued)*

*(continued)*

| Tool | Description |
|------|-------------|
| Show Members (SHOWMBRS.EXE) | Shows the usernames of members of a group. |
| SNMP Monitor (SNMPMON.EXE) | This utility is used on servers only. It can be used to create SNMP configuration files for monitoring and managing any SNMP MIB variables across any number of SNMP nodes. |
| SNMP Browser (SNMPUTIL.EXE) | Displays SNMP information from an SNMP host on the network. |
| Server Check (SRVCHECK.EXE) | Lists the nonhidden shares and enumerates the users on the ACLs for that share. |
| Server Information (SRVINFO.EXE) | This utility is used on servers only. Displays information about a remote server, including processes. |
| Switch User (SU.EXE) | Allows a process to run under an arbitrary user account. Based on the su (switch user) utility found on UNIX systems, it runs a new process in the security context of the specified user, given that the specified domain, username, and password are correct. The su service must be installed and enabled by the administrator before it can be used. |
| Substitute Access Control Information (SUBINACL.EXE) | Allows administrators to obtain security information on files, Registry keys, and services, and transfer this information from user to user, from local or global group to group, and from domain to domain. This utility is restricted to administrators. |
| Task Killing Utility (KILL.EXE) | Used to end one or more tasks or processes. The processes can be identified by their ID numbers, names, or window titles. Ending system-sensitive resources can cause system errors. |
| TCP/IP Remote Shell Service (RSHSVC.EXE) | Provides a command-line shell for remote users. Any computer with an RSH client can access this service, and there is no authentication in place. |
| Task List (TLIST.EXE) | Displays a list of tasks, or processes, currently running on the local computer— e.g., process ID number, process name, and title of window (when applicable). |
| TDI Tracing Utility (TDISHOW.EXE) | Allows individuals to collect and display the contents of packets being sent across |

*(continued)*

*(continued)*

| Tool | Description |
|------|-------------|
| | the Transport Driver Interface (TDI) layer. Use this utility only for troubleshooting purposes. |
| Telnet Server Beta (TELNETD.EXE) | Provides a terminal-emulation solution for running command-line utilities, scripts, and batch files from clients on a network, independently of a client's operating system. All network traffic between client and server is unencrypted and could be captured for analysis by an intruder. |
| User Stats (USRSTAT.EXE) | This utility is used on servers only. Displays the username, full name, and last logon date and time for each user in a given domain. |
| Web Administration of Microsoft Windows NT Server | Allows administration of Windows NT Server via web browsers. |
| Windows NT Auto Logon Setter (AUTOLOG.EXE) | Configures a Windows NT Workstation to log on as a specified user at boot time. No logon box is displayed; the specified user is automatically logged on. The logged on user cannot log off and allow another user to log on, unless AUTOLOG is disabled. |
| | This utility bypasses all authentication controls that exist in Windows NT. Anyone who turns on the computer has access to the machine and to any networks to which it is attached. Moreover, the password of the logged on user is stored in the Registry in plain text. |
| Windows NT C2 Configuration Manager (C2CONFIG.EXE) | Used to compare current system configurations with those needed for C2 compliance. Also, the utility allows configuration changes to be made. |
| Windows NT System Policy Editor (POLEDIT.EXE) | Sets administrative policies for a Windows NT system. |
| Command Line MSD (WINMSDPP.EXE) | Provides system configuration and status information. It reads the Registry and dumps this information to a text file named MSDRPT.TXT. The use of this utility is restricted to users with administrative privileges. The user must ensure however, that the permissions to the dump file restrict access to administrative users. |
| Extended CACLS (XCACLS.EXE) | Sets or modifies file-system security options or access control lists of files. It can be used to set appropriate file and directory permissions when installing a new system. |

# Glossary

## A

**Access Control Entries (ACE)** Specifies user or group account auditing and access permissions for a given object.

**Access Control List (ACL)** File and print servers check the Access Control List (ACL) of each resource before allowing a user to access a file or use a printer. If the user, or a group to which the user belongs, is not listed in the ACL, the user is not allowed to use the resource.

**access mask** Every ACE must have an access mask. An access mask tells the ACE which attributes are available for a particular object type. The ACE can then grant permissions based on that mask. For example, a file can set Read, Write, Execute, Delete, Take Ownership, and Change Permissions because an access mask defines these attributes. (See also **Access Control Entries**.)

**access methods** The rules governing the use of the physical network by various devices.

**account lockout** An NT security feature that can be set to lock out an account after a certain number of unsuccessful logon attempts. (Three bad attempts are common.) This feature prevents hackers from breaking into an account.

**account policies** Set from the User Manager application to change how passwords are used. Setting the account lockout policy helps to prevent the system from being hacked into.

**Administrator account** One of the two built-in NT user accounts. (See also **Guest account**.) The Administrator account man-ages the workstation's user accounts, policies, and resources. This account cannot be locked out or disabled. The Administrator account even has control over the files owned by other users.

**Alerter** Service used by the Server and other services. Alerter broadcasts the logged-on user name in the NetBIOS name table, which can be considered a security breach.

**alerts** Critical security controls that help perform real-time monitoring. Enabled by configuring the Performance Monitor.

**assets** Anything that is of value and needed for the operation of the corporation.

**auditing policies** An important component of the Effective Security Monitoring controls. Auditing measures the system against a predefined system setting to ensure that no changes have occurred.

**availability** Ensuring that information and vital services are accessible when required.

## B

**backup domain controllers (BDC)** After a domain has been created, the entire account database is mirrored on each BDC. The PDC keeps the information updated within five minutes by default. (See also **PDC**.)

**Bonk and Boink** Variations of the Teardrop attack. (See **Teardrop attack**.)

**Business Continuity Plan (BCP)** Plan for a corporation to continue the business processes needed for it to function after a disaster. A Business Continuity Plan would include or reference the Disaster Recovery Plan and build upon it. (See also **Disaster Recovery Plan**.)

## C

**C2** A security evaluation level assigned to a specific product, by the National Computer Security Center (NCSC), a division of the National Security Association (NSA), after a period of detailed product review and attestation. The C2 level of "trust" is one level that can be granted to an evaluated product. The defined levels of trust, in increasing levels of trust (or security), are D, C1, C2, B1, B2, B3, and A1. NT 3.5 with the Service Pack 3.0 has the C2 level of trust.

**Callback security** Security feature implemented within RAS. When a user is configured to use Callback and dials in to a RAS server, the server disconnects the session, and then calls the client back at a preset telephone number or at a number provided during the initial call.

**CIFS (Common Internet File Sharing)** An enhanced version of SMB services that is available for use over the Internet. (See also **SMB**.)

**Clipbook Viewer** Default service that supports the Clipbook Viewer application, allowing pages to be seen by remote Clipbooks.

**Computer Browser** Default service that maintains an up-to-date list of computers and provides the list to applications when requested. Provides the computer list displayed in the Select Computer and Select Domain dialog boxes; and in the main Server Manager window.

**confidentiality** The protection of information in the system so that unauthorized persons cannot access it.

**corporate security policy** Defines the assets of a corporation, risks to those assets, owners of the assets, and how to protect those assets. It includes creating security awareness among employees and having senior management support. Also defines the framework under which the entire corporation treats and reacts to attacks on its resources.

**corrective security controls** Used to correct security holes that have been exploited.

**Client Services for NetWare (CSNW)** One of the two installable network components, CSNW is the client redirector and NWLink is the IPX/SPX-compatible network transport protocol. (See also **NWLink**.)

**cryptography** See **public key cryptography, secret key cryptography,** and **symmetric cryptography.**

## D

**data striping** Process that allocates data evenly among the drives, improving reliability and access times. (See also **RAID**.)

**decision tree** A query-like structure that graphically represents the filter expression within the Network Monitor application. In a decision tree, statements are linked together by colored AND, OR, and NOT tabs. Combined, these statements specify the kinds of data the user wants to capture or display. (See also **filtering**.)

**denial of service attack** One of the most common security attacks on Windows NT, which attempts to prevent the use of a system either by using all available processor resources, memory resources, network resources, or by shutting down the system.

**detective security controls** Ascertain when security holes are in the process of being exploited.

**Dial-Up Networking (DUN)** Dialing-out service that is set up when RAS is installed as a service. DUN allows the user to connect to any dial-up server using the Point-to-Point protocol (PPP) as a transport mechanism allowing for TCP/IP, NetBEUI, or IPX/SPX network access over an analog modem, ISDN, or X.25 PAD devices.

**Dial-Up Networking Server** Allows Windows 98 to host a single dial-up network connection. Any client with PPP support can dial in using either IP, IPX, or NetBEUI as their connection protocol. Windows 98 can then act as a server sharing its files and printers just as it does on a LAN, or it can act as a gateway for an IPX or NetBEUI network.

**Directory Replication** An NT process utilizing the Directory Replicator service that makes an exact copy of a folder's contents and places it on another server.

**Directory Replicator** Default service that replicates directories and the files in the directories between computers.

**Disaster Recovery Plan (DRP)** Plan for recovery of necessary systems and data to support the core processes necessary to run the business.

**discretionary access** Access control when the person who created the file or folder is the owner and is responsible for securing those files and folders.

**domain** A group of computers containing domain controllers that share account information and have one centralized accounts database. The four domain models—single domain, complete trust, master domain, and multiple-master domain—represent various stages of growth and decentralization.

**domain controller** Serve two purposes in the NT environment: to authenticate users and to grant them access to other resources within the network. (See also **primary domain controller** and **backup domain controller**.)

# E

**Electronics Communications Privacy Act (ECPA)** Prevents the user from eavesdropping on the activities of an intruder, even if the user owns the system, unless the user posts a message to indicate that all activities are subject to being monitored.

**Emergency Repair Disk (ERD)** A disk that can be used to repair a Windows NT system. This disk can repair missing Windows NT files and restore the Registry to include disk configuration and security information back to the configuration the system had when the ERD was last updated.

**encrypted authentication** Methods for secure network transmission that include the simple Password Authentication Protocol (PAP), which permits clear-text passwords and the Shiva Password Authentication Protocol (SPAP) used by Windows NT workstations when connecting to a Shiva LAN Rover.

**Event Log** Default service that records system, security, and application events in the Event Log files.

**Event Viewer** The tool within Windows NT used to review logged and audited events. Event Viewer has three logs that record system, security, and application-related events, known as the System Log, the Security Log, and the Applications Log, respectively.

# F

**FAT (File Allocation Table) file system** The FAT file system is predominantly used for other operating systems such as Windows 3.x and Windows 95. To support backward compatibility,

Windows NT fully supports the FAT file system. This is also because of FAT's universal acceptance and accessibility through other operating systems. Does not support Windows NT Security features and does not offer any of the robust NTFS features. (See also **NTFS**.)

**FAT32** The Windows 98 32-bit upgrade to the FAT file system that originally came from DOS. The benefits of FAT32 include optimal use of disk space and larger partition sizes than the maximum 2 GB (gigabyte) size allowed by FAT. Windows 98 supports only FAT and FAT32 files systems and Windows NT does not support FAT32.

**fault tolerance** Recovery from operational failure control due to the system's ability to withstand hardware failures and software errors. Windows NT provides fault tolerance by allowing the redundancy of data by simultaneously writing files to multiple disks, and by replicating the contents of file directories to other servers on the network.

**filtering** An Effective Security Monitoring control used within the Network Monitor application that allows the system administrator to specify expressions to capture data either by protocol or network address. The filter expressions are represented by a decision tree. (See also **decision tree**.)

**finger** Tool used to gather information about users on any machine running a finger server.

**firewall** Software that prevents unauthorized traffic between two networks by examining the IP packets that travel on both networks. Firewalls look at the IP address and type of access the packet requires (such as FTP or HTTP) and then determine if that type of traffic is allowed.

**FTP Publishing Service** Default service that, in Windows NT 4.0, is part of Internet Information Server (IIS).

# G

**global groups** Created on domain controllers and used to assign local permissions to domain users. The sole purpose of a global group is to gather users together at the domain level so that they can be placed in the appropriate local groups. (See also **local groups**.)

**group accounts** Accounts used for grouping together users who perform the same function or require access to the same resources. If it were not for group accounts, access would have to be granted to resources on a per-user basis.

**Guest account** One of the two built-in NT user accounts. The Guest account is for the one-time or occasional user. (See also **Administrator account**.)

# H

**HARDWARE** Registry subtree that contains information about the hardware that is detected upon system startup. Such information might include device settings, interrupts, and information about hardware components.

# I

**impersonation** Technique for a server process to access objects that it doesn't have permissions to. If the client process has proper access permissions, the server process impersonates the client process in order to access the object.

**Integrity** The protection of information in the system from unauthorized, unanticipated, and unintentional modification ensuring data is accurate and complete.

**IPX/SPX** (Internetwork Packet Exchange/Sequenced Packet Exchange) Protocol used to connect Novell networks.

**IT Security control model** The relationship between corporate business objectives and IT Security controls or Windows NT Security features. An effective security model has three objectives: Confidentiality, Integrity, and Availability.

# L

**Land attack** A denial of service attack in which the source and destination SYN packets have the same address and the same port. This attack forces the computer to operate more slowly while trying to respond to packets sent to itself.

**Last Known Good Configuration** An option during bootup that allows the user to restore the system to the last working system configuration. When used, it discards any changes to the configuration since the last working system configuration.

**legal notice** Corporation-specific message that appears whenever a user logs on the system warning them that only authorized users may access the system and that they are being monitored. Set through the Registry Editor or System Policy Editor. (See also **Registry Editor** and **System Policy Editor**.)

**local groups** Defined on each machine and may have both user accounts and global groups as members but cannot contain other local groups. (See also **global groups**.)

**Local Security Authority** The heart of the NT security subsystem. It creates security access tokens, authenticates users, and manages the local security policy.

**logon scripts** Used to start applications or set environment variables for a computer upon logon.

# M

**mandatory logon** NT uses mandatory logon to force a user to logon before it grants that user access to the system.

**Messenger** Default service that sends and receives messages sent by administrators or by the Alerter service. This service is stopped when the Workstation service is stopped.

**Microsoft Challenge Handshake Authentication Protocol (MS-CHAP)** An encrypted logon protocol used by remote users.

**mirroring** Enables Windows NT to read files from, and write files to, two disks simultaneously. Entire disks (or sets of disks) can be mirrored or just partitions on each disk. If one drive fails, the second continues to function as normal.

**monitoring controls** Include violation and exception reporting which help management determine whether their systems are being compromised.

# N

**nbstat** Tool used to display the contents of the remote computer's NetBIOS name table. The information listed in the NetBIOS name table can be used to determine the Domain name or workgroup the machine is in and the currently connected users. The information may also be used to uncover the Administrator's account, due to the fact that account SIDs are displayed in the name cache.

**NetBEUI (NetBIOS Extended User Interface)** NetBEUI, the built-in protocol of Microsoft networking, supports communication in a Microsoft-only environment when the network is small and composed of a single network segment. NetBEUI is a nonroutable protocol, meaning that its packets contain no routing information and cannot pass through routers into other network segments. NetBEUI protocol is best suited for local area networks that do not connect to the Internet. (See also **NetBIOS**.)

**NetBIOS** Protocol used when Microsoft networking is required in a large multisegment network. NetBIOS has many similarities to NetBEUI except for the fact that it can be routed into other network segments when combined with either the TCP/IP or NWLink protocols in a form known as an encapsulated protocol. (See also **TCP/IP**, **NetBEUI** and **NWLink**.)

**Net Logon** Default service that performs authentication of account for primary domain and backup domain controllers, and also keeps the domain directory database synchronized between the primary domain controller and the backup domain controllers of the domain. For other computers running Windows NT, supports pass-through authentication of account logons. Used when the workstation participates in a domain.

**netstat** Tool used to display the status of the TCP/IP stack including what ports are open and what connections are active.

**Network DDE** Default service that provides a network transport as well as security for DDE (Dynamic Data Exchange) conversations.

**Network DDEDSDM** Dynamic Data Exchange Share Database Manager manages the shared DDE conversations. It is used by the Network DDE service.

**Network Monitor** Tool used to monitor packets of information that are sent from or received by the computer where the program is running, including broadcast and multicast frames. The Microsoft System Management Server includes an advanced Network Monitor tool, which allows the user to capture frames sent to and from any computer on the network, edit and transmit frames on the network, and capture frames from remote computers running Network Monitor Agent on the network.

**NTFS (New Technology File System)** The file system exclusive to Windows NT 4.0. Utilizes Windows NT File and Directory Security features so it is more secure than FAT. (See also **FAT [File Allocation Table] file system**.)

**NT LM Security Support Provider** Default service that provides Windows NT security to RPC (Remote Procedure Call) applications that use transports other than named pipes.

**NWLink** Microsoft's implementation of the IPX protocol that allows connectivity between the Windows NT and the Novell NetWare environments. (See also **CSNW**.)

# O

**Out-of-Band attacks** Attacks where data is sent outside the normal expected band that has been shown to affect Windows NT. This attack may cause Windows NT to have trouble handling any network operations.

# P

**pass-through authentication** Occurs when the user chooses a domain to log on from an NT computer, but the computer doesn't have an account in that domain.

**Performance Monitor** Tool configured to monitor system performance, to gather vital information on system statistics, and to analyze and graphically display information. Can also be configured to send alerts when a hacker may be attempting to compromise security. There are four ways to view the information gathered by the Performance monitor: chart, alert, log, and report.

**PING (Packet InterNet Groper)** A standard TCP/IP network utility that sends packets from one machine to another in order to determine if there is a valid network route between them.

**Ping-of-Death attack** A security attack involving Ping. Issuing a Ping packet of larger than normal size set at 64 Kbytes causes the Ping-of-Death. This attack effectively takes the system off-line until rebooted.

**Ping-of-Death 2 attack** A variation on the original Ping-of-Death whereby multiple packets of either greater than 64 K in size or multiple 64 K fragmented packets are sent, crashing the receiving system.

**Point-to-Point Protocol (PPP)** Enables links between two points with no devices in between.

**Point-To-Point Protocol Multilink Protocol (PPP-MP)** An Internet standard allowing multiple protocols, such as NetBEUI and IPX, to be encapsulated within IP datagrams and transmitted over public backbones such as the Internet.

**Point-to-Point Transmission (PPT)** Many computer networks use point-to-point transmission methods, where there may be one to dozens of points between the two ends (e-mail is a good example of this). Each point is only concerned with transferring data from itself to the next point downstream.

**Point-to-Point Tunneling Protocol (PPTP)** Microsoft PPTP is a transport mechanism under which remote users can connect to corporate networks through secure channels creating connections commonly referred to as Virtual Private Networks (VPNs). There are two implementations of PPTP today, one is a North American version featuring 128-bit encryption and the other is an exportable version with 40-bit encryption. (See also **Virtual Private Networks**.)

**preventative security controls** Ensure that security vulnerabilities are not exposed.

**PricewaterhouseCooper's Windows NT Security Audit Program (C&L-NTSAP)** Designed to assist the administrator in performing the systems audit process focusing on IT Security controls and Windows NT Configurable Security features. Primarily aimed at a Windows NT Server primary domain controller, but selectively applies to six different types of servers (domain controller, file and print member server, application server: web server, application server: database server, application server: remote access server, and workstation.

**primary domain controller (PDC)** The central server in the network that maintains the security database for that domain.

**Privacy Act** See **Electronics Communications Privacy Act (ECPA)**.

**protocols** Languages used by computers. In order for two computers to talk to each other they must speak the same language (use the same protocol).

**proxy server** A local server between the client workstation and the Internet itself.

**public key cryptography** Consists of a public key and a private key. The public key is given freely to anyone that needs it, and the private key is kept secret by the keys' owner and is stored in the user's security file.

# R

**RAID (Redundant Array of Inexpensive Disks)** Enables a system to segment data and store pieces of it on several different drives, using a process known as data striping. The principal reason for implementing RAID is for fault tolerance. (See also **data striping**.)

**REGEDT32.EXE** Executable that launches the Registry Editor. (See also **Registry** and **Registry Editor.)**

**Registry** NT's database that controls the computer by containing all the system and program configuration parameters. Contains the SAM and configuration data for applications, hardware, and device drivers. The Registry also contains data on user-specific information including settings from user-profiles, desktop settings, software configurations, and network settings.

**Registry Editor** A Microsoft tool for editing the Registry. Both the new tool (REGEDIT.EXE) and the traditional Registry Editor (REGEDT32.EXE) are included. Some of the new features of REGEDIT.EXE include improved search capabilities and a Windows Explorer interface. (See also **Registry**.)

**Remote Access Service (RAS)** A default service that enables users to connect over a phone line to a network and access resources as if they were at a computer connected directly to the network.

**remote control** A type of program that grants a user remote control so they can administer a server. This variation of external networking allows the client to take full control of the machine; all input devices, such as the keyboard and mouse, are routed to the remote client.

**remote node** The external networking method employed by Windows NT Remote Access Services (RAS). The Remote Node method allows a remote client machine to dial in to a server and attach itself to the network using various protocols. (See also **Remote Access Service**.)

**Remote Procedure Call (RPC)** Used by programmers to create an application consisting of multiple procedures; some run on the local computer, and others run on remote computers over a network. RPCs allow commands to be sent from one system to execute programs on another system.

**Remote Procedure Call (RPC) Locator** Default service that allows distributed applications to use the Microsoft RPC service and manages the RPC Name Service database. The server side of distributed applications registers its availability with this service. The client side of distributed applications queries this service to find available server applications.

**Remote Procedure Call (RPC) Service** Default service that is the RPC subsystem for Windows NT. It includes the endpoint mapper and other related services.

**resource domains** Process of sharing resources, such as printers and files, within a domain. Administered by the resource domain controller.

**risk** The measurement of exposure to possible harm or loss. The threat could be from a variety of sources, including market forces, disgruntled employees, competitors, or one's own inefficient and outdated processes.

**roaming user** A user who logs on the network at different times from different computers.

# S

**SAM (Security Access Manager)** (1) A database that maintains all user, group, and workstation accounts in a secure database. (2) Registry subtree that contains all account and security information for local users on a non-domain controller and for all users in the current domain on a domain controller.

**Schedule** Default service that must be running if the AT command is to be used. The AT command can be used to schedule commands and programs to run on a particular date and time.

**secret key cryptography** Secret key encrypts and decrypts messages using a single secret key called a bulk encryption key in the Key Management Server. Two examples of secret key cryptography are DES and CAST. The Key Management Server supports CAST 40 and CAST 64. DES and CAST 64 are available only in North America.

**Secure Attention Sequence** Invoked at logon by pressing CTRL+ALT+DELETE, this feature requires the user to acknowledge the notice by clicking the OK button in the message box before continuing.

**SECURITY** Registry subtree that contains security information for the local machine on non-domain controllers and for the entire domain on domain controllers.

**security descriptors** Describes the security attributes for an object, and has the following parts: Owner Security ID: identifies the owner of the object, which allows that person to change the permissions for the object; Group Security ID: only used by the POSIX subsystem; Discretionary Access Control List (ACL): identifies the groups and users who are allowed and denied access.

**Security Identifier (SID)** Used to uniquely identify each user, NT Workstation, and Server on the network.

**Security Log** A report where suspicious information can be filtered and tracked.

**Security Reference Monitor** Verifies that the user has permissions to access the requested object, and then performs that action.

**Server** Default service that provides Remote Procedure Call (RPC) support, and file, print, and named piping sharing using SMB services.

**Server alerts** Used to send notification messages to users or computers. Server alerts are generated by the system, and relate to server and resource use. They warn about security and access problems, user session problems, printer problems, and server shutdown because of power loss when the UPS service is available.

**Server Manager** A utility not only for managing servers, but also for managing workstations and the domain. Allows the administrator to control most domain activity, including domain controller administration, setting up shares, configuring replication settings, modifying services, and monitoring user connections.

**services** Processes that run in the background of a Windows NT environment and may be started automatically at boot time or manually started and stopped by the administrator or server operators. Services typically run under the System account, but they may also run under a user-defined account. There are two types of services: those that operate as part of the system kernel, and those that operate under the Win32 subsystem.

**share** Created by granting a particular resource a share name. This name is what other users or devices recognize as the entity with which they have permission to access. (See also **share-level security**.)

**share-level security** Used to give other users access to your hard drive via the network. The four types of share permissions are No Access, Read, Change, and Full Control.

**Simple Network Management Protocol (SNMP)** An Internet standard for monitoring and configuring network devices. An SNMP network is composed of management systems and agents.

**SLIP (Serial Line Internet Protocol)** An older protocol used to carry TCP/IP over low-speed serial lines.

**SMB (Server Message Block)** Services that form the backbone of Microsoft networking in the Windows NT environment. All file and printer sharing in Windows NT operate using the SMB services.

**SOFTWARE** Registry subtree that contains software configuration information pertaining to the local computer.

**Spooler** Provides print spooler services.

**symmetric cryptography** So named because both the sender and receiver use a single key.

**SYN Flood attack** A flood of TCP connection requests (SYN) that can be sent to a server, effectively tying it up and causing the server to respond with a reset to all further connection requests.

**SYSTEM** Registry subtree that contains all data that is essential for starting the system.

**System Policy Editor** Tool that provides the ability to configure and maintain the environment and actions of users, groups, and computers. Controls the same configurations as the Registry Editor. (See also **Registry Editor**.)

**System User Access Form** Defines the appropriate level of access depending on the user's job responsibilities.

**Systems Security audit** An independent examination designed to determine whether adequate controls exist to ensure the following corporate IT objectives: Effectiveness, Efficiency, Compliance, Reliability of Information, Confidentiality, Integrity, and Availability.

# T

**TCP/IP (Transmission Control Protocol/Internet Protocol)** An industry-standard suite of protocols designed for local and wide-area networking. Widely used for Internet communication.

**Teardrop and Teardrop 2 attacks** Attacks that can cause a system to halt by using up all available memory in the kernel.

**Telnet** Terminal emulation for character-based communicating.

**tftp (trivial file transfer protocol)** Tool that allows unauthenticated file transfer to any tftp server.

**tracert** Traces the path that a packet follows to its destination server.

**trigger** Conditions that must be met before an action occurs.

**trust** There are two possible trust configurations, the one-way trust and the two-way trust. In a one-way trust, one domain trusts the users in the other domain to use its resources. A two-way trust is actually comprised of two one-way trusts. Each domain trusts the user accounts in the other domain.

**trusted domain** Domain in which your workstation has an account. A user in one domain also can be authenticated to another domain by establishing trust relationships. (See also **trust**.)

**trust relationship** A one-way administrative and communicative link between two domains allowing one domain (the trusting domain) to honor authentication requests from users of another domain (the trusted domain). (See also **trust** and **trusted domain**.)

# U

**UPS (Uninterruptable Power Supply)** A device consisting of a standalone power source (a battery or a generator) and circuitry which will automatically and instantaneously switch from building power to backup power in the case of an outage.

**user account**  Represent users who access the resources on the domain. User accounts do not have to represent individuals; they can also be accounts for services, such as an SQL Server account.

**User Manager for Domains**  The administrative tool used to manage user accounts, groups, and policies. User Manager has the ability to copy, rename, or delete user accounts. The User Manager for Domains tool contains three policies that can be customized for different security needs, Account Policies, User Rights, and Auditing Policies. (See also **account policies**, **user rights**, and **auditing policies**.)

**User Mode**  The location of most of Windows NT code. It is often referred to as a nonprivileged processor mode. This is also where applications and the various subsystems are run. User Mode is designed to prevent applications from bringing down the operating system.

**user rights**  Allow the administrator to control which operations a user or group performs. Each right enables the user to perform specific operations on the computer.

# V

**Virtual LANs (VLANs)**  Restrict where the data can travel by configuring communications equipment to route data across specific paths.

**Virtual Private Networks (VPNs)**  Allows remote users to access internal network resources, including multiple protocols and applications, through virtual connectivity to the internal network.

# W

**war dialers**  Programs that rapidly dial a range of phone numbers defined by a hacker to determine what numbers have modems connected. After the hacker determines which numbers have modems, they attempt to log in the system connected to that modem.

**Windows NT Diagnostics**  Utility to view various system, resource, and environment information. Also used to monitor possible breaches of security.

**Workstation**  Default service that provides network connections and communications.

# Index

References to figures, screen shots, and tables appear in italic font.

## Symbols and Numbers

* (asterisk), 150
$ (dollar sign), 159

## A

A1 trust rating, 28
Ability to Recovery from Operational Failure control, 6, 7, 203–19, 249–52
Access Computer from the Network user right, 133, 135
Access Control Lists (ACLs), 133
access rights. *See also* permissions; user rights
  granting/removing, 21–22
  physical security and, 62
  procedures for, 21–22
Access through Share Permissions dialog box, 158
Account button, 116, 121
Account dialog box, 121, *122*
Account Disabled option, 116, 117, 170
Accounting domain, 71
Account Operators local group, 96, 104, 107
Account Policy dialog box, 123, *124,* 125–27
accounts. *See also* groups
  creating/modifying, 108–22
  deleting, 109
  lockout of, 127–28, 130–31, 242
  policies for, 123–40, *131,* 242
  receivable, 19, 20
ACLs (Access Control Lists), 133
Act as Part of the Operating System user right, 137, 139

Active Users command, 85
Add & Read permission, 150, 151, 152
Add Key command, 185
Add Names field, 111
Add permission, 151, 152
Address command, 41
Address Database dialog box, 41
Address Expression dialog box, 41
Address List, 41
Add to Alert command, 31
Add to Alert dialog box, *31*
Add to Chart command, 30
Add to Log command, 33
Add to Report command, 34
Add Trusted Domain dialog box, 71
Add Trusting Domain dialog box, *70*
Add Users and Groups dialog box, *48, 111,* 145, 148
Add Value command, 185
Add Workstations to the Domain user right, 133, 135
Administrators group, 22, 96, 127
  backups and, 214
  basic description of, 98, 106–8
  external networking and, 90
  server security and, 165–68, 175
  shared permissions and, 157, 158, 159
  workstations and, 13, 116
Advanced button, 74
air conditioning, 204
alarms, security, 62, 63
Alert command, 31, 35
Alerter service, 177, 179, 209
Alert If field, 32
Alert Options dialog box, 31, *32*
alerts, 6, 182, 244. *See also* Alert View
  adding/setting, 31, 35–36
  basic description of, 29–32, 174–75
  for full Event Logs, 195
Alerts dialog box, 174, *175*
Alert View. *See also* alerts
  basic description of, 30, 31–32
  information from, saving, 36
All Events command, 55
AllocateCDROM Registry value, 194, 247, 250

AllocateFloppies Registry value, 194, 247, 250
Allow Any Authentication option, 81, 91
Allow Changes Immediately option, 126
Allow XX Users radio button, 158
ALPHA systems, 143
AND tab, 41
Applications Log, 54, 57–59
  Event Log wrapping settings for, *58*
  securing, 59
  size recommendations, *58*
assets, protection of, 16, 17–23
asterisk (*), 150
Asynchronous Transfer Mode (ATM), 80
AT command, 176
ATM (Asynchronous Transfer Mode), 80
auditing, 134, 229, 242. *See also* Audit Log; Event Viewer
  backups and, 195–96
  basic description of, 43–59
  enabling, 195–96, 247
  printer, 51, 52, 230
  protocols, 232–33
  recommended settings, 44–48
  Registry, 49, *50, 51,* 230
  Remote Access Server (RAS), 46, 53, 198, 230–31
Audit Log, 25, 108, 195, 231. *See also* auditing
  basic description of, 43–59
  deleting, 107
  securing, 58–59
  taking time to generate, 15
Audit Policy dialog box, 56, 57
Audit These Events button, 44
Authenticated Users group, 102, 103
authentication
  auditing and, 53
  credentials, caching of, 194, 247
  Microsoft Encrypted Authentication, 91, 92
  pass-through, 68–69
  PPTP (Point-to-Point Tunneling Protocol) and, 76
  Remote Access Server (RAS), 12, 80–81

AutoAdminLogon value, 194, 247
AUTORUN.INF, 198
availability, 4, 6–8

## B

B1 trust rating, 28
B2 trust rating, 28
B3 trust rating, 28
Back Up Files and Directories user
    right, 133, 135
Back Up Files and Folders user
    right, 155
Backup Information dialog box,
    212, *213*
Backup Local Registry option, 205,
    213
Backup Operators group, 97–98,
    104, 159, 214, 251
backups
    auditing and, 195–96
    basic description of, 209–19
    Registry, 204–5
    strategies for Enright bank, 7–8
    tape backups, 62–63, 204
    with Windows NT Backup, 205,
        210–14, 251
badges, identification, 62
Bad Logon Attempts field, 127
Bad Logon Attempts option, 124,
    127, 128–29
batch files, 119
BCP (Business Continuity
    Planning), 216, 218–19, 252
BDCs (backup domain controllers),
    10, 66, 93, 181, 232. *See also*
    domain controllers
Binary command, 185
Boink attacks, 78, 79
Bonk attacks, 78, 79
booting
    to DOS system disks, 143
    from floppy disks, 63
Buffer Space option, 42
Buffer Space Then Pattern Match
    option, 42
Bypass Traverse Checking user
    right, 137

## C

C1 trust rating, 28
C2 trust rating, 27–28
cables, 62, 63
CachedLogonsCount Registry
    value, 194, 247
caching, authentication credentials
    of, 194, 247
CAD (Computer Aided Design),
    90–91
CADATA, 90–91
Call Back option, 13, 64, 85, 92,
    122
cameras, security, 62
Capture Filter dialog box, *40–41*
Capture menu
    Address command, 41
    Display Captured Data
        command, 39
    Filter command, 40
    Find All Names command, 41
    Start command, 39
    Triggers command, 42
Capture Trigger dialog box, *42*
case sensitivity, 125
category information, in the Event
    Viewer, 56
CD-ROM drives
    automatic program execution
        for, 198
    disabling, 193, 247, 250
Challenge Handshake
    Authentication Protocol
    (CHAP), 13, 81, 89, 91
Challenge Response authentication,
    196
Chamoun Company, 91, 130–31
Change Password button, 43
Change permission, 146, 150–52,
    155, 158–59, 192
Change Permissions permission,
    49, 52–53, 146, 149
Change Settings option, 57
Change the System Time user right,
    133, 135
CHAP (Challenge Handshake
    Authentication Protocol),
    13, 81, 89, 91
Chart View, 30–31, 36

CIFS (Common Internet File
    Sharing) protocol, 75
cipher locks, 62
ClearPageFileAtShutdown Registry
    value, 198, 248
Clipbook Viewer service, 177, 179
clock dependency, 222
Close button, 87
CMD.EXE, 139
commands
    Active Users command, 85
    Add Key command, 185
    Address command, 41
    Add to Alert command, 31
    Add to Chart command, 30
    Add to Log command, 33
    Add to Report command, 34
    Add Value command, 185
    Alert command, 31, 35
    All Events command, 55
    AT command, 176
    Binary command, 185
    Computer command, 36
    Create Report command, 36
    Delete command, 185
    Display Captured Data
        command, 39
    Filter command, 40, 55
    Find All Names command, 41
    Log command, 33
    Log Settings command, 57
    MultiString command, 185
    New Global Group command,
        112
    New Local Group command,
        109
    New User command, 115
    Open command, 119
    Properties command, 144, 146,
        152, 157
    Report command, 34
    Save As command, 56
    Start command, 39
    String command, 185
    Triggers command, 42
    Update Now command, 33, 34
Comment field, 157
Communication Port dialog box,
    *83*
communications room, 62–63, 231–
    32

compatibility, 142
competitiveness, 18
compliance, 4
compression, 142
Computer Browser service, 178, 179
Computer command, 36
Computer field, 30, 32, 34
computers
    import computers, 169, 173–74
    information about, in the Event Viewer, 56
    laptop computers, 64
    mainframe computers, 61
    properties for, 164–75, 244
    rooms for, 62, 203–4, 231–32, 249
ComSpec variable, 139
confidentiality, 4–7, 43, 49, 65, 81
Configure button, 74, 87, 89
Configure Port Usage dialog box, 87, 89
Confirm Password field, 115
consistency, 5
Control Panel
    handling passwords with, 43
    handling protocols with, 72, 74
    handling Remote Access Server settings with, 80–82, 86–89
    Monitoring Agent applet, 43
    Network applet, 72, 74, 80–81, 86–89
    Services applet, 170
    system security management and, 183
"cookie-cutter" security configuration, 9
copying data, 63, 155
corporate security policy
    auditing and, 45
    awareness of, 16, 24–25
    commitment to, 16, 24–25
    developing, 15, 16–26
    exceptions to, 21
    management of, 16, 25–26
    Microsoft Office and, 227
    review of, 16, 25–26
    standards for, 22–23
cost/benefit analysis, 19–20, 24
Counter Definition field, 31
Counter field, 30, 32, 34

counters, 29–32, 34–35
CPUs (central processing units), 34, 37, 78
crashes, 31, 57–58, 78–79, 195, 247
"Crash On Audit Fail" flag, 58
CrashOnAuditFail Registry value, 195, 247
Create a Page File user right, 137, 140
Create a Token Object user right, 137, 140
Create Link option, 51
Create Link permission, 50–51, 191
Create Permanent Shared Objects user right, 137, 140
Create Report command, 36
Create Subkey option, 51
Create Subkey permission, 50, 191
credentials, 101, 194, 247
Current Startup Configuration feature, 215

## D

D trust rating, 28
DAC (discretionary access control), 50, 51
data
    compression, 142
    copying, 63, 155
    forging, 19, 20
    integrity of, 4–7, 62, 65, 203, 209
    recovery, 209–19, 251–52
    striping, 208
database servers, 10, 12
    physical security and, 62
    security monitoring and, 35, 44, 45, 46
Data Encryption Standard (DES), 81
Date field, 55
dates
    Event Viewer information on, 55
    expiration, for accounts, 121
Debug Programs user right, 138, 140
decentralization, of resources, 62
decision trees, 40–41
Delete command, 185
Delete option, 51

Delete permission, 49–53, 146, 149, 156, 191
deleting
    Audit Logs, 107
    files, 156
    groups, 96
    shared permissions, 158
    trust relationships, 71
denial of service attacks, 18, 57, 77–79, 128, 234
DES (Data Encryption Standard), 81
Description field, 110, 113, 115
desktop, look and feel of, 13
Diagnostics (Windows NT), 36–43, 186
    analyzing computer environments with, 226
    recommended settings, 37–38
    starting, 36
    tabs, 37
Dialin button, 116, 122
Dialin dialog box, 122
Dial Out Only radio button, 87, 89
Dial Out Only service, 87–89
Dial Out option, 87, 89, 90, 92
Dial-Up Networking, 89
directories. See also file systems
    copying, 155
    home, 119–20
    locking, 172
    moving, 155
    ownership of, 152
    permissions for, 144–51, 152–53, 154–60, 242, 245–46
    physical security and, 63
    profiles and, 118
    Registry, securing, 189–90
    replication of, 169, 170–72, 173–75, 244–45
    shared, 99
Directory Auditing dialog box, 47
Directory field, 48, 147
Directory Permissions dialog box, 146, 147–48, 158
Directory Replication dialog box, 169
Directory Replicator service, 170–75, 178, 179, 181–82
Disabling Call Back option, 85

Disaster Recovery Planning (DRP), 216–19
Disconnect All button, 166
Disconnect button, 166
Disconnect User button, 83, 86
disgruntled employees, 18
disk. *See also* ERDs (Emergency Repair Disks)
  duplexing, 207
  mirroring, 7, 12, 206–8
Disk Administrator, *207,* 208, 216,
Display Captured Data command, 39
Display tab, 37
dollar sign ($), 159
Domain Administration control, 65
Domain Admins global group, 66, 101, 106
domain controllers, 46, 58, 69, 96–98. *See also* PDCs (primary domain controllers)
  backup (BDCs), 10, 66, 93, 181, 232
  basic description of, 10, 11
  rights/capabilities for, *236–38*
  storage of, in computer rooms, 62
Domain Guests global group, 101
Domain Member Server option, 92
domains
  administration of, 65–66
  auditing and, 46, 49
  basic description of, 66
  master, 10–11, 13
  names of, 101
  trust relationships and, 66–72
Domain Users global group, 101, 106
Do Not Keep Password History option, 126
Do Not Overwrite Events option, 57
DontDisplayLastUserName Registry value, 194, 247
Don't Log option, 214
DOS (Disk Operating System)
  file systems and, 131, 142
  logon scripts and, 119
  Remote Access Server (RAS) and, 80
  system disks, booting to, 143

Drives tab, 37
DRP (Disaster Recovery Planning), 216–19
DWORDs, 53, 75, 173, 185, 197–98

# E

earthquakes, 19, 20, 203
eavesdropping, 27, 63
ECPA (Electronic Communications Privacy Act), 27
Edit Address button, 41
Edit menu
  Add to Alert command, 31
  Add to Chart command, 30
  Add to Log command, 33
  Add to Report command, 34
effectiveness, definition of, 4
Effective Security Management control, 227
Effective Security Monitoring control, 40, 43–59
efficiency, definition of, 4
electronic key cards, 62
e-mail, 53
employees
  disgruntled, 18
  physical security and, 62, 63
  rights/responsibilities of, in corporate security policy, 23
  temporary, 121
Enable Security option, 74
encapsulated protocols, 73
encryption, 37, 63, 64
  MD4 encryption, 81, 91
  protocols and, 72, 76
  RC4 encryption, 76, 81, 89, 91
  Remote Access Server (RAS) and, 13, 81–82, 89, 92
  SAM and, 187
Enright Bank, 3–4, 5, 7–8
Enumerate Subkey permission, 50, 191
environmental protection, 203–4, 249. *See also* physical security
Environment tab, 37
environment variables, 139, 140
ERDs (Emergency Repair Disks), 27, 203–5, 215–16, 251–52
errors

counters for, 35
  input, 19, 20
  recording, with the Event Viewer, 54–57
Errors Access Permissions counter, 35
Errors Granted Access counter, 35
Errors Logon counter, 35
Ethernet, 62
European Commission ITSEC (Information Technology Security Evaluation Criteria), 28
evaluation levels, 27–28
Event Detail dialog box, *55–56*
Event IDs, 56
Event Log
  full, alert message for, 195
  secure viewing of, 198, 248
  service, 178, 179, 209
  settings, *57*
  wrapping options, 57, 58
Event Log Settings dialog box, *57*
Event Log Wrapping option, 57, 58
Event Viewer, 43–45, 53–58, 231–32. *See also* auditing
  Applications Log, 54, 57–59
  basic description of, 54–57
  categories, *56*
  recommended settings, 57–58
  Security Log, 6, 44, 54, 57–59, 134, 135
  starting, 54
  System Log, 54, 57–59
Everyone group, 102–3, 153, 155
EXE (executable) files
  logon scripts as, 119
  permissions and, 155–56
Execute Command Line option, 42
Execute permission, 49, 137, 146, 149, 206
expiration dates, for accounts, 121
Explain button, 31
Explorer, 156, 216, 245–46
  enabling auditing with, 47
  setting permissions with, 144, 145, 146, 147, 157
export servers, 169, 170–72, 174
expressions, locating/adding, 41
external networking, 7, 79–91, 233–35

## F

FAT (File Allocation Table) file system, 63, 144, 156–60
  basic description of, 141, 143
  NTFS vs., *142*
FAT32 file system, 141
fault tolerance, 206–9, 250–51
F-C2/E3 trust rating, 28
FDC (File Delete Child) permission, 150
Fecha Manufacturing Corporation, 9–13, 62, 200–202
  network security management and, 73, 74, 76
  security monitoring and, 31, 34–35, 41–49, 51–53, 55
Feinmerica, Inc., 90–91, 129–31
FER (Final Evaluation Report), 28
fields
  Add Names field, 111
  Alert If field, 32
  Bad Logon Attempts field, 127
  Comment field, 157
  Computer field, 30, 32, 34
  Confirm Password field, 115
  Counter Definition field, 31
  Counter field, 30, 32, 34
  Date field, 55
  Description field, 110, 113, 115
  Directory field, 48, 147
  File field, 145
  Full Name field, 115
  Group Name field, 110, 113
  Initial Password field, 70
  Instance field, 30
  List Names From field, 111
  Log Event in Application Log field, 32
  Members field, 110, 113
  Network Alert field, 32
  Not Members field, 113
  Object field, 30, 32, 34, 35
  Owner field, 145, 147
  Password field, 71, 115
  Run Program on Alert field, 32
  Share Name field, 157
  Switch to Alert View field, 32
  Trusted Domains field, 70, 71
  Trusting Domains field, 70, 71
  Update Time field, 32

  Username field, 115
File and Directory auditing, 46–49, 51
File and Object Access auditing, 45–53
File field, 145
File menu
  Computer command, 36
  Create Report command, 36
  Open command, 119
  Properties command, 144, 146, 152, 157
filenames
  character restrictions for, 143
  extensions for, 45
  support for, NTFS vs. FAT, 142
File Permissions dialog box, *144–45*
files. *See also* filenames; file servers; file systems
  batch files, 119
  compression of, 142
  copying, 155
  deleting, 156
  moving, 155
file servers, 10, 11–12, 44, 62
file systems. *See also* directories; NTFS (Windows NT File System)
  basic description of, 141–43
  converting between, 143
  FAT (File Allocation Table) file system, 63, 141, *142*, 143–44, 156–60
  recommendations for choosing, 143
Filter command, 40, 55
filtering, 40, 41–42
  with the Event Viewer, 55
  password, 125, 130, 196, 248
  TCP/IP packet, 73–74
Find Account dialog box, 111
Find All Names command, 41
Finger, 77
fire suppression systems, 204
firewalls, 63
fixes, to patch security weaknesses, 23
floods, 19, 20, 203
floppy drives, 63, 193, 247, 250

Force Shutdown from a Remote System user right, 133, 136
Forcibly Disconnect Remote Users option, 124, 128–29
FPNWCLNT.DLL, 196
FTP (File Transfer Protocol), 41, 63, 74, 178, 179
FTP Publishing service, 178, 179
Full Control permission, 52–53, 135, 146–55, 158–62, 190–93
Full Detail option, 214
Full Name field, 115
FullPriviledgeAuditing Registry value, 196, 248
fund transfer systems, 17, 18

## G

general ledgers, 19, 20
Generate Security Audits user right, 138, 140
GetAdmin, 134
Global Group Membership dialog box, 111, *114*, 117
global groups. *See also* group accounts
  basic description of, 94, 99–101
  built-in, 101
  creating, 112–13
  managing, 113–14
  scenarios for, *105*
  trust relationships and, 66, 72
Grant All button, 84
Grant Dial-in Permission to User option, 84, 122
graphical user interface (GUI), 185, 198
group accounts. *See also* groups, global; groups, local
  basic description of, 93, 94–105
  creating, 109–10
  managing, 109–14
  memberships in, *100*, 117, *118*
  securing, considerations/ recommendations for, 103–5
  special, 101–2
Group Memberships dialog box, 117, *118*
Group Name field, 110, 113
Group Properties dialog box, 113
group shares, 11, 13

groups, global. *See also* group
  accounts
 basic description of, 94, 99–101
 built-in, 101
 creating, 112–13
 managing, 113–14
 scenarios for, *105*
 trust relationships and, 66, 72
groups, local. *See also* group
  accounts
 adding users to, 110–11
 basic description of, 94, *95*, 96–
  103
 creating, 109–10
 managing, 113–14
 memberships in, 99, *100*, 101
 scenarios for, *105*
Groups option, 170
guards, security, 62
Guests group, 13, 97, 98, 106, 108
GUI (graphical user interface), 185,
 198

**H**

hackers
 auditing and, 44–45
 Call Back feature and, 85
 Event Viewer and, 56–57, 58–59
 guessing of passwords by, 44,
  53, 90, 127, 130–31
 knowledge of user names by,
  preventing, 194
 physical security and, 63–64
 shared permissions and, 160
 use of war dialers by, 88
 user accounts and, 117
HAL.DLL, 143
Halon, 204
handles,185
HARDWARE key, 186
 SAM key, 186–87
 SECURITY key, 187–88
 SOFTWARE key, 191–95, 232,
  246, 250, 277
 SYSTEM key, 75–76, 160, 195–
  98, 230–31, 245–48
Hardware Recognizer, 186
heat detectors, 204
help desks, 130
hexadecimal addresses, 41

hidden shared permissions, 159–
 60. *See also* shared
 permissions
HKEY_CLASSES_ROOT subtree, 51,
 187, 188
HKEY_CURRENT_CONFIG subtree,
 188
HKEY_CURRENT_USER subtree,
 188
HKEY_DYN_DATA subtree, 188
HKEY_LOCAL_MACHINE subtree,
 51, 53, 173, 184, 189
HKEY_USERS subtree, 184, 188,
 193, 247
hot-swappable disks, 208
Hours button, 116, 120
Hours option, 116, 120, 170
HTTP (Hypertext Transfer
 Protocol), 74
humidity control, 204

**I**

identification badges, 62
IDs, 22, 56, 63. *See also* SIDs
 (security identifiers)
import computers, 169, 173–74
Increase Quotas user right, 138,
 140
Increase Scheduling Priority user
 right, 138, 140
Initial Password field, 70
input errors, 19, 20
installation disks, protective
 storage of, 62
Instance field, 30
integrity, of data, 4–7, 61–62, 65,
 203, 209
Interactive group, 103
internal network connections, 7,
 233–35
IP (Internet Protocol) addresses,
 spoofing, 78
IPX (Internet Packet Exchange)
 protocol, 73, 76–77, 89
ISDN (Integrated Services Digital
 Network), 80
ISPs (Internet Service Providers),
 76
IT (Information Technology)
 Security Control Model

basic description of, 1–8
objectives of, 1, 2–3
security controls, *2*
Windows NT security features
 and, 7–8
ITSEC (Information Technology
 Security Evaluation Criteria),
 28

**J**

JJ's Widget, Inc., 91–92

**K**

kernel, 37. *See also* memory

**L**

Land attacks, 78, 79
LanManager Challenge Response
 authentication, 196, 248
LANs (local area networks), 9, 63,
 79, 196, 248
laptop computers, 64
Last Know Good Configuration
 feature, 215, 252
launching
 Event Viewer, 54
 Network Monitor, 38
 Performance Monitor, 30
 Registry Editor, 49
 Remote Access Server (RAS), 83
 Windows NT Diagnostics, 36
legal notices, 26–27, 194–202, 227,
 247
LegalNoticeText Registry value,
 195, 247
List Names From field, 111
List permission, 151, 152
LMCompatibilityLevel Registry
 value, 196, 248
Load and Unload Device Drivers
 user right, 138, 140
Local Group Properties dialog box,
 113, *114*
local groups. *See also* group
  accounts
 adding users to, 110–11
 basic description of, 94, *95*, 96–
  103

creating, 109–10
managing, 113–14
memberships in, 99, *100,* 101
scenarios for, *105*
Local Guest group, 116
LocalSystem account, 171
Lockout Duration option, 124, 128
Lock Pages in Memory user right,
    138, 140
Log command, 33
Log dialog box, 33
Log Event in Application Log field,
    32
log files. *See also* logs
    for backups, 213–14
    deleting, 59
    size recommendations for, 57,
        58
Log menu
    Log Settings command, 57
    Save As command, 56
logoff, 44, 46, 56
logon
    audit feature, 46
    banners, 194–202
    information, in the Event
        Viewer, 56
    legal notices at, 26–27, 194–202,
        227, 247
    null credentials, 102, 197
    scripts, 119, 174
    security monitoring and, 35–38,
        44–45, 46, 56
    user management and, 102, 103,
        119–20
Log On As A Batch Job user right,
    138, 140
Log On As A Service user right,
    138, 140, 174
Log On As option, 173, 177
Logon Hours dialog box, *120*
Log on Locally user right, 134, 136
Log On to Change Password
    option, 124, 129
Logon To dialog box, 120, *121*
logs. *See also* log files; Log View
    Applications Log, 54, 57–59
    Security Log, 6, 44, 54, 57–59,
        134, 135
    System Log, 54, 57–59
Log Settings command, 57

Log View
    basic description of, 30–34
    information from, saving, 36

## M

mainframes, 61
Manage Auditing and Security Log
    user right, 134, 136
Manage button, 172
Manage Documents permission,
    102, 161, 162
Manage Exported Directories
    dialog box, *172–73*
Manage Imported Directories
    dialog box, 173, *174*
manuals, outlining security
    policies, 24
Manual Update option, 34
marketing, corporate, 2, 3, 12
Master Domains, 10–11, 13
Maximum Allowed radio button,
    157
Maximum Log Size option, 57
Maximum Password Age option,
    116, 124–25, 129, 131, 242
Megan's Children Hospital, 2–3, 5
Members button, 111
Members field, 110, 113
memory
    caching of authentication
        credentials in, 194, 247
    kernel, 37
    monitoring, 31, 37
    page files, 37, 138, 197, 248
Memory tab, 37
memos, security, 25
Messenger service, 178, 179, 209
Microsoft Encrypted
    Authentication, 91, 92
Microsoft IIS (Internet Information
    Server), 12, 103
Microsoft Office, 221–52
Microsoft SQL Server, 153
Microsoft System Management
    Server, 38
Microsoft Windows 95, 141, 143
Microsoft Windows 98, 141
Microsoft Windows NT Server, 9,
    38, 51–52, 66, 169
    logon scripts and, 119

permissions and, 156, 159–60
    SMB services and, 76
Microsoft Windows NT
    Workstation, 9, 156
Minimum Password Age option,
    124, 125, 129, 131, 242
Minimum Password Length option,
    124, 125–26, 131, 242
MIPS (millions of instructions per
    second) systems, 143
mission statements, 3, 16
modems, 13, 63–64, 122
Modify Firmware Environment
    Variables user right, 139,
    140
Monitoring Agent applet, 43
MS-CHAP (Microsoft Challenge
    Handshake Authentication
    Protocol), 13, 81, 89, 91
MS-DOS
    file systems and, 131, 142
    logon scripts and, 119
    RAS and, 80
    system disks, booting to, 143
multiple-layered security controls,
    107
MultiString command, 185

## N

National Computer Security Center
    (NCSC), 27
national defense applications, 17
National Security Association
    (NSA), 27
natural disasters, 19, 20, 203–4
Nbtstat, 76
NCSC (National Computer Security
    Center), 27–28
NetBEUI, 72–73, 75, 77, 89, 92
NetBIOS, 41, 73, 76, 78, 177
Net Logon service, 178, 179
Netstat, 77
NetWare (Novell), 73, 196
network access points, 62, 64, 232
Network Alert field, 32
Network applet, 72, 74, 80–81, 86–
    89
Network button, 87, 88
Network Configuration dialog box,
    *88–89*

Network DDEDSM service, 178, 179
Network DDE service, 178, 179
Network group, 103
network jacks, 64
Network Monitor, 38–39, 43, 229
Network Monitor Agent, 38, 43
Network Monitor dialog box, 38, *39*
Network tab, 37, 38
New Global Group command, 112
New Global Group dialog box, *112–13,* 114
New Local Group command, 109
New Local Group dialog box, 109, *110*
New User command, 115
New User dialog box, *115–16*
No Access permission, 146, 151–52, 155–56, 158–59, 161
No Account Lockout option, 127
No Call Back radio button, 84
non-domain controllers, 98–101, *237–40*
NOS (Network Operating System), 9
Not Members field, 113
Not Shared radio button, 157, 158
NOT tab, 41
Nothing option, 42
Notification Packages Registry value, 196, 248
Notify option, 51
Notify permission, 50, 191
NSA (National Security Association), 27
NTCONFIG.POL, 200
NTFS (Windows NT File System), 7, 21, 63, 119, 152. *See also* file systems
  auditing and, 48
  basic description of, 141, 142
  FAT vs., *142*
  permissions for, 144–47, 156–60, 188
NTFSDOS, 143
NT LM Security Support Provider service, 178, 179
NT Server. *See* Microsoft Windows NT Server
NTUSER.DAT, 118

Null Credentials logon, 102, 197
NULL session connections, 102, 197
NWLink, 73, 72

## O

object access information, in the Event Viewer, 56
Object field, 30, 32, 34, 35
objectives, in corporate security policy, 16
Office. *See* Microsoft Office
OLE (Object Linking and Embedding), 187
Open command, 119
Open Resources dialog box, *168–69,* 181, 244
operational failure, recovering from, 6, 7, 203–19, 249–52
options (listed by name)
  Account Disabled option, 116, 117, 170
  Allow Any Authentication option, 81, 91
  Allow Changes Immediately option, 126
  Backup Local Registry option, 205, 213
  Bad Logon Attempts option, 124, 127, 128–29
  Buffer Space option, 42
  Buffer Space Then Pattern Match option, 42
  Call Back option, 13, 64, 85, 92, 122
  Change Settings option, 57
  Create Link option, 51
  Create Subkey option, 51
  Delete option, 51
  Dial Out option, 87, 89, 90, 92
  Disabling Call Back option, 85
  Domain Member Server option, 92
  Do Not Keep Password History option, 126
  Do Not Overwrite Events option, 57
  Don't Log option, 214
  Enable Security option, 74

Event Log Wrapping option, 57, 58
Execute Command Line option, 42
Forcibly Disconnect Remote Users option, 124, 128–29
Full Detail option, 214
Grant Dial-in Permission to User option, 84, 122
Groups option, 170
Hours option, 116, 120, 170
Lockout Duration option, 124, 128
Log On As option, 173, 177
Log On to Change Password option, 124, 129
Manual Update option, 34
Maximum Log Size option, 57
Maximum Password Age option, 116, 124–25, 129, 131, 242
Minimum Password Age option, 124, 125, 129, 131, 242
Minimum Password Length option, 124, 125–26, 131, 242
No Account Lockout option, 127
Nothing option, 42
Notify option, 51
Overwrite Events as Needed option, 57
Overwrite Events Older than x Days option, 57
Ownership option, 162
Password Never Expires option, 116, 117, 170
Password Uniqueness option, 124, 126, 131, 242
Pattern Match option, 42
Pattern Match Then Buffer Space option, 42
Periodic Date option, 34
Preset To option, 84, 85
Print option, 52, 53
Process Tracking option, 45, 46, 57
Profile option, 170
Replace Auditing on Existing Files option, 47–48
Replace Auditing on Subdirectories option, 47–48

Replace Permissions on Existing Files option, 147, 155
Replace Permissions on Subdirectories option, 147
Require Data Encryption option, 81
Requiring Microsoft Encrypted Authentication option, 81
Reset Counter option, 124, 128
Restrict Access to Owner or Administrator option, 213
Set By Caller option, 84, 85
Set Value option, 50, 51, 191
Show Advanced User Rights option, 136
Startup Type option, 173
Summary Only option, 214
This Account option, 173
User Cannot Change Password option, 116, 117, 170
User Must Change Password at Next Logon option, 115, 117, 170
Verify after Backup option, 213
Options menu
    Log command, 33
    Read Only Mode command, 184
    Report command, 34
    Update Now command, 33, 34
Orange Book criteria, for C2 evaluation, 27
order entry, 19, 20
OR tab, 41
Original Equipment Manufacturer Service Release 2, 141
OS/2 operating system, 80, 141
Out-of-Band attacks, 78, 79
overheating, 62
Overwrite Events as Needed option, 57
Overwrite Events Older than x Days option, 57
Owner dialog box, 152
Owner field, 145, 147
ownership, 45, 134–35, 152, 162
Ownership option, 162

## P

page files, 37, 138, 197, 248

PAP (Password Authentication Protocol), 81, 89
parameters, 37, 53, 57, 198, 248
Parameters Registry value, 198, 248
partitions, 142–43, 146–47, 152
passfilt.dll, 125, 196
Passprop, 127
Password field, 71, 115
Password Never Expires option, 116, 117, 170
Password Uniqueness option, 124, 126, 131, 242
passwords, 6, 18, 63, 119
    account policies and, 124–27, 130–31
    auditing and, 53
    changing, 43, 71, 115–16, 124–25, 242
    character restrictions for, 125–27, 130
    expiration of, 116, 117, 170
    filtering, 196, 248
    guessing, 44, 53, 90, 127, 130–31
    network security management and, 71, 83–89, 90, 92
    Remote Access Server (RAS) and, 81–82, 83–89
    restrictions on, 124–26
    SAM and, 187
    statistics for, 38
    trust relationships and, 70–71
    uniqueness of, 124, 126, 131, 242
    user credentials and, 101
    user management and, 102, 108
    workstation lockout and, 202
Pattern Match option, 42
Pattern Match Then Buffer Space option, 42
PDCs (primary domain controllers), 10, 93, 106–7, 232. See also domain controllers
    auditing and, 45
    network security management and, 66, 69, 71
    promoting a BDC to, 181
    Registry backups and, 205
    server security and, 181, 182
    trust relationships and, 69, 71
    user rights and, 134

Performance Monitor, 6, 29–36, 30, 228. See also alerts
    Chart View, 30–31, 36
    Log View, 30–34, 36
    Report View, 30–31, 34
Periodic Date option, 34
permissions. See also permissions (listed by name)
    basic description of, 132
    group folder shares and, 11
    implementing, 144–55
    IT Security Control Model and, 5, 7
    logon scripts and, 119
    printer, 160, 161, 162
    recommended, 153–54, 155–56
    Registry, 188, 189, 190, 191–201
    resource security and, 141–62
    share permissions, 63, 155–57, 158–60
    special groups and, 101
    statistics for, 38
    trust relationships and, 72
    user management and, 94, 95, 99, 101–4, 119
    user rights vs., 132
permissions (listed by name)
    Add & Read permission, 150, 151, 152
    Add permission, 151, 152
    Change permission, 146, 150–52, 155, 158–59, 192
    Change Permissions permission, 49, 52–53, 146, 149
    Create Link permission, 50–51, 191
    Create Subkey permission, 50, 191
    Delete permission, 49–53, 146, 149, 156, 191
    Enumerate Subkey permission, 50, 191
    Execute permission, 49, 137, 146, 149, 206
    FDC (File Delete Child) permission, 150
    Full Control permission, 52–53, 135, 146–55, 158–62, 190–93
    List permission, 151, 152
    Manage Documents permission, 102, 161, 162

No Access permission, 146, 151–52, 155–56, 158–59, 161
Notify permission, 50, 191
Print permission, 161
Query Value permission, 50, 191
Read permission, 49–51, 146, 149–52, 155–59, 190–92
Set Value permission, 50, 191
Special permission, 190–91
Take Ownership permission, 49, 52, 53, 146, 149
Write DAC permission, 50, 51, 191
Write Owner permissions, 191
Write permission, 49, 146, 149
Permissions button, 146, 158
Permissions tab, 161
Permit All radio button, 74
physical security, 7, 61–64, 231–32
Ping (Packet Internet Groper), 78–79
Ping-of-Death 2 attacks, 78, 79
Ping-of-Death (large Ping packet) attacks, 78, 79
policy, corporate security
    auditing and, 45
    awareness of, 16, 24–25
    commitment to, 16, 24–25
    developing, 15, 16–26
    exceptions to, 21
    management of, 16, 25–26
    Microsoft Office and, 227
    review of, 16, 25–26
    standards for, 22–23
portability, 61
ports
    names of, 53
    secure RAS and, 82–83
    usage of, configuring, 87, 88
    Port Status button, 83
Port Status dialog box, 83
POSIX, 137, 139, 149–50
power supplies, 204. See also UPS (Uniterruptable Power Supply)
Power Users group, 98, 99, 158
PPTP (Point-to-Point Tunneling Protocol), 76
Preset To option, 84, 85
Preset To radio button, 84
preventative controls, 6

Printer Auditing dialog box, 52
Printer Permissions dialog box, 160
printers, 11, 36, 242. See also print servers
    auditing, 51, 52, 230
    color, 51
    managing, 160–62
    permissions for, 160, 161
    spooling and, 178, 180
Print Manager, 160–62
Print Operators group, 97, 99, 105
Print option, 52, 53
Print permission, 161
print servers, 10, 11–12, 44, 62
privacy rights, 23
Process Tracking option, 45, 46, 57
Profile button, 116, 118
Profile option, 170
Profile Single Process user right, 139, 140
Profile System Performance user right, 139, 140
Properties button, 86
Properties command, 144, 146, 152, 157
Properties dialog box, 47, 157–58, 164–65
proprietary systems, 27
protocols, 72–79, 89
    auditing, 232–33
    dial-out, 89
    encapsulated, 73
    finding/filtering, 41
    installing, 72
    selection of, 72–73
Protocols tab, 72, 74

Q
Quality Computer, 9
Query Value permission, 50, 191

R
RAID (Redundant Array of Inexpensive Disks), 12, 208
RAM (random access memory). See also memory
    locking pages in, 138
    monitoring, 31, 37

RAS (Remote Access Server), 12–13, 62, 234–35
    audit features for, 46, 53, 198, 230–31
    authentication, 12, 80–81
    Call Back options for, 122
    configuring, 86–89, 92
    remote node networking and, 80–81
    scenarios for, 90–92
    security monitoring and, 35, 36, 44, 46, 53
    user administration and, 83–89
RC4 encryption, 76, 81, 89, 91
Read permission, 49–51, 146, 149–52, 155–59, 190–92
recovery, of data, 209–19, 251–52
Recycle Bin, 156
Refresh button, 37
REGBACK.EXE, 204, 205, 251
REGEDIT.EXE, 183, 189. See also Registry Editors
REGEDT32.EXE, 26–27, 49, 183–84, 189–90, 245–46. See also Registry Editors
Registry. See also HKEY_LOCAL_MACHINE subtree; Registry Editors
    administrative shares and, 160
    auditing, 49, 50, 51, 230
    backups, 204–5
    "Crash On Audit Fail" flag in, 58
    edit commands/data types, 185
    enabling parameters in, 53
    examining the security of, 245–46
    HKEY_CLASSES_ROOT subtree, 51, 187, 188
    HKEY_CURRENT_CONFIG subtree, 188
    HKEY_CURRENT_USER subtree, 188
    HKEY_DYN_DATA subtree, 188
    key values, 193–202
    legal notices and, 227
    making changes to, updating the Emergency Repair Disk after, 27
    password filters and, 125
    permissions, 188, 189, 190, 191–201

restoring, 215
server security and, 173
SMB services and, 75–76
system security management
    and, 183–202

Registry Editors
    REGEDIT.EXE, 183, 189
    REGEDT32.EXE, 26–27, 49, 183–
        84, 189–90, 245–46
    setting legal notices with, 26–27
    setting up Registry auditing
        with, 49–50
    starting, 49
    system security management
        and, 183–84
Registry Key Auditing dialog box,
    49, 50
Registry Key Permissions dialog
    box, 189, 190
reliability, definition of, 4
Remote Access Admin, 82–84
Remote Access Admin dialog box,
    82–83
Remote Access Permissions dialog
    box, 84
Remote Access Service dialog box,
    80
Remote Access Setup dialog box,
    86–87
Remote Access Users dialog box,
    85, 86
remote control networking, 79–80
remote node networking, 79–91
Replace a Process Level Token user
    right, 139, 140
Replace Auditing on Existing Files
    option, 47–48
Replace Auditing on Subdirectories
    option, 47–48
Replace Permissions on Existing
    Files option, 147, 155
Replace Permissions on
    Subdirectories option, 147
Replication button, 169
Replication dialog box, 244
Replicator group, 97, 98
Replicator service, 119
Report command, 34
Report View, 30–31, 34
reports, 30–31, 34, 36

Require Data Encryption option, 81
Requiring Microsoft Encrypted
    Authentication option, 81
Reset Counter option, 124, 128
Resource Kit (Windows NT), 127,
    155, 205
resource security, 141–62, 243
Resources tab, 37
Restart audit feature, 45, 46
Restore Files and Directories user
    right, 134, 136
Restrict Access to Owner or
    Administrator option, 213
RestrictAnonymous Registry key,
    197, 248
RestrictGuestAccess Registry value,
    198, 248
Revoke All button, 84
rights, user. See also rights, user
    (listed by name); users
    advanced, 131–32, 136–37
    basic description of, 131–40
    recommendations for securing,
        135–36, 139–40
rights, user (listed by name). See
    also rights, user
    Access Computer from the
        Network user right, 133, 135
    Act as Part of the Operating
        System user right, 137, 139
    Add Workstations to the Domain
        user right, 133, 135
    Back Up Files and Directories
        user right, 133, 135
    Back Up Files and Folders user
        right, 155
    Bypass Traverse Checking user
        right, 137
    Change the System Time user
        right, 133, 135
    Create a Page File user right,
        137, 140
    Create a Token Object user
        right, 137, 140
    Create Permanent Shared
        Objects user right, 137, 140
    Debug Programs user right, 138,
        140
    Force Shutdown from a Remote
        System user right, 133, 136

    Generate Security Audits user
        right, 138, 140
    Increase Quotas user right, 138,
        140
    Increase Scheduling Priority user
        right, 138, 140
    Load and Unload Device Drivers
        user right, 138, 140
    Lock Pages in Memory user
        right, 138, 140
    Log On As A Batch Job user
        right, 138, 140
    Log On As A Service user right,
        138, 140, 174
    Log on Locally user right, 134,
        136
    Manage Auditing and Security
        Log user right, 134, 136
    Modify Firmware Environment
        Variables user right, 139,
        140
    Profile Single Process user right,
        139, 140
    Profile System Performance user
        right, 139, 140
    Replace a Process Level Token
        user right, 139, 140
    Restore Files and Directories
        user right, 134, 136
    Shut Down the System user
        right, 134, 195
    Take Ownership of Files or
        Other Objects user right,
        134–35, 136, 152
RISC-based systems, 143
risk assessment, 16, 17–20, 24–25,
    217
robust operating systems, 72–73
roles, definition of, in corporate
    security policy, 21
ROLLBACK.EXE, 185
rotation schedules, for backups,
    211
RPCs (Remote Procedure Calls), 77,
    178, 180
RSA Data Security
    MD4 encryption, 81, 91
    RC4 encryption, 76, 81, 89, 91
Run Program on Alert field, 32
RWXDPO special permissions,
    149–50

## S

SAM (Security Account Manager), 66, 186–87, 216
Samba service, 75
Save As command, 56
Save As dialog box, 119
Save button, 41
saving
  events to external files, 56
  Performance Monitor information, 36
  System Policy Editor settings, 200
Schedule service, 178, 180, 197, 248
scope, in corporate security policy, 16
screen savers, 202
Screen Saver tab, *202*
Search button, 111
SECEVENT.EVT, 59
Secure Attention Sequence, 26, 195
Security Account Manager database, 183
Security Log, 6, 54, 57–59
  auditing and, 44
  securing, 59
  user rights and, 134, 135
security policy, corporate
  auditing and, 45
  awareness of, 16, 24–25
  commitment to, 16, 24–25
  developing, 15, 16–26
  exceptions to, 21
  management of, 16, 25–26
  Microsoft Office and, 227
  review of, 16, 25–26
  standards for, 22–23
Security Policy Changes audit feature, 44–46
Security tab, 52, 146, 147, 152
Send Message button, 83, 86
Send To All button, 83, 86
senior management, 24–25
Server Manager
  alerts and, 174–75
  basic description of, 163–64
  considerations/recommendations for using, 181–82

export servers and, 170–72
promoting PDCs with, 181
Server Manager dialog box, 171
Server Operators group, 98, 99, 104, 157–59, 175
Server service, 75–76, 178, 180
Service Pack 2, 125
Service Pack 3, 13, 27, 75, 77, 103
services. *See also* services (listed by name)
  basic description of, 175–80
  examining, 244
  recommendations for, *179–80*
  startup accounts for, changing, 176–77
services (listed by name)
  Alerter service, 177, 179, 209
  Clipbook Viewer service, 177, 179
  Computer Browser service, 178, 179
  Dial Out Only service, 87–89
  Directory Replicator service, 170–75, 178, 179, 181–82
  FTP Publishing service, 178, 179
  Messenger service, 178, 179, 209
  Net Logon service, 178, 179
  Network DDEDSM service, 178, 179
  Network DDE service, 178, 179
  NT LM Security Support Provider service, 178, 179
  Replicator service, 119
  Samba service, 75
  Schedule service, 178, 180, 197, 248
  Server service, 75–76, 178, 180
  Spooler service, 178, 180
  Workstation service, 75–76, 178, 180
Services applet, 170
Services dialog box, *171, 176,* 177
Services tab, 37
Set by Caller option, 84, 85
Set By Caller radio button, 84
Set Value option, 50, 51, 191
Set Value permission, 50, 191
SHA-1 (Secure Hashing Algorithm), 76
Shared As radio button, 157

Shared Resources dialog box, *167–68*, 181, 244
Share Name field, 157
share names, 157
share permissions, 63, 155–57, *158–60. See also* permissions
Share Permissions dialog box, 158
Shares button, 167
Sharing tab, *157–58*
Show Advanced User Rights option, 136
Show Full Names button, 110
shut down
  auditing and, 45, 46, 195
  forced, 99, 133, 136
  page file clearing at, 197–98, 248
  user rights for, 133, 134, 195
  without logon, 195, 247
Shut Down the System user right, 134, 195
ShutdownWithoutLogon Registry value, 195, 247
SIDs (security IDs), 55, 76, 102, 106–7
  Account Disabled option and, 117
  creating new, 109
simple TCP/IP services, 76–77
SMB (Server Message Block) protocol, 75–76, 156
smoke detectors, 204
sniffing data, 43
SNMP (Simple Network Management Protocol), 77
source information, in the Event Viewer, 56
SPAP (Shiva Password Authentication Protocol), 81, 89
Special Access dialog box, *145–46*
Special Access permissions, 145
Special Directory Access dialog box, *148–49*
Special Directory Access permissions, *148–49,* 150, *151–52*
Special File Access permissions, 148–49
Special permission, 190–91
spoofing, 78

Spooler service, 178, 180
stand-alone systems, 65, 95
Standard Directory Access
        permissions, 148, 150
Standard File Access permissions,
        145
standards
    development of, 22–23
    ideals and, gap between, 25–26
Start command, 39
starting
    Event Viewer, 54
    Network Monitor, 38
    Performance Monitor, 30
    Registry Editor, 49
    Remote Access Server (RAS), 83
    Windows NT Diagnostics, 36
startup accounts, for services, 176–
        77
Startup button, 170
Startup Type option, 173
static electricity, 203
statistics, 37
Statistics button, 37
Stop Capture radio button, 42
Stop Log button, 33
String command, 185
striping, data, 208
Summary Only option, 214
SUP (Single Use Password) card,
        81–82
Switch to Alert View field, 32
SYN Flood attacks, 78, 79
SYSEVENT.EVT, 59
SYSKEY.EXE, 187
SYSTEM.INI, 183
System Log, 54, 57–59
System Policy Editor, 26–27, 118
    basic description of, 198–200
    creating/updating policies with,
        199–200
    examining policies with, 248–49
    features, 201–2
System Properties dialog box, 139
System Security Management, 183–
        202, 245–46
System tab, 37
system time, 99, 133, 135
System User Access form, 22

T
Take Ownership button, 162
Take Ownership of Files or Other
        Objects user right, 134–35,
        136, 152
Take Ownership permission, 49,
        52, 53, 146, 149
tape backups, 62–63, 204. See also
        backups
TCP/IP (Transmission Control
        Protocol/Internet Protocol),
        13, 82, 91–92
    basic description of, 73–77
    configuring, 89
    packet filtering and, 73–74
    Ping and, 78
    RPCs and, 77
    services, simple, 76–77
Teardrop attacks, 78–79
Telnet, 41, 63, 78, 79
text file format, 36
This Account option, 173
time, system, 99, 133, 135
TNI (Trusted Network
        Interpretation), 28
tolerance strategy, 7
Tracert, 76
triggers, 41–42
Triggers command, 42
Trojan Horses, 155, 192, 196. See
        also viruses
Trusted Domains field, 70, 71
Trusting Domains field, 70, 71
trust ratings. See also trust
        relationships
    A1 trust rating, 28
    B1 trust rating, 28
    B2 trust rating, 28
    B3 trust rating, 28
    C1 trust rating, 28
    C2 trust rating, 27–28
    D trust rating, 28
    F-C2/E3 trust rating, 28
trust relationships. See also trust
        ratings
    basic description of, 27, 66–72
    C2 level of, 27–28
    creating, 70–71, 72
    deleting, 71
    global groups and, 99, 101

non-transitive, 68
one-way, 67, 68, 70–71
securing, considerations/
        recommendations for, 71–72
two-way, 67, 68, 71
types of, 67–68
user accounts and, 121
Trust Relationships dialog box, 70
type information, in the Event
        Viewer, 56

U
UDP (User Datagram Protocol), 74,
        78–79
Unicode, 142
UNIX, 75
Update Now command, 33, 34
Update Time field, 32
UPS (Uniterruptable Power
        Supply), 178, 180, 208–9,
        250, 251
UPS dialog box, 209
Use of User Rights policies, 44, 46
User Account button, 86
User Account Databases, 10, 45,
        115
user accounts
    basic description of, 93, 114–22
    creating, 115–16
User and Group Management audit
        feature, 44–45, 46, 56
User Cannot Change Password
        option, 116, 117, 170
User Environment Profile dialog
        box, 118
User Manager, 93, 101
User Manager for Domains, 44,
        170–73, 183–84
    basic description of, 83–89, 93
    creating/modifying accounts
        with, 108–22
    creating trust relationships with,
        70–71
    opening the Account Policies
        dialog box with, 123
    opening the User Rights Policy
        dialog box with, 132
User menu
    New Global Group command,
        112

New Local Group command, 109
New User command, 115
User Must Change Password at Next Logon option, 115, 117, 170
Username field, 115
usernames, 53, 101, 115, 194
user profiles, 118, 119
User Properties dialog box, 113
user rights. *See also* user rights (listed by name); users
  advanced, 131–32, 136–37
  basic description of, 131–40
  recommendations for securing, *135–36, 139–40*
user rights (listed by name)
  Access Computer from the Network user right, 133, 135
  Act as Part of the Operating System user right, 137, 139
  Add Workstations to the Domain user right, 133, 135
  Back Up Files and Directories user right, 133, 135
  Back Up Files and Folders user right, 155
  Bypass Traverse Checking user right, 137
  Change the System Time user right, 133, 135
  Create a Page File user right, 137, 140
  Create a Token Object user right, 137, 140
  Create Permanent Shared Objects user right, 137, 140
  Debug Programs user right, 138, 140
  Force Shutdown from a Remote System user right, 133, 136
  Generate Security Audits user right, 138, 140
  Increase Quotas user right, 138, 140
  Increase Scheduling Priority user right, 138, 140
  Load and Unload Device Drivers user right, 138, 140
  Lock Pages in Memory user right, 138, 140

Log On As A Batch Job user right, 138, 140
Log On As A Service user right, 138, 140, 174
Log on Locally user right, 134, 136
Manage Auditing and Security Log user right, 134, 136
Modify Firmware Environment Variables user right, 139, 140
Profile Single Process user right, 139, 140
Profile System Performance user right, 139, 140
Replace a Process Level Token user right, 139, 140
Restore Files and Directories user right, 134, 136
Shut Down the System user right, 134, 195
Take Ownership of Files or Other Objects user right, 134–35, 136, 152
User Rights Policy dialog box, *132, 136*
users. *See also* user rights
  administering, 83–89
  disconnecting, 124, 128–29, 166, 176, 242
  monitoring, 85–86
  server security and, 165–66, 176
User Security Management, 235, *236–42*
User Sessions dialog box, *165–66,* 168, 169, 181, 244
Users group, 98, 105, 106–8

**V**

variables, environment, 139, 140
Verify after Backup option, 213
Version tab, 37
viable, use of the term, 18
View menu
  Alert command, 31, 35
  All Events command, 55
  Filter command, 55
  Log command, 33
  Report command, 34

viruses, 63, 155, 192, 205–6, 250.
  *See also* Trojan Horses
VLANs (Virtual LANs), 63
VPNs (Virtual Private Networks), 76

**W**

WANs (wide area networks), 73, 79
war dialers, 88
warning messages, 27, 54–57
web servers, 10, 12
  physical security and, 62
  security monitoring and, 34–35, 44, 46
Win32 subsystem, 175
Windows 95 (Microsoft). *See* Microsoft Windows 95
Windows 98 (Microsoft). *See* Microsoft Windows 98
Winsock, 81, 91
wireless network connectors, 64
workstations, 10, 13, 97, 116, 120–21
  audit features for, 46
  C2 trust rating and, 27–28
  lockout of, 202, 249
  network security management and, 76, 77, 79, 87
  physical security and, 62, 63–64
  security of, questions for assessing, 232–33
  server security and, 164, 169, 178, 180
Workstation service, 75–76, 178, 180
Write DAC permission, 50, 51, 191
Write Owner permissions, 191
Write permission, 49, 146, 149

**X**

X.25 packet switched networks, 80

**Y**

Y2K issues, 222, *223–24*

**James Jumes** is a Senior Manager of PwC's Operational Systems Risk Management practice. He has over 10 years' experience in information technology strategy, business system selection and implementation, and security. James is the author of *Windows NT 3.5 Guidelines for Security, Audit, and Control*. He earned an M.B.A. from Lehigh University and an M.Ed. and B.A. in Psychology from Boston College.

**Neil Cooper** is a Senior Technical Manager of PwC's Technology Risk Services practice, and has over 16 years experience in data processing. He has primary responsibility for leading the Windows NT Security service line for PwC, and is part of PwC's technical team for UNIX, Windows NT, and Internet Security Services. Neil earned an M.S. in Geology from the University of Delaware and a B.S. in Geology from Pennsylvania State University. Neil is a Certified Information Systems Security Professional.

**Paula Chamoun** is a Senior Technical Specialist in PwC's Computer Assurance Services Technology Risk Services practices. Her background includes networking, developing applications using genetic algorithms and neural networks, and programming in C and C++. At PwC, she has performed an array of IT assurance services for large financial services and manufacturing clients. Paula is a Certified Information Systems Auditor and Certified Information Systems Security Professional. She earned an M.S. in Management Information Systems from the University of Virginia and a B.S. in Computer Science from Pace University.

**Todd Feinman** is a Senior Technical Specialist in PwC's Technology Risk Services practice. Todd's technical focus is on Windows NT, Internet and Electronic Commerce Security including network privacy, cryptography, firewalls, and protection strategies. He has reviewed system configurations and network topologies, and assessed the appropriateness of the related security controls. Todd earned a B.S. in Accounting from Lehigh University.

The manuscript for this book was prepared and galleyed using Microsoft Word 97. Pages were composed by Microsoft Press using Adobe PageMaker 6.52 for Windows, with text in Garamond and display type in Franklin Gothic. Composed pages were delivered to the printer as electronic prepress files.

Interior Graphic Designer:     James D. Kramer
Principal Compositor:          Laura Shellhase
Principal Proofreader:         Mildred Rosenzweig
Indexer:                       Liz Cunningham

# http://mspress.microsoft.com/reslink/

## Look
## beyond
## the kits!

If you deploy, manage, or support Microsoft® products and technologies, here's a hot link to the hottest IT resources available—http://mspress.microsoft.com/reslink/. Microsoft Press® ResourceLink is an essential online information resource for IT professionals—the most complete source of technical information about Microsoft technologies available anywhere. Tap into ResourceLink for direct access to the latest technical updates, tools, and utilities—straight from Microsoft—and help maximize the productivity of your IT investment.

For a **complimentary 30-day trial CD** packed with Microsoft Press IT products, order via our Web site at http://mspress.microsoft.com/reslink/.

**Microsoft** Press

# Register Today!

Return this
*Microsoft® Windows NT® 4.0 Security, Audit, and Control*
registration card today

## Microsoft® Press
**mspress.microsoft.com**

---

## *Microsoft® Windows NT® 4.0 Security, Audit, and Control*

_____  _____  _____
FIRST NAME                MIDDLE INITIAL         LAST NAME

_____
INSTITUTION OR COMPANY NAME

_____
ADDRESS

_____

_____  _____  _____
CITY                                       STATE       ZIP

_____  (   )
E-MAIL ADDRESS                             PHONE NUMBER

U.S. and Canada addresses only. Fill in information above and mail postage-free.
Please mail only the bottom half of this page.

*For information about Microsoft Press®*

*products, visit our Web site at*

**mspress.microsoft.com**

**Microsoft®** Press

---